Modernism, Theory, and Responsible Reading

Modernism, Theory, and Responsible Reading

A Critical Conversation

Edited by
Stephen Ross

BLOOMSBURY ACADEMIC
LONDON • NEW YORK • OXFORD • NEW DELHI • SYDNEY

BLOOMSBURY ACADEMIC
Bloomsbury Publishing Plc
50 Bedford Square, London, WC1B 3DP, UK
1385 Broadway, New York, NY 10018, USA
29 Earlsfort Terrace, Dublin 2, Ireland

BLOOMSBURY, BLOOMSBURY ACADEMIC and the Diana logo are trademarks of
Bloomsbury Publishing Plc

First published in Great Britain 2022
This paperback edition published 2023

Copyright © Stephen Ross, 2022

Stephen Ross and contributors have asserted their rights under the Copyright, Designs and
Patents Act, 1988, to be identified as Authors of this work.

For legal purposes the Acknowledgments on pp. vii–viii constitute an
extension of this copyright page.

Cover design by Eleanor Rose
Cover shows Leni Akcelrud at the National Institute for Technology in Rio, 1968.
Photograph by Clara Aguinsky Ackelrud

All rights reserved. No part of this publication may be reproduced or transmitted
in any form or by any means, electronic or mechanical, including photocopying,
recording, or any information storage or retrieval system, without prior permission
in writing from the publishers.

Bloomsbury Publishing Plc does not have any control over, or responsibility for, any
third-party websites referred to or in this book. All internet addresses given in this
book were correct at the time of going to press. The author and publisher regret any
inconvenience caused if addresses have changed or sites have ceased to exist, but
can accept no responsibility for any such changes.

A catalogue record for this book is available from the British Library.

A catalog record for this book is available from the Library of Congress.

ISBN: HB: 978-1-3501-8581-4
PB: 978-1-3501-8641-5
ePDF: 978-1-3501-8582-1
eBook: 978-1-3501-8583-8

Typeset by Newgen KnowledgeWorks Pvt. Ltd., Chennai, India

To find out more about our authors and books visit www.bloomsbury.com
and sign up for our newsletters.

Contents

Acknowledgments — vii

1 Introduction: Responsible Reading — 1
  Stephen Ross

Part I Theory — 21

2 The Positive of the Negative: Joycean Post-Structuralism as Felskian Critique — 23
  Robert Baines
3 Responsible Reading of Theory — 41
  Fabio Akcelrud Durão
4 Modernism, Critical Theory, and Affect Theory *Avant La Lettre* — 59
  Yan Tang
5 The Case for Prosthetic Thinking — 79
  Kathryn Carney

Part II Method — 91

6 Beyond the Search Image: Reading as (Re)search — 93
  Daniel Aureliano Newman
7 On the Advantages of Saying "No" (to Binaries, Totalizations, "Weakness," "Modesty," "Humility") — 111
  Cristina Ionica
8 Weak Theory, "Responsible" Reading, and Literary Criticism — 131
  Masami Sugimori

Part III Practice — 151

9 Absolutely Small: Sketch of an Anarchist Aesthetic — 153
  Roger Rothman

10	Adorno as a Reader: Writing the Mediation of Literature and Philosophy *Matthew Gannon*	169
11	Writing from Somewhere, Reading from Anywhere: New Criticism and (Neo)liberal Globalization *Sonita Sarker*	189
12	Too Literal Translation: Some Poems of Roger Fry *Rivky Mondal*	207
13	Afterword: Necessary–Impossible and Responsible–Irresponsible Reading *Paul K. Saint-Amour*	225

| Notes on Contributors | 235 |
| Index | 239 |

Acknowledgments

A volume like this takes a village to build. Apologies to those who wish these thanks were briefer. First, I would like to thank the Modernist Studies Association for continuing with the seminar format at their conferences. This book grew out of initial conversations facilitated by that format, and owes its dialogic impulse—and commitment to responsible reading—to it. Continuing that theme, I want to thank all the participants in the seminar on "Modernism and Theory" at the 2019 MSA conference in Toronto. Not all of them appear in this volume, and not all who appear in the volume were in the seminar, but the original group provided powerful inspiration in their generous and nuanced contributions. I spoke to Ben Doyle at Bloomsbury about this book at that same conference and he expressed interest from the start. He has been a stalwart supporter and savvy co-developer of it all along; I'm grateful to him and his team at Bloomsbury for their aid the whole way.

This book simply would not exist were it not for the good offices of Deborah Ogilvie, whose perspicacity and attention to detail more than made up for my general lack of both. It's thanks to her that we have a full manuscript and that correspondence was handled so quickly and with such aplomb. Her own research assistant, Grant, was a support in turn, I'm sure, and deserves a nod here as well.

I owe a debt of gratitude to those colleagues with whom I (seemingly endlessly) bashed out the details and challenges of thinking through weak theory, *pensiero debole*, critique and post-critique, weak modernism, affect, ethics, and responsibility. Paul K. Saint-Amour's special issue on "Weak Theory, Weak Modernism" started it all, nudging me out of a rut to think about things anew. I would like to single out J. Allan Mitchell, whose prior work on post-critique was invaluable in my own process. Amy Tang, Graham Jensen, Christopher Douglas, Nicholas Bradley, Erin Ellerbeck, Kevin Tunnicliffe, Misao Dean, Joe Grossi, Marina Bettaglia, and basically anyone else who wandered too close to where I was sitting in the campus coffee shop (hello Munchie Bar!) while I was thinking through these issues. If I've missed your name here, it's not because our conversations were not valuable, but rather due to the shortage of perspicacity mentioned above. David James and María del Pilar Blanco provided timely and unbelievably useful feedback on a draft of the introduction, and continue to inspire my thinking in these lines (hello to William). I am grateful to them for taking the time to read, respond, and then chat online about it all.

Last, but never least, I want to thank my family. They put up with it all, as usual, and kept me healthy and strong by insisting that we get outside every day, play on the ocean and in the woods, and take time to squabble and laugh every day. Stephanie, Kathleen, Adam: none of this matters without you.

1

Introduction: Responsible Reading

Stephen Ross

Seriously? Do we really need yet another <adjective> reading? We already have a superabundance of approaches—close reading, distant reading, middle reading, mere reading, surface reading, micro-sociological reading, reparative reading, paranoid reading—and that's without the various critical orientations that themselves name characteristic methods: feminist reading, critical race reading, historicist reading (old and new), post-structuralist reading, psychoanalytic reading, Marxist reading and post-Marxist reading, phenomenological reading, and so on. We're not exactly hurting for options, here. So, why introduce another option—yet another possible way of understanding what we do and should do as literary and cultural critics? What is to be gained here, aside from incremental career advancement and, perhaps, if all goes well, a brief moment in vogue before the Next Big Thing? The contributors to this volume and I thought about these questions at length before deciding it was worth it after all. In a series of conversations, both *en groupe* and in smaller sub-sets, we decided that it was worth the work to intervene in a debate that seemed to us to have missed something essential. In broad terms, that debate is between something called critique and something else called post-critique, and what seems to have gone missing in action is a middle ground, a principled approach that we are calling responsible reading.

This term—responsible reading—picks up a thread that has been dropped by both contemporary practitioners of critique and theorists of post-critique. As I will outline below, what goes by the name of critique today has devolved into a purely destructive enterprise that ignores the drive toward justice embedded in critique as it develops from Kant through Marx to Nietzsche, Freud, the Frankfurt School, Foucault, Butler, and others. If the animating energy of critique is essentially dialectical, pushing for what Marx called the "ruthless critique of all that is," it does so in the name of clearing ground for a better future, a more just stage of development. The critical practice identified by Felski, Latour, and others as critique today, by contrast, only focuses on destruction, on eviscerating works with cultural currency and status but without attending at the same time to their ameliorative potentials. It is distinctly non-dialectical in its baby-with-the-bathwater approach, selectively targeting works for their ideological sins (often anachronistically), and casting them out in toto rather than considering whether there might also be elements worth saving, worth developing, worth allowing to seed and grow.

By a swing of the pendulum in the other direction, Latour and Felski push for a move beyond critique itself, rather than a judicious analysis of its failings and its affordances that would seek to limit the former and cultivate the latter. Importantly, and generatively for this volume, both Latour and Felski seem at least passingly aware that in doing so they are bypassing the middle ground of responsible, or fair, reading.[1] For Latour, the prospect of fair reading appears only to be dropped immediately when he posits a third alternative between what he calls the fact and fairy positions: "why not add a third position, a *fair*² position?" (243). Why not indeed? But he doesn't. The impetus of his challenge to corrosive critique is too great to stop here and formulate this alternative. Instead, Latour pursues the trajectory away from corrosive critique toward its opposite number, for him "matters of concern." Felski follows suit, introducing the possibility of a more just approach—and naming the alternative we advocate for in the present volume—only to drop it without further thought. Noting that practitioners of corrosive critique tend to "ignore or brush aside the question of what constitutes a fair or responsible reading" (115), Felski seems to imply that post-critique embraces this option, though she never again raises it in these terms. Moreover, as with many elements of post-critique, fair or responsible reading is defined only negatively, as a bad practice to be foregone, rather than as an opportunity to articulate a positive alternative. In this logic, ironically, it replicates precisely the corrosive nature of critique as Felski, Latour, Sedgwick, Anker, and others characterize it.

Perhaps the first question to address is what we mean when we say "critique." As the key term in the debate, critique is remarkably slippery ground. Much of this slipperiness emerges from the dual mode in which critique's critics have approached it: on one hand, they have simply identified the reductive "caricature" (Saint-Amour n.p.) of critique outlined just below, while on the other, they have accepted this version of critique and made it their target without bothering to nuance or challenge its validity. Thus, though Felski allows that there are "varying hues and shades of meaning" (2) to the term, and recognizes that the term has a much longer and more nuanced history, she and other advocates of post-critique brush such distinctions aside to generate a more useful—but arguably less responsible—stark opposition.[3] In the resulting Manichean opposition of critique versus post-critique, critique is presented as little more than scholarly character assassination, if we can adopt Amanda Anderson's characterological description of critical modes for the moment. Critics such as Eve Sedgwick, Bruno Latour, Rita Felski, Elizabeth Anker, Stephen Best and Sharon Marcus, and Heather Love present a version of critique which reads paranoiacally, suspiciously, to uncover the hidden ideological maneuvers of cultural products, in the process mastering them and exposing them as tools of oppression: "The task of the social critic is now to expose hidden truths and draw out unflattering and counterintuitive meanings that others fail to see. The modern era ushers in a new mode of militant reading: what Ricoeur calls a *hermeneutics of suspicion*" (Felski 1). Certainly, this can be true, as any number of published articles and books illustrates. As Anker and Felski rightly note, such critiques—corrosive critiques—leave "little room ... for attention to contradictions or qualitative differences in social or political conditions (15). Anthony Julius's 1995 exposé of anti-Semitism in T. S. Eliot's poetry, and the critical firestorm it ignited, is a case in point. Exposing the anti-Semitism running through some of Eliot's poems, Julius seemed to invite a wholesale condemnation of the poet himself as an unredeemed anti-Semite whose work perhaps ought no longer to be read. In his "critique," Julius thus appeared to sacrifice all of Eliot on the altar of political activism, grotesquely reducing both the complexity of Eliot's work and the subtlety of political critique. In doing so, such corrosive critiques also betray an inflated sense of political efficacy:

> Impatient with incremental or piecemeal political change, critique insists that real-world, pragmatic progress is nothing but a strategy for disguising the persistence of structural inequality, rendering any form of optimism at best overly credulous or misplaced and at worst a craven capitulation. At the same time, critique's commitment to exposure can exaggerate its own power to transform the social world, a tendency that is especially evident among literary and cultural critics. (Anker and Felski 15)

In this mode, critique is but little concerned with responsibility to the wider complexity and challenge of cultural objects, their producers, and their consumers—of the expansive ecology of relationships they produce.[4]

What, then, do we mean when we write, "post-critique"? According to Felski, post-critique and its surrogates attempt to meet the cultural object on its own terms and to recover something of the reason we read in the first place, even if we can't recover the experience of first reading itself. As Stephen Best puts it, post-critique is

> a mode of reading that declines to unmask, demystify, interrogate, subvert, or expose the literary text (the habit of generations of recent critics). Postcritique means to expand the uses of literature beyond that of marking an absence or an insufficiency, returning readers to the values that drew them to the literary work of art in the first place ("aesthetic pleasure, increased self-understanding, moral reflection, perceptual reinvigoration, ecstatic self-loss, emotional consolation, or heightened sensation" [188]). (338)

Sympathy replaces cynicism in a range of reading methods that attend to the pleasures of reading, to the ecstasy and transport—the wonder—that ostensibly drew us all to become critics in the first place. Glenn Willmott has done some of the most insightful and compelling work in this line already, crisscrossing the boundary between what he calls "reading for wonder" and taking seriously the reading practices of nonacademic audiences. His work should be extended. Led by, rather than sneering at, popular reading practices, post-critique accepts and validates aesthetic experience and affect as ends in themselves, as reason enough to read without imagining that our readings are key to the imminent revolution, to social justice, to overthrowing the oppressive regimes of modernity.

As Stephen Best points out, however, post-critique, at least as Felski describes it, is decidedly short on examples, explicitly avoiding close analysis in its articulation and staying vague on method throughout (339). And though we have one or two good indications of how to do this sort of work—Wai Chee Dimock's essay on Henry James and Colm Tóibín is perhaps the best-known example—the precise method (or range of methods) that would animate post-critique remains rather vague. I wonder, for example, what it would look like to try a post-critical reading with *Heart of Darkness*. Would Felski—would anyone—dare to recover the ecstasy of the first experience with that particular book? How could we read it reparatively, to recover its constructive dimensions and to honour its efforts to gather us together? Is it possible to "place ourselves in front of the text, reflecting on what it unfurls, calls forth, makes possible" (Felski 12) in this case? Or is *Heart of Darkness* somehow *hors de combat* now, thanks precisely to corrosive critiques like Achebe's? Is it beyond reparation? Felski approaches this issue when she asks why we are "so hyperarticulate about our adversaries and so excruciatingly tongue-tied about our loves?" (13). It's a valid question, but too simple for much of modernism, where our adversaries may also be our loves.

I have, of necessity, been all too brief in sketching out the extreme poles of the current debate, though I have sought to be responsible in my brevity. There is, of course, a great deal more going on with both critique and post-critique, a great deal more nuance and variety to account for than I can here. But perhaps we can proceed with this rough schematization for the immediate purpose of saying how and why what the contributors to this volume call responsible reading is worth advancing. My point thus far has not been to trouble or challenge either "critique" or "post-critique," but to establish them as points of orientation for our notion of responsible reading. Both terms still desperately need more focused analysis in the present context, as does the precise nature of the relationship between them. In the present volume, Durão, Tang, Ionica, Sugimori, and Gannon begin this work most directly. We still await a contemporary companion to Horkheimer and Adorno's *Dialectic of Enlightenment*, however—a *Dialectic of Critique* that would trace how critique became a perverse parody of itself, at least in some contexts, for some writers.

The value of responsible reading lies in its dual articulation of (1) a middle ground between critique and post-critique, and—more importantly—(2) a principle upon which to proceed regardless of one's critical orientation. As both the contributors to this volume and the mode in which we have assembled it (about which more below) indicate, responsible reading helps identify what the humanities can do that nothing else can—and why it matters. Instead of the corrosive mode of critique identified by Latour and Felski, for example, but equally instead of the predetermined ameliorative modes of post-critique, responsible reading asks what cultural objects think. Rather than exercise critique indiscriminately, responsible reading entertains the notion that cultural objects themselves may be doing the work of critique, post-critique, something entirely else, or all of these in turn—or even in tension, conflict, and overlap. It refuses to instrumentalize cultural objects any more than necessary (taking them up at all seems to entail a certain degree of instrumentalization), and instead to work at detecting and laying out the internal thinking-feeling that cultural objects do so we can understand the types of thought and affect they produce in specific contexts. These contexts, in turn, are as vast as our curiosity.[5] At its best, responsible reading means *thinking-with* cultural objects: thinking through wicked problems with the new perspectives such objects provide, and joining them in their own processes of thinking through wicked problems of their own.

Responsible reading is thus a mode of what Saint-Amour calls weak theory. It retains the value of critique as Vattimo describes it, consisting "less in an unmasking of the hidden (which would bring it closer to a certain notion of hermeneutics as the 'school of suspicion') than in an effort to reconstruct a non-partial point of view" (40). Instead, responsible reading partakes of a more dialectical model, one that "accepts and develops the heritage of dialectics, conjoining it to difference" (48). In this dialectical frame, responsible reading adheres to the complexity of critique and diverges from Vattimo's characterization of weak theory as a means by which we can "grasp totality as such" (40). Responsible reading opts instead for the interminable logic of nonidentity, of self-overcoming, that underwrites weak theory more broadly. As a practice, it corresponds to weak theory's commitment "to know but not necessarily to know better than its object" (Saint-Amour n.p.): not to know it finally or completely, of course, but to be guided by what it knows, how it thinks, and what it feels. To treat it as something like a subject in its own right, a product not just of impersonal forces—economic, political, linguistic, even psychological—but also of a living breathing person capable of inconsistency, contradiction, passion, and change over time. As such, responsible reading emphasizes the ethical and scholarly imperative to try always to know just a little bit better the object as a nexus of subjective and objective forces, and to be forthright and honest in how we meet that responsibility. It requires us to respond to the complexity of the object's appeal: aesthetic, affective, intellectual, and, crucially, ethical. It tries to put these principles into practice, activating in concrete ways Felski, Vattimo, and Saint-Amour's sense of the value of weakness: that we are called to let the object take the lead, seeking neither to master it nor to dominate it. Anything but a "verbal icon" to be approached in splendid isolation from its various contexts, the cultural product is always already part of an infinite ecology of relations that includes us, anticipates our engagement, and negotiates its own reading. As a concrete practice of weak theoretical criticism, responsible reading's open-endedness equally means attending to the utopian potential, the constructive, compositional, productive elements of cultural objects: "Weak thought would be the means by which those so far unworlded ruins might gain our compassion and charge us to make radically new social formations become world. Weakness would be the strait gate through which newness would enter" (Saint-Amour n.p.). This utopian potentiality is consistent with Vattimo's preservation of the positive dimensions of critique as central to responsible reading, and forms a central element of queer theory's use of critique as well (see Love 366; cf. Castiglia).

There is, then, strength in weakness, but not in the way that Saint-Amour worries it will appear. Instead, it is the strength of resilience, of recognizing the dialectic of negation and creation as fundamental to the hermeneutic project (as Felski finally delivers it to us) and, if we are being honest, to the project of living ethically at all.

In this respect, responsible reading means an interminable process of interpretation across a range of approaches, affects, and modes—its fundamentally weak polarity means that it can never foreclose alternatives. Contra Felski's scorn for the New Ethics' insistence on the irreducible alterity of the literary work, and her dismissal of critique's tendency toward "*endless rumination on a text's hidden meanings or representational failures*," responsible reading means refusing ever to be done with a cultural object, never considering its interpretive and experiential potentials to have been exhausted or even satisfactorily accounted for (28, 174). It insists upon the complexity and even incoherence of significant cultural objects as instances of thinking-feeling—of thinking-feeling as an activity without terminus that embraces an ever-changing and potentially infinite array of influences and possible outcomes. From this perspective, responsible reading views Latour and Felski's version of critique as worse than inadequate. The critical practice of seeking and destroying cultural objects for thought-crimes is, in this regard, the crudest mode of instrumentalization. It betrays the complexity of not just the objects themselves, but of our engagements with them, often over decades. As we live with them, meeting them frequently for a time, then perhaps again after long absences, they become something more than mere objects in the world to us.

James Simpson underscores this shifting affective relationship in his typology of critical orientations toward texts: stranger, lover, friend. Though Simpson downplays the intersubjectivity—the relationship not just to the text, but to its author and its myriad other readers—thus implied, Mark Wollaeger slyly reintroduces it when he adds an additional orientation that seems to me even more appropriate: the familial. He passes it off as a bit of a joke, but as with all jokes, there is a kernel of truth, and in this case it is important. That kernel of truth is that we often deplore the things our family members do, get angry with them, ignore them, even shut them out for a time, though we continue to love them. Such complex affective states are part and parcel of most family dynamics, as are unconditional love, acceptance, support, and help with navigating challenging times. The cultural objects we study and the ecologies we join when we do so bear some affinity to this familial ambivalence and complexity. These critical ecologies blur the lines between objectivity and subjectivity, inter-objectivity and intersubjectivity. They include objects—texts, paintings, sculptures, manifestos, compositions, performances, and so on—and producers, authors, artists, scholars, critics, and students. Critical exposé may be valid—it may sometimes be necessary—but it is never sufficient. Simply to focus on what we interpret as an individual person's, work's, or object's ideological errors so we can reduce them to those errors, compartmentalize them, and be done with them is just not responsible. It ignores our mutual obligation to honor the overflowing variety of the person (or work or object), to maintain an ethical comportment toward them. Doing so may lack the rush of righteousness that comes with condemnation, and it is almost never satisfactory, but that's the proper terrain of the humanities.

Responsible Reading and Modernism

A special relationship obtains between modernist studies and responsible reading practices, as it does between modernism and theory more generally. Saint-Amour has already pled this case in slightly different terms, aligning weak theory with modernist studies, at least in its latest incarnation.[6] As he makes plain, modernism was "made both necessary and possible in the west by theory's weakening" (n.p.). In practice, "epistemological humility and weakness-in-theory did not happen to modernism after the fact but happened as and through modernism" (n.p.). And, finally, modernist studies since the last decade of the twentieth century at least has "been weakening its immanent theory of modernism" (n.p.). In brief, as Saint-Amour makes inescapably clear, weak thought has been a cornerstone of modernism from its inception. Modernism emerged as a mode of weak thought in the first instance, and modernist studies has rediscovered that tendential weakness in the field's recent move to open-endedness and contingency.

And yet, as Saint-Amour also acknowledges, no general statement about modernism can stand long without running into counterexamples. Modernism's deep affiliation with weakness must contend with its self-declared strength in the words and works of Pound, Lewis, Eliot, and Marinetti, for example. Such figures not only trouble the link between modernism and weakness—they would challenge anyone who made such claims to a fight. Accounting for this contradictoriness is at the very root of responsible reading (and teaching, and publishing) of modernism today. This goes not just for claims about modernism's aesthetic elements, but its periodization, its pattern of spread and influence, and its politics. At least since the feminist and postcolonialist interventions of the

1970s, modernist studies has had to confront the broad—often unsavory, if not outright repellent—variety and complexity of its objects, figures, movements, and legacies. As scholars of modernism, we've been held to account for decades now, sometimes laughingly challenged to explain how we can bear to work on someone so unredeemable as Wyndham Lewis, and at other times directly called racist or anti-Semitic for our continued interest in, say, Mary Butts. How do we justify continuing to work on Woolf not only when her classism is brought up, but when her anti-Semitism is quoted at us, or, perhaps worse, when the casual racism of the Dreadnought Hoax is mentioned? What about Piet Mondrian's grotesque record of misogyny? What of Le Corbusier's career of trampling Indigenous peoples' values, ideas, and preferences in designing whole cities with little regard for geographic, cultural, and climatic specifics? Perhaps worse still, what happens when Hitler's speech on degenerate art becomes part of a widely adopted anthology of modernist materials (i.e., Rainey)? There is, perhaps, a *frisson* of daring in assigning Hitler to a class of undergraduates—if only to establish modernism's anti-fascist cred by showing how much the Nazis hated modernism—but the fact remains that we're still assigning Hitler. Work in the field has for a long time now been fraught with pitfalls, apologetics, excuses, and painful reckonings—at the same time as it has continued to generate joy, pleasure, insight, and gratification. The field's decisive rejection of the "men of 1914 model" and subsequent explosion in popularity from the 1990s on attests to modernism's ongoing appeal, precisely because we as a community have had to find ways to model responsible reading practices in complex, nuanced, and sometimes contradictory ways.

To do modernist studies for the last several decades has meant that we have to figure out how to explain ourselves and our enduring interest in—and desire to introduce students to—works that might outwardly appear to be simply too *outré* to engage. Thus, though Saint-Amour maintains that the "developments and provocations" of weak theory "have been slow to impact modernist studies, in part because their initial epicentre was in nineteenth-century studies" (n.p.), I would argue that modernist scholars have been practicing weak approaches for a long time. Just as modernist artists explored aesthetics and ideas that would only find explicit articulation in theory several decades later, so scholars of modernism were practicing weak approaches to their field's key objects long before we discovered the current critical language to describe them. We have had to be responsible for our ongoing interest in them, and for finding ways forward that neither repeat nor celebrate the irresponsibility of some modernists, some formulations of modernism, and some modes of modernist study.

This drive to responsible reading has been affectively charged in key ways, as well. Where feelings like shame, disgrace, and regret may drive corrosive critiques of some works, feelings like love, appreciation, and delight may also adhere to the same works. If we really had embraced a detached affect of critique, would we not have abandoned writers such as Conrad, Pound, Eliot, Lewis, even Woolf and Butts? Why do we keep returning to them, if not out of a powerful sense of appreciation and, yes, affection? Certainly, there is a push to decenter such figures, and a powerful drive to break open the canon—precisely what Saint-Amour means by "weak modernism"—but there is little call to get rid of ideologically undesirable artists altogether. How we do what we do—our methodology—is far more often the target of valid critique than which objects we choose to work on. And though we have definitely not displaced the old High Modernists as much as we might like to think we have, there can be no question that we have at least begun to try. We have registered the appeal of modernism's historical complexity by trying to make our field responsive to modernist works' breathtaking range and nuance. We have responded to the otherness against which modernism was for so long set (mass culture, philistinism, bourgeoisification, Victorianism, capitalism, commercialism, etc.) partly by accepting those "others" as valid elements of modernism (illegitimately othered in the first place), and partly by rethinking modernism itself weakly. Such "respons-ibility" is central to how our field has evolved for forty or more years at this point, and will be its key mode as it continues to develop. It is the ethical principle behind our ongoing commitment to works we might otherwise feel justified in abandoning to the dust heap of history, and to the embrace of new works already ignored for far too long. Such responsibility is not a purely theoretical notion, then, but an affective, daily, part of our scholarly practice. It animates the essays gathered here and orients them specifically toward modernist studies' vital weakness. It is also deeply ethical.

Ethics

At the very core of the notion of responsible reading is an ethical stance, a belief that there are more and less ethical ways to read. This insistence on ethics as the first principle of a reading method separates responsible reading from both corrosive critique and post-critique. This is not to say that either critique or post-critique is inherently unethical, but only that they all too easily lose sight of their responsibility to the cultural object and its ecologies, subordinating critical humility to an agenda. Both corrosive critique and post-critique risk instrumentalizing the work as a means of aggrandizing the critic. Friedman usefully sums up these two positions: corrosive "critique, Felski suggests, lionizes the scholar as hero and scholarship as demystification" (345). By contrast, "*The Limits of Critique* argues for a new mood and mode of reading, one that recognizes the agency of the text to arouse the emotions and imaginations of its readers as it circulates through time and space" (Friedman 345). Though Felski's approach apparently preserves "the agency of the text," it does so in a minor key, subordinating that agency to the affective states the work produces for readers. There is little question in either approach of attending to the text's semi-autonomy, to its ability to think for itself, to be a record of thinking-feeling *en procés* (i.e., both in process and on trial). Both approaches all too often instrumentalize the cultural object, treating it as a means to an end that ultimately takes its significance from what it does for the critic. In corrosive critique, the work is the occasion for the critic to demonstrate mastery, but even in post-critique the work as a complex object—an "actor" in Latour's sense—is still subordinated to the affect it produces in the attuned reader.

By contrast, responsible reading presupposes an ethical obligation to honor the complexity, dynamism, and even incoherence of the cultural object. Emmanuel Levinas's work on responsibility is illuminating in this regard. In "Ethics as First Philosophy," Levinas first describes the process of knowledge in terms that sound very much like those of corrosive critique: "in knowledge there also appears the notion of an intellectual activity or of a reasoning will [...] an activity which *appropriates* and *grasps* the otherness of the known" (76). The knower overcomes the alterity of what is known, either reducing its difference to a mode of knowable and controllable sameness, or else annihilating it. It's an unethical process, one that fails in the call to respond to the appeal of the other in their otherness. The ethical alternative for Levinas lies in resting uneasily in incomplete knowledge: "beyond knowledge and its hold on being, a more urgent form" emerges: "that of wisdom" (78). This wisdom is ethical. It respects the alterity of the other, fearing "injustice more than death" (85). It makes responsibility to the other—whatever shape it takes—the primordial affect, the condition of possibility for subjectivity, sociality, and thought: ethics as first philosophy.

A reading practice on this basis would perforce accept the ultimate elusiveness of the object being read. It would never have done with any work and never be able to rest easy in its account of it. It would operate constantly with a sense of what Levinas calls *mauvaise conscience*: "it has no intentions, or aims, and cannot avail itself of the protective mask of a character contemplating in the mirror of the world a reassured and self-positing portrait. It has no name, no situation, no status" (81). This approach might seem to accord with the "New Ethics" as Felski defines it, but I think this is something different: the indeterminacy I see here has nothing to do with an ultimately untouchable otherness of the cultural object so much as with the perpetual work of interpretation (see Felski 28). If we credit Anderson's reading of theoretical approaches as character types, then this description gains further traction as a prescription for properly ethical reading. What is irreducibly other about literature is not some sacred kernel of alterity, but precisely its dynamism in tandem with our own, its propensity to shift significations with contexts and to yield new insights at every new inspection.

I have retained the original French for *mauvaise conscience* to keep its dual significations, otherwise difficult to render concisely in English. Most intuitively, *mauvaise conscience* indicates a bad conscience, a sense of guilt, and this is certainly part of how Levinas uses it. But it is more complicated than that, expressing a stance that is "not guilty, but accused; and responsible" (Levinas 81). As Masami Sugimori points out in this volume, Levinas's use of "responsible" animates the term's larger etymology, beginning with thirteenth-century Anglo-Norman legal uses indicating "entitled to an answer … answerable, required to answer" and originating in the Latin respons-, respondere "respond" "promise in return," from re- "back" + spondere "to pledge" (*Oxford English Dictionary*). "Responsible" thus always indicates dialogism, a return that entails a pledge, promise, or even compulsion. It is *en procés*, unresolved, unsettled, incomplete. It describes a state of being regarded by the other (here, the work or object) and being compelled to respond to it without ever being able to do so adequately. More importantly, *mauvaise conscience* likewise signifies faulty knowledge, a bad consciousness, a consciousness that is not fully present, healthy, robust, and complete. It betrays our sense always that we do not quite understand the other/work, that something in it evades us at any given instant, in any given reading. As an ethical-critical stance, *mauvaise conscience* recognizes the responsibility always to respect the critic's inability ever to account finally for the richness and complexity of a cultural object and its wider ecology. An ethical criticism is definitionally responsible to the object worlds it seeks not to know (in Levinas's sense) but about which—perhaps even from which—to acquire wisdom. As critics, we must be willing to think with and through the affective and intellectual dynamics of the aesthetic experience as an inherently ethical arena. We must accept that works have the status of actors: they are others toward which we are oriented, which regard us (in the dual sense of seeing us and pertaining to us), and to which we owe a just response. Just such an orientation is what we seek in this volume as we variously work through the implications of weak theory, weak modernism, post-critique, and the legacies of critique both corrosive and dialectical.

Responsible reading also entails an affective and critical stance within the larger community of scholars. It means not just citing one another accurately but doing so generously and productively. It means recognizing that scholarly work is a mode of composition, even when that larger project includes moments of dispute, even conflict. One of the things that makes scholarship so valuable is its commitment to responsible engagement. As we respond to others' work, we are responsible for our words—we must be willing and able to answer for them. To that end, I'd like to advocate for adjectives, which are often scorned as insufficiently objective or distanced in critical discourse. If we accept, as I think we must, that critical discourse is inherently affective, then adjectives provide privileged ways to register it. If someone's contribution is especially insightful, say so. If it is brilliant, say so. More: when you read an article you really like, or that you find especially helpful, contact the author and say so. Far, far too much of the time we write and wonder whether anyone ever reads our work. Instead of thinking about it as networking, consider it as community building: the affective orientation is all. We wait for reviews, references, citations—but even these don't tell us much necessarily about how our work is being received. A truly wrongheaded article might, for example, have an enviably high citation index because every subsequent article invokes it only to repudiate it. The quality of our work's reception is at least as important as its quantity. More, qualitative assessment is where the humanities live, and where we should stake out our territory. We can build our community with simple acts of communication, of composition, that do not preclude critique by any means, but that certainly do depend upon us behaving humanely toward one another. Doing so is a key feature of responsible reading, and one we hope will gain momentum going forward. Responsible reading as we conceive of it is at once ethical, practical, political, and humane; it describes a principled attitude, a commitment to read in ways that are characteristically humanist and that showcase the value of the humanities.

As with all work in the humanities, responsible reading must be thought in terms of its wider contexts, in this case perhaps most pertinently the long history of imperialism and its lasting legacies of racism and bigotry. If, as is so often declared, modernism is the literature of modernity, then we must equally understand that modernity is coextensive with European global imperialism and the racist discourses that both sustain it and are perpetuated by it. For the captured Africans who chose death by drowning over slavery in the Middle Passage to the too-many who still die because they "can't breathe" under contemporary policing practices, modernity—modernist studies—is responsible. We must take seriously the roles played by cultural production in it, as well as against it, and through it. Race, racialization, and racism are embedded in the DNA of modernist cultural production, from the Triangular Trade in slaves and commodities that fuelled modernity's surge to global prominence to the painfully recent scandals of residential schools in Canada, the UK's grotesque treatment of the Windrush Generation (from the moment of arrival in 1948 to the scandal of 2018 and after), and including state-sponsored racism throughout the Commonwealth, British and American slavery, and the institutional reinvention of slavery in the American prison-industrial complex. It's a long history, comprising 400+ years of brutality, othering, oppression, and violence, alongside the more commonly adduced rise of empiricism, rationalism, industrialization, the germ theory of disease, the invention of vaccines, and humanism. These movements are mutually dependent: they chart multiple vectors of influence, contradiction, and reinforcement that crisscross, recede and resurge, conflict and converge, often unpredictably, across time and space. They disrupt uniform understandings of spatiality and temporality themselves, layering each historical moment with times and places that are not alien to that moment, but define it. In doing so, they produce cultural objects that engage with, navigate, and make sense of them. Some of these objects are sophisticated and complex in their own right. Others are simple and direct but no less worthy of study for that. All are embedded in complexity and contradiction; all condense and articulate overlapping matrices of influence, agency, and overdetermination. As scholars of the cultural production of this crazy maelstrom, we have deep responsibilities to its complexities and contradictions. To read modernism responsibly—to read responsibly at all—today, is to acknowledge and deal with this history.

As Holocaust-survivor Levinas would have it, we have an infinite responsibility to the millions upon millions of others in whose place we stand and upon whose pasts our present is erected: who have made possible our presence by their absence. The claims of these infinite historical others are upon all of us as scholars of modernism today. "Other" and "us" have multiple valences in this context, merging and diverging as we alter scale, perspective, and the identity of the perceiver. Most broadly, the "others" to whom we must respond are the legions of the (as-yet) unknown others whose lives are the very stuff of modernity. Most locally, they are our colleagues, students, teachers, friends, and nemeses—the essential "others" whose presence enables community per se. These terms denote shifting relationships of co-constitution rather than binary opposition.

The Atlantic slave trade, genocide of Indigenous peoples, and systemic racism around the world are part of this relationality, but so are professional precarity, race- and gender-homogenous panels and publications, and the simple right to move about one's habitus in safety and security. There is no question of not responding to these "others" and the histories they bear, since ignoring them is itself a response. Rather, we—*all* scholars of modernism and theory—can only determine what our response will look like.

This is heavy stuff, and the burden can feel immense, overwhelming, whatever affects attach to it: guilt, shame, exuberance, optimism, fear, righteousness, rage, sadness. The foregoing has been focused on our responsibilities as scholars of modernism, but lurking on the periphery is something of a huge problem we have yet to face head on. As David James and María del Pílar Blanco pointed out to me, the discourse of political and ethical responsibility in scholarly circles has a tendency to overestimate the power of scholarly practice in terms of political effectiveness. Anker and Felski actually make this one of the most salient parts of their critique of critique, when they note that "critique's commitment to exposure can exaggerate its own power to transform the social world, a tendency that is especially evident among literary and cultural critics" (15). Several questions arise: What, really, is the political power of literary or cultural criticism? Though I agree that it is important in scholarly terms to unearth marginalized works, along with the histories and rhetorics of their marginalization, what political effect does doing so actually have? What kind of responsibility do we have *as literary scholars* to take political action, to reform our institutions, to march in the streets, to riot when nothing else seems likely to work—and how far can we legitimately view our scholarly work as commensurate with, if not as a catalyst for, such activities of reconstitution, mobilization, and protest? Is it enough, for instance, to change the scholarly record, to move the field in ever more inclusive directions, to raise up subsequent generations in traditions of thought at once critical (of inequality) and creative (of potential solutions)? As professional writers, most of us will be able to find a rhetoric to match our affective states, to lend heft to our words so that they seem like taking urgent action. But are we kidding ourselves? What is the nature of our responsibility in this frame? Are our words enough? Would they be enough if we stopped overselling their revolutionary power?

Some readers will recall the scandal and outrage that erupted in July 2000 when Edward Said joined pro-Palestinian protestors and threw a rock at an Israeli guardhouse. For Said, the answer to the above questions seemed clear: commitment in the scholarly realm, if it were to be authentic, also meant activism, even violent protest. It was not just a question of scholarly commitment, but of a holistic ethics and politics, the sort of thing that precludes charges of being a faux revolutionary like the anarchists in Joseph Conrad's *The Secret Agent*. The separation between theory and practice in this context is itself viewed askance as a way out, a way to talk the talk but not walk the walk, as it were. Ought we, if we are to be responsible scholars of modernism, theory, modernity working within these histories of inequality, "take it to the streets"? Do we risk being called hypocrites for anything less than total commitment to the cause, or is there a middle ground? And if there is a middle ground, where is it and who gets to say? To be sure, everyone has limits to their commitment—few enough have the sort of full-blooded enthusiasm of Nelson Mandela or Martin Luther King, Jr. We all have lines we prefer not to cross, and others we absolutely will not. But we whose work directly addresses long histories of inequality must be able to answer for the tension between what we say our work does and how we live the rest of our lives.

For some—for many whose experience of those long histories of inequality are intimate, personal, immediate, lived daily—there is little tension: scholarship is coextensive with political activism, even if that scholarship is conducted in institutions that are themselves part of those long histories of inequality. For others, it is enough to reshape the field in ever more inclusive terms, to change how we view the history of the field, to challenge the institutional apparatuses that sustain inequality and intolerance still. I confess I don't have an answer. It's a problem I struggle with constantly. I'm a straight, white, man with tenure at a Canadian university. I do not know how to navigate these claims, counterclaims, and complications. But I do know that they can't be ignored. The claim they lay upon us is undeniable. We must each respond to them in measure with our sense of commitment and uncertainty. We must accept *mauvaise conscience* as perhaps the sine qua non of scholarship today, and of a constant need to calibrate our words with our actions—as the ethico-political horizon toward which future work must tend.

Structure, Sign, and Play

From the start, we have sought to make *Responsible Reading* something more than just a collection of papers on a shared topic, but a performance of the principles we are trying to formulate. The book began one optimistic afternoon when, temporarily freed from a lingering sense of apathy about the profession in the spring of 2019, I proposed a seminar on the topic of Modernism and Theory for the Modernist Studies Association conference in Toronto. I had been motivated in large part by Saint-Amour's "Weak Theory,

Weak Modernism" cluster on the *Modernism/modernity* Print Plus platform. That said, as my own response to that cluster suggested, I remained dubious, even concerned about the discredit being heaped upon critique and the ambiguity around post-critique. So, even though the topic seemed to have been well-mined by that spring of 2019, I thought, "Well, why not? Let's find out if there's more to say." The participants in that seminar produced some electric contributions, presenting a much wider array of opinion and insight than I had expected. Initially concerned that we would simply spend three hours doing corrosive critique on the notion of post-critique, I soon found that my interlocutors were thoughtful, generous, accommodating—in a word, responsible. They sought really to inhabit and understand the arguments they engaged, and to see how they might respond to them in ways I can only think of as deeply ethical. In the midst of it all, Daniel Aureliano Newman suggested the term "responsible reading" to describe the as-yet inchoate perspective we all seemed to be fumbling toward.[7] It rang true as soon as he said it and quickly provided an intellectual infrastructure for our subsequent investigations.

Not all the contributors to *Responsible Reading* were in that seminar, and not all the seminar participants are present in the volume, but the foundational idea has only gained force as we have assembled this volume. Each contributor has written a major chapter of approximately 7,000 words and been assigned to write a much briefer response to someone else's chapter. Though we could not include the responses in this volume, they will appear on Bloomsbury's web site. This has been a process, at times, even, *un procés*. Original contributions were responded to, then revised and resubmitted so that the responses could be revised and enhanced in turn. Multiple long-term dialogues have emerged from this process. Pushing things further, once the full manuscript was assembled— all the main chapters and all the responses in more or less final state—it was circulated to all the contributors. At this point, everyone was invited to revise their work one more time, adding in references to other contributions: responses, challenges, advances, and appreciations. The result is a whole that is deeply interrelated, coherent in n-dimensions (which is, perhaps, to say that it is ultimately incoherent in ethical ways), and self-referential (in a good way). It has both print and digital components, performing cross-media responsiveness and inviting extended conversations. We have tried, throughout, to model responsible reading in as many modes as possible, and to capture in print a formative moment in responsible reading *en procés*. With luck, these papers will find yet more lively respondents and generate yet more scholarly dialogue. Ideally, the process of responsible reading is interminable: let the games begin!

Notes

1 Though our use of the term "responsible reading" does not come directly from Felski, we acknowledge its presentation in her work, and want to embrace its potential.
2 Unless otherwise noted, all emphasis is in original.
3 For a powerful rejoinder to this reductive version of critique, see Castiglia in Anker and Felski.
4 Throughout this introduction I will use "object" as a shorthand to designate the cultural artifact in its wider ecology, not as a "verbal icon" or static entity, but as a dynamic intensity, a shifting node where multiple forces and influences overlap—often but not always anchored to a material artifact or punctual event—to produce an aesthetic experience. This conception gives the lie to the conventional boundaries that have long allowed critical separation of such objects from their manifold interpenetrating contexts, and instead reads the broader matrix as integral to the object-event to which we attend: it enfolds but is not limited to the book, say, or the opera or painting or happening, but also its producers, consumers, political, cultural, historical, psychological, economic, ideological, biological, infrastructural, philosophical, and potentially infinite other crosscurrents.
5 As Daniel Newman suggests, and as Amy Tang takes up in this volume, curiosity is a key disposition in both critique and post-critique, one that can underwrite multiple methods and approaches, while entailing sustained vulnerability and interest on the part of the reader/critic.
6 Interestingly, Felski claims that modernism itself is partially responsible for the prevalence of paranoid reading practices: "Suspicious readers are preceded and often schooled by suspicious writers" such as Kafka and Beckett (42).
7 As is often the case with memory, this version is a collective product: I recall the term coming from Masami Sugimori, he recalls it coming from Newman, and Newman recalls it coming from me. I am only sure that I did not coin it, and Sugimori seems certain he did not either.

References

Anderson, Amanda. *The Way We Argue Now: A Study in the Cultures of Theory*. Princeton UP, 2006.

Anker, Elizabeth S., and Rita Felski. "Introduction." *Critique and Postcritique*, edited by Elizabeth S. Anker and Rita Felski. Duke UP, 2017, pp. 1–30.

Best, Stephen. "La Foi Postcritique, on Second Thought." *PMLA/Publications of the Modern Language Association of America*, vol. 132, no. 2, 2017, pp. 337–43, DOI:10.1632/pmla.2017.132.2.337.

Best, Stephen, and Sharon Marcus. "Surface Reading: An Introduction." *Representations*, vol. 108, no. 1, 2009, pp. 1–21.

Castiglia, Christopher. "Hope for Critique?" *Critique and Postcritique*, edited by Elizabeth S. Anker and Rita Felski. Duke UP, 2017, pp. 211–29.

Dimock, Wai Chee. "Weak Theory: Henry James, Colm Tóibín, and W. B. Yeats." *Critical Inquiry*, vol. 39, no. 4, Summer 2013, pp. 732–53.

Felski, Rita. *The Limits of Critique*. U of Chicago P, 2015.

Friedman, Susan Stanford. "Both/and: Critique and Discovery in the Humanities." *PMLA/Publications of the Modern Language Association of America*, vol. 132, no. 2, 2017, pp. 344–1, DOI:10.1632/pmla.2017.132.2.344.

Latour, Bruno. "Why Has Critique Run out of Steam?" *Critical Inquiry*, vol. 30, Winter 2004, pp. 225–48.

Levinas, Emmanuel. "Ethics as First Philosophy." *The Levinas Reader*, edited by Seán Hand, translated by Seán Hand and Michael Templé. Blackwell, 1989, pp. 75–87.

Love, Heather. "Close but not Deep: Literary Ethics and the Descriptive Turn." *New Literary History*, vol. 41, no. 2, 2010, pp. 371–91.

Love, Heather. "Critique Is Ordinary." *PMLA/Publications of the Modern Language Association of America*, vol. 132, no. 2, 2017, pp. 364–70, DOI:10.1632/pmla.2017.132.2.364.

Marx, Karl. Letter to Arnold Ruge, September 1843, https://www.marxists.org/archive/marx/works/1843/letters/43_09-alt.htm. Accessed February 17, 2021.

Saint-Amour, Paul. "Weak Theory, Weak Modernism." *Modernism/modernity*, Print Plus, vol. 3, no. 3, 2018, https://modernismmodernity.org/articles/weak-theory-weak-modernism. Accessed February 17, 2021.

Sedgwick, Eve Kosofsky. "Paranoid Reading and Reparative Reading; or, You're So Paranoid, You Probably Think This Introduction is About You." *Novel Gazing: Queer Readings in Fiction*, edited by Eve Kosofsky Sedgwick. Duke UP, 1997, pp. 1–37.

Simpson, James. "Interrogation Over." *PMLA/Publications of the Modern Language Association of America*, vol. 132, no. 2, 2017, pp. 377–83, DOI:10.1632/pmla.2017.132.2.377.

Vattimo, Gianni. *Weak Thought*. State U of New York P, 2012.

Willmott, Glenn. *Reading for Wonder: Ecology, Ethics, Enchantment*. Palgrave Macmillan, 2017.

Wollaeger, Mark A. "Reading Felski: Playfulness, Politics, Pedagogy." *PMLA/Publications of the Modern Language Association of America*, vol. 133, no. 1, 2018, pp. 221–3, DOI:10.1632/pmla.2018.133.1.221.

Part I

Theory

2

The Positive of the Negative: Joycean Post-Structuralism as Felskian Critique

Robert Baines

In *The Limits of Critique*, Rita Felski defines her conception of critique as

> a spirit of skeptical questioning or outright condemnation, an emphasis on its precarious position vis-à-vis overbearing and oppressive social forces, the claim to be engaged in some kind of radical intellectual and/or political work, and the assumption that whatever is *not* critical must therefore be *un*critical. (2)

Within the field of Joyce studies, the major critical mode that most fully adheres to the above definition is that of post-structuralism. This essay will explain how Joycean post-structuralism operates as Felskian critique and why this makes it valuable to contemporary Joyce studies. In doing so, the essay will focus primarily on readings of *Finnegans Wake* because post-structuralist Joyce critics usually engage with that work.

The post-structuralist reading of Joyce has its origins in Jacques Derrida's 1962 *Edmund Husserl's Origin of Geometry: An Introduction*. There, in Derrida's first major discussion of Joyce, he contrasts Husserl's desire for univocity against the equivocity of Joyce's writing. According to Derrida, Joyce's "endeavor" is to

> repeat and take responsibility for all equivocation itself, utilizing a language that could equalize the greatest possible synchrony with the greatest potential for buried, accumulated, and interwoven intentions within each linguistic vocable, each word, each simple proposition, in all worldly cultures and their most ingenious forms (mythology, religion, science, arts, literature, politics, philosophy, and so forth). And, like Joyce, this endeavor would try to make the structural unity of all empirical culture appear in the generalized equivocity of a writing that, no longer translating one language into another on the basis of their common cores of sense, circulates throughout all languages at once,

accumulate their energies, actualizes their most secret consonances, discloses their furthermost common horizons, cultivates their associative syntheses instead of avoiding them, and rediscovers the poetic value of passivity. (102)

As Sam Slote observes, in considering the notion of equivocity that Derrida is using here, one needs to keep in mind the distinction that he makes a few pages earlier between two different kinds of equivocity (403). According to Derrida, "There is a *contingent* plurivocity or multisignificance and an *essential* one" (100). One can understand this distinction by drawing upon the *OED*'s definition of the "equivocal" as "Of words, phrases, etc.: Having different significations equally appropriate or plausible" ("Equivocal, Adj. and n."). On one side of Derrida's distinction is a form of equivocity characterized by contingently different significations of equal plausibility and, on the other, is a version of equivocity defined by essentially different significations of equal plausibility. To quote Slote, the pun would be an example of the former (403). The latter, which is the form of equivocity that Derrida associates with Joyce, involves equivocations that are essential rather than contingent. By this Derrida means equivocations that, instead of being deliberate constructs, are the products of words having different meanings in different languages.

Derrida makes this point more clearly in his 1982 essay "Two Words for Joyce" through the use of an example from *Finnegans Wake*. What is conspicuous about this example is that it is not one of *Wake*'s many complex portmanteau words and phrases, but rather the very simple phrase "he war" (FW 258.12). This phrase exemplifies the essential form of equivocity that Derrida associates with Joyce because, as Derrida puts it, "It *was* written *simultaneously* in both English and German." In saying this, Derrida refers to the fact that "[w]ar is a noun in English, a verb in German" ("Two Words for Joyce" 155).

When one understands the form of equivocity that Derrida associates with Joyce, one can see that Derrida's interest lies less in defining the exact nature of Joyce's writing and more in using that writing to make larger points about the nature of language. This is why, in Derrida's discussion of Joyce in his book on Husserl, he eschews specifics and speaks in broad, often hyperbolic terms. The consequence of this is that, while Derrida does identify a number of the important features of Joyce's writing—its excess of meaning; its rejection of the boundaries between different languages and forms of discourse; its exposure of linguistic convention—his claims regarding those features are wild overstatements. That being said, one can fully understand why Derrida's enthusiastic depiction of Joyce as supreme linguist and visionary cultural analyst inspired so many critics.

Subsequent post-structuralist readings of Joyce would focus on the features of Joyce's writing that Derrida highlights and would be influenced by his tone. The reason those readings are more negative, and thereby more in keeping with Felskian critique, is that, while Derrida celebrates Joyce's extraordinarily powerful writing, those readings would consider how the reader is supposed to cope with such writing.

Derrida's discussion of Joyce in his book on Husserl drew the attention of Philippe Sollers, one of the founders of the influential avant-garde journal *Tel Quel*. Sollers played a key role in the creation of the post-structuralist Joyce because, in 1972, he commissioned one of the works that would define that conception of Joyce, Stephen Heath's "Ambiviolences: Notes for reading Joyce." In that essay, Heath focuses on *Finnegans Wake* and argues that that text cannot be viewed as "the simple carrier of a message (a meaning)":

> The writing of *Finnegans Wake* … develops according to a fundamental incompletion; the text produces a derisive hesitation of sense, the final revelation of meaning being always for "later." The writing opens out onto a multiplicity of fragments of sense, of possibilities, which are traced and retraced, colliding and breaking ceaselessly in the play of this text that resists any homogenization. (31–2)

As in Derrida's characterization, Joyce's writing is here defined as excessive, mobile, and unfettered. On this occasion, however, rather than sparking wonder, that writing poses a challenge. It is not that the language of the *Wake* refuses to yield any meaning but rather that it rejects the reader's attempts at imposing stable, conclusive meanings upon it. It will not be mastered. All readers can do is to play with the shifting, unstable "fragments of sense" that they glean from the text.

Heath's reading of the *Wake* offers an example of what Felski calls "*literature as critique*." This occurs when a work of literature is "lauded for its power to defamiliarize and demystify, to lay bare the banality of the commonplace, to highlight the sheer contingency and constructedness of meaning" (Felski 16). However, while Heath's reading certainly meets this definition, it also exceeds it. Terms of exposure like "demystify" and "lay bare" don't capture the violence of Heath's version of the *Wake*. That version has more in common with Felski's primary definition of critique, the definition that begins this essay. To use the terms of that definition, Heath's *Wake* is so "radical" and so "skeptical" that, rather than simply exposing the conventions by which meaning normally operates in literature, it smashes those conventions to pieces (Felski 2). In doing so, Heath argues, the *Wake* also renders useless the tools by which traditional literary criticism locates and defines meaning. Staid conceptions of how author, text, and reader function offer no aid in interpreting such a text. For Heath, it is the revolutionary ideas of post-structuralist thinkers such as Julia Kristeva, Roland Barthes, and, of course, Derrida that explain how meaning operates in the *Wake*, and he consistently presents Joyce as anticipating, supporting, and demonstrating those ideas. By utilizing Joyce in this manner, Heath is able to ascribe his own critique of traditional literary criticism to the infallible Joyce.

Yet, while Heath's reading of the *Wake* is dominated by critique, it also at times adopts the approach that Felski opposes to critique, that of "postcritical reading." To be a post-critical reader is to conceive of reading as "an act of composition—of creative remaking—that binds text and reader in ongoing struggles, translations, and negotiations" (Felski 182). Heath echoes this language when he argues that "[t]he practice of writing-reading in Joyce's texts is the recognition of the text not as absolute origin or source (expression of 'Reality,' expression of the Author, etc.) but as intertextual space, dialogue of forms which write it as it writes them" (39). In sentences like this, when Heath draws upon Barthes and Kristeva to assert the creative agency of the reader, he demonstrates that his post-structuralist reading of Joyce is willing to tolerate some production amidst all the destruction.

Since Heath's essay was written in English, it marks the entry of the post-structuralist Joyce into English-language Joyce criticism. In the years that followed, a number of Anglo-American critics began to engage with the conception of Joyce. The year 1978 saw the release of the most canonical Anglo-American post-structuralist reading of Joyce, Colin MacCabe's *James Joyce and the Revolution of the Word*. MacCabe's conception of Joyce's writing is in many ways similar to that of Heath, and he also highlights the idea that Joyce's texts critique the traditional concepts and methods of literary criticism. There are, however, two important new elements within MacCabe's version of the post-structuralist Joyce.

One is an increased focus on the politics of Joyce's writing. MacCabe makes explicit the political ideology that is implicit in Heath's discussion of Joyce's revolutionary aesthetics. He does so most clearly in the concluding chapter of the book, a chapter titled "Joyce's Politics," when he asserts that "Joyce's writing becomes a more and more desperate attempt to deconstruct those forms of identification which had allowed the triumph of the national revolution to mean the very opposite of a liberation of Ireland" (MacCabe 170). In defining Joyce's writing in this manner, MacCabe reinforces the idea of that writing as critique.

As Felski observes, "'critique' is a term commonly associated with a progressively oriented politics" (140).

The other new element in MacCabe's reading of Joyce is a heightened emphasis on Joyce's anti-realism:

> Joyce's texts, however, refuse the subject any dominant position from which language could be tallied with experience. *Ulysses* and *Finnegans Wake* are concerned not with representing experience through language but with experiencing language through a destruction of representation. (4)

MacCabe here defines Joyce not as critiquing the conventions of literary realism but as seeking to destroy the very notion that language can represent experience. This conception of Joyce is difficult to square with the hyper-realism of much of his fiction and MacCabe seems aware of this. It is conspicuous that the first sentence speaks of "Joyce's texts" and the second of "*Ulysses* and *Finnegans Wake*." While those two novels certainly push the boundaries of literary realism more than Joyce's prior works, MacCabe's claim regarding Joyce's anti-realism is so strong that even they cannot fully support it. MacCabe ends up demonstrating that there are limits to the extent to which Joyce's works, even *Ulysses* and *Finnegans Wake*, can function as critiques of literary convention.

In turning from the 1970s to the 1980s, one sees the post-structuralist Joyce moving into the mainstream of Joyce criticism. As Geert Lernout observes, that conception of Joyce became ever more prominent across the International Joyce Symposiums in Dublin in 1982, in Frankfurt in 1984, and in Copenhagen in 1986 (183). As the 1980s began to draw to a close, however, Joyce critics started to move away from post-structuralism. To quote Len Platt, "Joyceans in the late 1980s began to work from very precise historical materials to produce a Joyce much more animated in relation to Irish, English and, indeed, wider European politics and culture" (113).

When Joyce studies as a whole began to leave post-structuralism behind, many were not sad to see it go. This is because one of the consistent features of post-structuralist Joyce criticism is that it attacks older modes of criticism and labels them naïve, quietist, and ineffective. In keeping with Felski's definition of critique, Joycean post-structuralism very much holds "the assumption that whatever is *not* critical must therefore be *uncritical*" (2). Understandably, this aspect of the post-structuralist Joyce did not sit well with the scholars in many of the other fields of Joyce studies. Indeed, it is a sign of the opposition that the post-structuralist Joyce sought and received that the classic history of the post-structuralist Joyce, Lernout's *The French Joyce*, is also a critique of that conception of Joyce. Lernout offers his central objection to the Joyce of the post-structuralists in the conclusion of his book:

> Their problem is that their reading is always already established: Joyce … escapes, deconstructs, differs. The norm may be science, phallocentrism, or metaphysics, and the deconstruction feminist, masculinist, Marxist, or Freudian, but the a priori structure is always one of exception; in each case the attempt to describe the aberration is impossible by definition. No text could really (absolutely) escape, and if there were such a text, one could not write about it. (239–40)

Lernout's objection to Joycean post-structuralism resembles that of Felski to critique: "My objection is not to the existence of norms as such—without which thinking could not take place—but to the relentless grip, in recent years, of what we could call an antinormative normativity: skepticism as dogma" (Felski 9). Both Lernout and Felski dislike readings with preordained anti-normative positions. Since those readings already know what they want to say, they do not listen, they do not respond, and so cannot be responsible. Lernout's objection to one particular form of critique effectively supports Felski's broader objection to critique because it is compelling. It is certainly the case that, from its inception, the post-structuralist Joyce has been a construct designed to unite and personify particular related principles from the fields of politics, philosophy, and aesthetics. Furthermore, Lernout is quite right to observe that post-structuralist readings of Joyce are often so hyperbolic that they make claims as to how Joyce's texts function that could not possibly be proven—for example, in "Ambiviolences" when Heath speaks of the *Wake* as being a "text that resists any homogenization" (31–2). Lernout's negative view of the post-structuralist Joyce is one that has been held by many Joyce scholars in the last three decades and this is why the post-structuralist Joyce is now largely a historical figure.

The end of the post-structuralist Joyce was not the end of critique within Joyce studies. As noted, when the post-structuralist Joyce waned in the late 1980s, Joyce studies shifted its focus to readings concerned with Joyce's engagements with the history, politics, and culture of his age. Those readings, especially the postcolonial readings, frequently adhere to Felski's definition of *"literature as critique"* (16). While Joyce studies today retains a strong interest in locating Joyce within the events and ideologies of his time, the dominant mode within Joyce studies for at least as long as I've been involved in that field, which is about fifteen years now, has been that of genetic criticism. The best means of judging the current relevance of the post-structuralist Joyce, and thereby the mode of critique it offers, is therefore by defining the relationship between Joycean post-structuralism and Joycean genetic criticism.

To quickly gain a sense of the operative conception of genetic criticism within contemporary Joyce studies, it is helpful to look at the 2004 book *Genetic Criticism: Texts and Avant-Textes*, which was edited by the noted Joyce scholars Jed Deppman, Daniel Ferrer, and Michael Groden. In the introduction to that book, Ferrer and Groden offer this definition of genetic criticism:

> Like old-fashioned philology or textual criticism, it examines tangible documents such as writers' notes, drafts, and proof corrections, but its real object is something much more abstract—not the existing documents but the movement of writing that must be inferred from them. Then, too, it remains concrete, for it never posits an ideal text beyond those documents but rather strives to reconstruct, from all available evidence, the chain of events in a writing process. (2)

Such a mode of criticism is clearly a long way from Felskian critique. Indeed, not only is genetic criticism not discussed in *The Limits of Critique*, it is also the case that, when Felski lists some of "many scholars who choose to cultivate quite different gardens" to critique, she includes those who work in the related field of "textual editing" (26). Given the extent to which Joycean post-structuralism adheres to Felski's definition of critique, it is clearly quite different to Joycean genetic criticism. But this is not to say that the two are unrelated.

One can understand the connection between Joycean genetic criticism and Joycean post-structuralism by examining that between the two larger critical modes of which they are Joycean variants. As one might infer from Ferrer and Groden's description of genetic criticism as "striving to reconstruct" the "chain of events in a writing process," they regard that critical mode as "a true child of the French structuralist movement" (2). In saying this, Ferrer and Groden seek not to define genetic criticism as a mode of structuralism but rather as a product of structuralism. From their perspectives, genetic criticism is by no means antithetical to post-structuralism. In fact, Ferrer and Groden regard post-structuralism as an influence on genetic criticism and provide these two characterizations of the nature of that influence:

> [Genetic criticism] grows out of a structuralist and poststructuralist notion of "text" as an infinite play of signs, but it accepts a teleological model of textuality and constantly confronts the question of authorship. (2)

> The decisive fertilizing influence (and necessary foil) was the complex conception of text introduced by structuralism and poststructuralism in the 1960s and 1970s

> ... theorists such as Roland Barthes and Jacques Derrida saw texts as mobile, multistranded, and overflowing with referential codes ... Genetic criticism took up the notion of writing's mobility but observed that a text conceived as methodologically separate from its origins and from its material incarnation can lead to a paradoxical sacralization and idealization of it as *The Text*. (5)

In both quotes, Ferrer and Groden point to the "structuralist and poststructuralist notion of 'text'" (2). By this, they primarily mean the notion of "Text" introduced by Barthes in his 1971 essay "From Work to Text" (523). As is often the case with Barthes's work, it is difficult to rigidly align that piece with either structuralism or post-structuralism. The ideas within it derive from the former and are developed into the latter. This being the case, what can at least be said is that the conclusions of the essay are post-structuralist. This reading is supported by the fact that the notion of "Text" offered in Barthes's essay is frequently utilized in post-structuralist readings of Joyce. Heath's essay, for example, frequently echoes it.

Within "From Work to Text," the notion of the "Text" operates in opposition to that of the "work." While the latter is the traditional conception of the literary text, the former is something quite different. Barthes offers a number of characterizations of the "Text," and the most helpful takes the form of an extended metaphor:

> [T]he reader of the Text might be compared to an idle subject ...: this fairly empty subject strolls ... along a hillside at the bottom of which flows a wadi ...; what he perceives is multiple, irreducible, issuing from heterogeneous, detached substances and levels: lights, colors, vegetation, heat, air, tenuous explosions of sound, tiny cries of birds, children's voices from the other side of the valley, paths, gestures, garments of inhabitants close by or very far away; all these incidents are half identifiable: they issue from known codes, but their combinative operation is unique, it grounds the stroll in a difference which cannot be repeated except as *difference*. (525)

Within this metaphor as within much of the essay, Barthes defines the "Text" as ideal and the "work" as material. The "Text" is here the sum of the sensations apprehended by the stroller and each sensation can be understood as a signifier. The "work" is the sum of the objects that have caused those sensations. What is important to realize is that what is perceived by the stroller is not simply the sum of the received sensations but rather the product of the unique operation by which the stroller has united those sensations. This complex perception represents the reader's conception of the text.

Barthes's extended metaphor explains why Ferrer and Groden speak of the "Text" as being "multistranded" and "overflowing with referential codes" (5). In the sentence that contains those terms, Ferrer and Groden also describe the "Text" as being "mobile" (5). This word points to the idea that, just as the stroller's perception of the hillside develops over the course of their walk, so the reader's conception of the "Text" changes and evolves as the reader moves through it. In the other of the two previously quoted passages in which Ferrer and Groden speak of the "Text," they refer to it as an "infinite play of signs" (2). To understand this phrase, one needs to know that Barthes's preferred term for the process by which the reader engages with the "Text" and so produces his/her/their conception of it is "play" (526). One of the purposes of this term is to highlight the idea that the reader's conception of the "Text" is not merely the result of the active reader's examination of the passive text but rather the product of an interaction between "Text" and reader in which both are active. If this sounds familiar, that is because Heath and Felski both draw upon the notion of "play" in their models of reading. For Barthes, the reason the "play" of the "Text" is infinite is that, as he makes clear in his description of the reader's metaphorical nature walk, each act of reading is a singular, subjective event and so none can be definitive.

When one has a clear sense of the Barthesian "Text," one can see how different it is to the text of genetic criticism. The former is an infinite, ideal text within the mind of the reader. The latter is a finite, material text on the page of the author. These two conceptions of textuality both regard the text as a complex construct, but each privileges a different constructor and a different mode of language. Barthes clarifies the difference between the two in "From Work to Text" when he contrasts the metaphor of the "Text" with that of the "work": "The metaphor of the Text is here again detached from the metaphor of the work; the latter refers to the image of an *organism* which grows by vital expansion, by 'development' ...; the metaphor of the Text is that of the *network*" (525). As Barthes explains elsewhere in the essay, what he means by "network," is "a system without end or center" (524). In defining the "network" against the "organism," Barthes contrasts the open, fluid structure of the post-structuralist "Text" against the bounded, determined structure of the text of genetic criticism. Naturally, the metaphor of text as organism is built into the term "genetic criticism."

The difference between the Barthesian "Text" and the text of genetic criticism makes it difficult for Ferrer and Groden to argue for the post-structuralist influence on genetic criticism. For example, to return to an earlier quote, after discussing Barthes's distinction between "Text" and "work" in "From Work to Text," Ferrer and Groden assert that "[g]enetic criticism took up the notion of writing's mobility but observed that a text conceived as methodologically separate from its origins and from its material incarnation can lead to a paradoxical sacralization and idealization of it as *The Text*" (5). The problem with the idea of genetic criticism holding both of these positions is that the notion of "writing's mobility," as it functions in Barthes's essay, is a product of the immateriality of the "Text." One cannot have one without the other. Genetic criticism does engage with "writing's mobility," but it does so within its own conception of textuality by examining "the movement of writing" within a composition process (Ferrer and Groden 5, 2). This example shows that post-structuralist notions of how texts function cannot be applied to the text of genetic criticism because they are predicated upon a very different model of textuality.

In considering the relationship between genetic criticism and post-structuralism, one can see why Joycean genetic criticism and Joycean post-structuralism differ so much. To call genetic criticism and post-structuralism opposed would be inaccurate since the former focuses on the material text and the latter on the ideal, but it is the case that the structural models through which they understand their respective texts are opposed. Post-structuralism defines itself in part through its critique of the structuralist models of textuality that underpin critical modes like genetic criticism.

However, for all their differences, Joycean genetic criticism and Joycean post-structuralism have much to say to one another and should be more in dialogue with one another within Joyce studies as a whole and especially within the subfield in which both achieve their most powerful effects, *Wake* studies. In *The French Joyce*, Lernout demonstrates how the principles of textual modes of criticism like that of genetic criticism can benefit Joycean post-structuralism. His critique of the post-structuralist Joyce is productive and helpful because it points to significant errors and lacunae within that conception of Joyce and so indicates to post-structuralist Joyceans how they can amend and improve their critical approach. In the last part of this essay, I will adopt a similarly constructive approach to the relationship between Joycean genetic criticism and Joycean post-structuralism but view it from the opposite perspective to that of Lernout. Joycean post-structuralism has much to offer Joycean genetic criticism and this is because of rather than despite its mode of critique. There are three central means by which Joycean post-structuralism can benefit Joycean genetic criticism.

The Value of the Equivocal

Post-structuralist readings of Joyce define his works as critiquing the manner in which meaning normally functions in works of literature. Such readings further hold that, in doing this, Joyce's works also critique the means by which critics conventionally engage with the meanings of literary texts. When one knows the history of the post-structuralist Joyce, one can see that the true target of the critiques that post-structuralists ascribe to Joyce is simplification. Behind all the images of destruction and incapacity that one finds in post-structuralist readings of Joyce lies the Derridean vision of Joyce's texts as vast, overflowing, all-encompassing works whose meanings transcend and unite. In attacking other critical modes on the grounds of meaning, the goal of Joycean post-structuralists is to make other Joyce critics fully and deeply engage with the abundance, complexity, and fluidity of meaning to be found in Joyce's works.

For all its hyperbole and theatricality, Derrida's conception of Joyce's writing is relevant and useful to Joycean genetic criticism and especially to genetic readings of the *Wake*. This is because such readings often use Joyce's notes and drafts to reveal the conventional words and phrases from which Joyce's *Wake*an portmanteaus derive. For example, in discussing the dialogue between Paddrock and Balkelly in book four of *Finnegans Wake*, genetic scholars frequently point out that Balkelly's Kantian phrase "the Ding hvad in idself id est" derives from the phrase "this thing in itself," which appears in the middle of this entry in notebook VI.B.3: "Culter of this thing in itself see the grass (r+o+y+g+b+i+v)" (FW 611.21. VI.B.3: 64–5; JJA 29: 212). When one knows that "the Ding hvad in idself id est" is an adaptation of "this thing in itself," it is all too easy to privilege the latter phrase as the meaning or essential signification of the former and so to overlook, or at least relegate the significance of, the other words and phrases that can be found in "the Ding hvad in idself id est." These include the German "ding" [thing], the Danish "hvad" [what], the Latin "id est" [that is], and the Freudian "Id."

The question raised by Derrida's discussion of equivocity is that of the value of each signification. As noted, for a word to be "equivocal" is for it to have "different significations" that are "*equally* appropriate or plausible" ("Equivocal, Adj. and n."; emphasis added). This certainly challenges the idea that there can be one signification of a word or phrase that is substantially more essential than the others. In my view, when looking at the significations of a word or phrase in the *Wake*, the reader should neither privilege one at the expense of the others nor view all as equal but rather take a mediate approach and construct a hierarchy of signification by judging and relating the values of the different significations. This approach can be illustrated through the prior example, "the Ding hvad in idself id est" (FW 611.21). It is certainly the case that "thing in itself" is not only the root but also the primary signification of this phrase (VI.B.3: 64–5; JJA 29: 212). When one knows this, one can see the importance of the word "ding." Not only does it reference Kant's original German phrase, "Ding an sich," of which "thing in itself" is a translation, but it also counterpoints the notion of the unitary "*thing* in itself" by demonstrating the multiple ways in which that notion can be expressed (emphasis added). This is why "ding" is the secondary signification. To go one step further, since the phrase in question is concerned with interiority—that which things are in themselves rather than that which they appear to be—the Freudian "Id" is the tertiary signification. The idea that Joyce is referencing that notion is supported by the fact that Joyce combines "id" and "self" in the word "idself" (FW 611.21).

When Joycean post-structuralism pushes Joycean genetic criticism into more complex models of meaning such as this, it does so through both its critique of the models of meaning it regards as simplistic and its assertion of the complex model of meaning it supports. Both approaches are needed because each relies on the other.

Remember the Reader

When Joycean post-structuralists critique more traditional critical approaches to Joyce's works, one of the reasons they often do so is because they regard such criticism as positing a model of meaning in which Joyce puts his meanings into the text and then the reader discovers those meanings. For Joycean post-structuralists, this model underestimates the agency of the reader. Such critics regard the reader and the text as working together to create the meanings that the reader apprehends when engaging with the text. As noted, this aspect of the post-structuralist Joyce resembles Felski's notion of post-critical reading. Just as Felski clears the space for that notion through her critique of critique, so Joycean post-structuralists make room for their model of reading by challenging the idea of the author as the locus of meaning.

The privileging of reader over author within Joycean post-structuralism is a key factor within its relationship to Joycean genetic criticism because the latter takes the opposite approach. This makes sense given that Joycean genetic criticism focuses on the writing process rather than the reading process. Understandably, the consequence of each approach is that either the author or the reader is overlooked. Just as post-structuralist readings often speak of Joyce's intentions while denying that it is possible to access them, so genetic readings frequently neglect to acknowledge that Joyce's texts are constructed by their readers as well as by their author. Indeed, to even speak of those two processes of construction as separate is an error. As Ferrer and Groden point out, the "real object" of genetic criticism is "not the existing documents but the movement of writing that must be inferred from them" (2). Such inference can be conducted only by a reader.

Joycean genetic criticism is much more effective when it unites its own interest in the author with the post-structuralist interest in the reader. A good recent example of this is Finn Fordham's *Lots of Fun at Finnegans Wake*. In that book's extensive and illuminating introduction, Fordham defines multiple critical approaches to *Finnegans Wake* and then locates his own genetic approach amongst them. In doing so, Fordham defines himself as a reader and outlines both the capacities and limitations of his own critical method. While Fordham is by his own admission no post-structuralist, the humility and self-consciousness of his critical approach incorporates many of the best qualities of post-structuralism.

What needs to be emphasized about the positivity of the conception of the reader that operates within Joycean post-structuralism is that it is by no means anomalous. That aspect of the post-structuralist Joyce is a product of its critique of the agency of the author. If one views the model of reading advocated by Joycean post-structuralism as a form of, to use Felski's term, "postcritical reading," then the prefix "post" there means "from" rather than "after" or "against."

Beyond the "Teleological Model of Textuality"

Ferrer and Groden say of genetic criticism that it "accepts a teleological model of textuality" (2). When that model is used in Joycean genetic criticism, it is commonly used to show how a piece of text evolves as it passes from a source text into a notebook and then across multiple drafts and often multiple publications before landing in the final work. If post-structuralism were consistent, it would feel no need to oppose this model because it relates to the material text of the author rather than the ideal text of the reader. Yet, as Barthes's "From Work to Text" demonstrates, this is not the case:

> The intertextuality in which any text is apprehended, since it is the intertext of another text, cannot be identified with some *origin* of the text: to seek out the "sources," the "influences" of a work is to satisfy the myth of filiation; the quotations a text is made of are anonymous, irrecoverable, and yet *already read*: they are quotations without quotation marks. (525)

Barthes here challenges the "teleological model of textuality" by arguing against the idea that one can locate the origins of a text. It follows that if one cannot locate those origins, one cannot chart the text's movement toward its final form. To make this argument, however, Barthes must conflate the ideal readerly "Text" and the material authorial "work" through the term "text." At the start of the sentence, he speaks of "the intertextuality in which any text is apprehended," which is the intertextuality of the "Text." This form of intertextuality relates to the texts that a reader perceives to be quoted or referenced within a particular text. In the second clause of that sentence, however, Barthes goes on to talk about "the 'sources,' the 'influences' of a work." This is a different form of intertextuality that relates to the texts that an author draws upon in creating a new text. The purpose of this shift is to allow Barthes to depict the origins of a material authorial "work" as being as impossible to locate as those of an ideal readerly "Text." What is purposefully overlooked here is that, while the particular spark of inspiration that inspired any one work of literature cannot be fully recovered, many authors leave behind large quantities of *avant-textes* of different forms—drafts, notes, outlines, and so on—that enable critics to gain relative understandings of how the material composition processes of those authors began. Nonetheless, it remains the case that post-structuralism critiques the "teleological model of textuality" and one need only look to Heath or MacCabe to see that this is very much the case with post-structuralist Joyce criticism (Ferrer and Groden 2).

When one turns from the theoretical to the practical, however, one can see that there is little need to make the case that Joycean genetic criticism should cast out the "teleological model of textuality." In *Wake* studies and beyond, Joycean genetic criticism frequently transcends that model. Thanks in part to the ongoing debate surrounding Hans Walter Gabler's synoptic edition of *Ulysses*, it is today generally the case that Joyce scholars have little faith in the notion of a stable, final text. One can see this in *Wake* studies. While editions of *Finnegans Wake* tend to be more uniform than those of *Ulysses* and most share the same text and pagination, the text of the *Wake* that appears in most editions is rarely regarded as the end of that work's textual evolution. One of the main reasons for this is that that text is known to contain so many errors of so many different kinds that those errors have in themselves become a significant source of critical interest.

Just as the idea of the *Wake* as a telos is frequently challenged, so the notion of pieces of text travelling along a singular, linear path from their source texts to the *Wake* is often complicated. One of the recent books to most effectively do this is Dirk Van Hulle's *James Joyce's "Work in Progress": Pre-Book Publications of* Finnegans Wake *Fragments*. This book highlights the notion that, when Joyce published fragments of the *Wake* in journals and as books, these publications were ends in themselves as much as they were steps toward the publication of the entire work. This notion is very helpful because it allows one to view the composition of the *Wake* both as one coherent process and as the sum of multiple, overlapping, intertwined composition processes.

In critiquing the "teleological model of textuality," the most important idea that Joycean post-structuralism has to offer *Wake* studies, and indeed Joyce studies more broadly, relates neither to the end nor the middle of the composition process but rather to its beginning (Ferrer and Groden 2). One of the standard tasks of Joycean genetic criticism is that of locating the source texts for Joyce's notes. This arduous, labor-intensive work is incredibly valuable to Joyce studies as a whole. That being said, there is also validity to the post-structuralist objection to the notion of the source text. That notion marks such texts as points of origin, but, when one actually reads Joyce's source texts, one often finds that they are not direct expressions of original thought but rather nonfiction works that are full of quotes, paraphrases, and summaries. As a consequence of this, it is frequently the case that a Joycean note does not derive directly from its ascribed source text but rather from a work referenced in that text. While it is not necessary to cast out the idea that Joyce's notes have origins and instead embrace an infinite intertextuality, there is a need for a new terminology that recognizes that a piece of text often passes through multiple works before inspiring a Joycean note. Such terminology would need to be able to define grades of mediation as well as genuine points of origin.

Clearly, while Joycean post-structuralism strays beyond its boundaries in critiquing the "teleological model of textuality," that critique is useful because it encourages the complication and expansion of that model. Joycean genetic criticism already gains from responding to that critique and would benefit from doing so more fully.

To conclude, Joycean post-structuralism bears many of the essential qualities of Felskian critique: skepticism, radicalism, political intent, intolerance of alternate approaches. Because of this, Joycean post-structuralism has a number of the flaws that Felski locates within critique, most notably its predefined anti-normative stance. At the same time, however, Joycean post-structuralism also challenges Felski's negative view of critique by demonstrating the virtues of such an approach. In critiquing models of meaning, authorship, and textuality that it deems reductive, Joycean post-structuralism creates the space for its complex, thought-provoking conceptions of Joyce's texts. This important and necessary work makes Joycean post-structuralism relevant and useful to the genetic approach that prevails in contemporary Joyce studies. One need not brush aside its excesses and limitations to recognize the value of its critique.

References

Barthes, Roland. "From Work to Text." *Literary Theory: An Anthology*, edited by Julie Rivkin and Michael Ryan. John Wiley, 2017, pp. 522–7.

Derrida, Jacques. *Edmund Husserl's* Origin of Geometry: *An Introduction*, translated by John P. Leavey, Jr. U of Nebraska P, 1989.

Derrida, Jacques. "Two Words for Joyce." *Post-Structuralist Joyce: Essays from the French*, edited by Derek Attridge and Daniel Ferrer. Cambridge UP, 1984, pp. 145–59.

"Equivocal, Adj. and n." *OED Online*. Oxford UP, http://www.oed.com/view/Entry/63848. Accessed June 2, 2020.

Felski, Rita. *The Limits of Critique*. U of Chicago P, 2015.

Ferrer, Daniel, and Michael Groden. "Introduction: A Genesis of French Genetic Criticism." *Genetic Criticism: Texts and Avant-Textes*, edited by Jed Deppman, Daniel Ferrer, and Michael Groden. U of Pennsylvania P, 2004, pp. 1–16.

Fordham, Finn. *Lots of Fun at* Finnegans Wake: *Unravelling Universals*. Oxford UP, 2007.

Heath, Stephen. "Ambiviolences: Notes for Reading Joyce." *Post-Structuralist Joyce: Essays from the French*, edited by Derek Attridge and Daniel Ferrer. Cambridge UP, 1984, pp. 31–68.

Hulle, Dirk van. *James Joyce's "Work in Progress": Pre-Book Publications of* Finnegans Wake *Fragments*. Routledge, 2016.

Joyce, James. *Finnegans Wake*, edited by Robbert-Jan Henkes et al. Oxford UP, 2012.

Joyce, James. *The James Joyce Archive*, edited by Michael Groden et al. Garland, 1978–9.

Lernout, Geert. *The French Joyce*. U of Michigan P, 1992.

MacCabe, Colin. *James Joyce and the Revolution of the Word*. Macmillan, 1979.

Platt, Len. "'Now, Just Wash and Brush up Your Memoirias': Nation Building, the Historical Record, and Cultural Memory in *Finnegans Wake* 3.3." *Memory*

Ireland: Volume 4: James Joyce and Cultural Memory, edited by Oona Frawley and Katherine O'Callaghan. Syracuse UP, 2014, pp. 112–24.

Slote, Sam. "'Après Mot, Le Déluge' 2: Literary and Theoretical Responses to Joyce in France." *The Reception of James Joyce in Europe*, vol. 2, edited by Geert Lernout and Wim Van Mierlo. Thoemmes Continuum, 2004, pp. 382–410.

3

Responsible Reading of Theory

Fabio Akcelrud Durão

In the last fifteen years or so literary studies have been passing through a radical process of self-questioning. Contrary to former waves of change, at stake today is not just a matter of new trends—not new concepts, movements, or even areas—but rather a full reconsideration of the very foundations of the discipline. It's not that, say, "multitude" replaces "différance," or that suddenly postcolonialism appears sharper and more powerful than new historicism; nor is one concerned about which noun will next precede that curious particle "studies": a dispositive that transforms contents into fields. Instead, critics are challenging basic methodological issues, most clearly identified in recent considerations of reading and critique as *practices*. As we know, opposing the conception of the former as "close" and "deep" there are now calls for "distant," "surface," "casual," and "with-the-grain" reading. As for critique, the proposal is for an overcoming, albeit a strategic or nonbelligerent one, through what has been termed "post-critique."[1] These are reformulations that can significantly alter the whole edifice of literary studies, with implications that go beyond everyday practice in the classroom to involve institutional setups and the social legitimacy of literary study. In sum, then, we have to do here with nothing less than a thorough reshaping of the self-representation of literary studies.

I propose that we approach this heated and potentially exasperating debate by way of a detour, which at the same time is a return, namely, to the problem of Theory, properly capitalized for reasons that will be explained below. If we agree that the present crisis has its roots in the challenges Theory posed to literary study, canon formation, and the notion of culture in the 1970s–2000s, then it makes good sense to reassess theoretical discourse to ask what a responsible reading of Theory today might be. My intention is to evade the controversy spurred by such volumes as Corral and Patai's *Theory's Empire*, which tend to organize the discussion as an impoverishing opposition between accusers and defenders. My first contention, then, is that the present crisis paradoxically furnishes a propitious opportunity to rethink Theory with the benefit of hindsight regarding its unfulfilled promises and of foresight in relation to what current alternatives seem to project for the future. A responsible reading of Theory must avoid the two most obvious paths: those of proposing either an alternative to Theory or its sheer continuation, pretending nothing serious is really happening. This third way must displace the opposition of the new versus the same, an objective I think we can achieve if we consider Theory as a *genre*. This chapter is an initial step in that direction. It is divided into three parts: (1) a conceptual frame to characterize Theory as genre by investigating its founding contradiction, experiential ground, discursive rearrangements, material support, and symbolic function; (2) the risks Theory presents to itself; and finally (3) two reading strategies for reading Theory responsibly, maintaining it, but with a change. Of course, this framework should not be taken as exhaustive, but rather as an exercise, in both senses of the word, of theoretical imagination.

I

Let's start with a still common form of reading: Bakhtin without Dostoyevsky and Rabelais, Deleuze without Proust and Kafka, Derrida without Rousseau (and many others), Lacan without Freud, Freud without Sophocles, and so on. It won't do to assume a moralist posture—"our students (or colleagues!) don't read literature anymore"; it is much more fruitful to accept as a fact that for many scholars, students, and even nonacademics, Theory has an appeal of its own, above and beyond the objects it might be supposed to explain. Publishing houses have long realized this, as I first became aware many years ago as I saw a German edition of *Elective Affinities* in which the text of the novel preceded Walter Benjamin's essay like an introduction, a secondary text. Or, more recently, when I found Foucault's complete works edited by Gallimard's *Biblioteque de La Pléiade*, in the same collection with Racine, Baudelaire, or Proust (needless to say, I bought them all, Goethe—or was it Benjamin?—and Foucault). The most obvious case is the *Norton Anthology of Theory and Criticism*, which extends to theorists the whole scholarly approach normally reserved to the literary monuments of the past. Here each author has their own biographical introduction, bibliographic set of references (quite often commentary of commentary), and footnotes which frequently feel strained: by explaining what seems unnecessary or irrelevant they give the impression of just fulfilling a formal role, of being there to justify anthologization and the philological treatment of critics.[2] There are, then, abundant signs that theory has lost its supposed ancillary role—its status as a subordinate discourse whose primordial mission would be to elucidate a given text. So here is a first idea, not so much a discovery as an observation of a state of affairs, though one that has not received as much attention as it deserves, namely that *theory has passed through a process of (semi) autonomization and increasing self-sufficiency and self-referentiality, thus becoming Theory.*

I hate parentheses expressing ambiguity, but in the case of Theory's (semi) autonomy they are unavoidable. On the one hand, as was already mentioned, Theory seems often enough to be impatient with objects. How many articles have you read in which you feel that the whole impetus of the writing is to employ as many times as possible one or more buzz notions? To use the Russian Formalists' term, reality becomes the motivation of the device for terminological innovation—as for instance the impression one has at times that for Žižek the world exists to explain Lacan. On the other hand, no matter how independent Theory may aim to be, it never manages to become really intransitive: theory is always theory *of* something. Much of Theory's controversial character arises from this impasse resulting from the drive toward autonomy, which we will see is not devoid of reason, and its impossible concretization.

Let's agree that for a new genre to emerge at least two conditions must be fulfilled: one paradigmatic and the other syntagmatic. No new genre can take shape without connections to determinate forms of experience, which it then helps solidify and make visible. However, no new genre can become consistent without borrowing from already existing ones and/or rearranging their contents in new configurations. In order to approach the former, one must characterize Theory historically, which is indeed a thorny problem, given the potential suppleness of the object. For Rodowick, Theory can be traced back all the way to ancient Greece, while the essays collected by Herman occupy the opposite point of the spectrum by linking specific theoretical trends to quite punctual historical occurrences. An intermediary case is that of North's political history, which associates the current crisis of literary studies to a prevalence of scholars over critics in a tension that has followed the incorporation of literature in the university since the nineteenth century (the distinction is discussed by Graff). As with a number of other fluid objects, periodization here is best conceived as part of the object it analyzes: the validity of its temporal structuring should be judged together with the cogency of its analysis.

The story I would like to propose starts with the social transformations of postwar Europe, especially France, and which includes three main elements: the emergence of a generation whose ties with its immediate past were severed; a remarkable expansion of the educational system, especially at the university level, and including the humanities; and a new level of commodification of culture, allowing for the consolidation of high-culture industry. From this conjuncture arose a new kind of intellectual, quite different from the philosopher and the *homme de lettres* (Kauppi): the theorist. At first identified with structuralism, the theorist, claimed to speak in the name of science, could have a conflict-laden relationship to existing academic institutions, but would not shy away from speaking to a general audience. An avant-garde ethos, too, helped give a sense of momentous novelty and change to Theory's pronouncements. *Tel Quel*'s case is paradigmatic here: founded by young privileged writers in their mid-twenties,[3] the journal was immensely successful. It was never associated to academic institutions, which were spurned, though a considerable part of its sales were due to university libraries' subscriptions, and its successive phases were always ushered in with a feeling of urgency and beginning from scratch.

All of this is to say that there was a *cultural substratum* or structure of feeling, if you want, in which Theory thrived and which it also reinforced. Ideas were not just things one organized into arguments; instead, they invited ways of being and of interacting with other people. Take *écriture*, for instance: it was not just a term in an intellectual debate, nor was it a simple tool for understanding reality. Rather, it was a concept with a promise, a harbinger of a possible reconfiguration of the world, joining language, desire, and economy in the same term. Again, in however attenuated and modified a fashion, Theory carried on something of an avant-garde, perhaps even revolutionary ethos. As a living illustration of this, we can turn to the narrative Philipp Felsch tells of Peter Gente, the founder of Merve Verlag, in his *Der lange Sommer der Theorie*. In its summer, "theory was more than a succession of thoughts in the brain [*Kopfgedanken*]; it was a claim to truth, an article of faith and part of a lifestyle"[4] (Felsch 12). Merve's founders and their friends saw themselves before anything as impassioned readers, and theirs "was not only a publishing house, but rather a reading group and a community of fans [*Fangemeinde*]—in sum: a reception nexus [*Rezeptionszusammenhang*]" (19). In short, then, for a considerable time, editing books couldn't be described as a job, not even as work properly speaking, for it seemed to represent an adventure with new ways of unveiling and imagining the world. Even though universities functioned as catalysts, bringing people together, the decisive aspect was that ideas appeared to broaden one's horizon of experience at the same time that they elucidated reality: cafés, restaurants and bars vied with auditoria. It's no coincidence that this period witnesses the emergence of the paperback theory book, like Seuil and Suhrkamp's *Theorie* series, and Merve's. The paperback theory book is particularly revealing: as a small and cheap object it can be carried and read anywhere. It's not the kind of book you read in the library, but in a park, train, or study group. More than that, it desacralizes the book as a vehicle of knowledge. To conclude, and to play it low, let's agree that theory was at the very least *exciting*.[5]

The discussion so far helps us formulate some hypotheses regarding the textual rearrangements effected by Theory as a genre. The main one is that Theory has been converted into a problematically separate realm by demarcating a space which is strictly speaking neither that of philosophy nor that of literary criticism anymore, even though it is closer to the latter and may seem indistinguishable from it. In relation to philosophy, Theory downplays the role of tradition and of history. Individual philosophers are dealt with on their own, without recourse to the long succession of answers to fundamental philosophical questions. Once concepts are wrenched from the long conversation that constituted them, they acquire something of a prêt-à-porter character, the possibility of being easily mobilized in new situations and for new objects. As far as Theory is concerned, breaking up traditions, both the philosophical and the literary, is as unavoidable and structural as the number of hours of study is limited.[6] Important here for the mediation between philosophy and criticism was the emergence of language as the central theoretical problem, which allowed for a relatively smooth inclusion of philosophers and literary scholars in a common ground, and which was only further reinforced by a renewed central role assigned to literary works in philosophical reflection. In relation to literary criticism, the main transformation brought about by Theory, as has been suggested already, lies in the primacy given to conceptual elaboration in textual analysis, which now becomes much more sophisticated and productively self-conscious.

The formation of a culture of theory was an important factor for its rise as a genre; another one was its institutionalization in the academy, which redirected and reshaped such culture. Only after theory fully entered the university did it make sense to refer to it with a capital "T" to mark its conversion into a field of inquiry, however nebulous, self-contradictory, and self-denying it may conceive itself to be.

If in France and Germany theory thrived in a public sphere in tandem with the university, when it travelled to the Anglophone world it reached a broader audience only after it was institutionalized. This doesn't mean that it lost its capacity to excite and captivate—which incidentally reminds how porous the university can be. The academic circumstances were however different. Even if it dislodged philosophy, theory in Europe remained closely related to it; after crossing the Atlantic however, it found hostile departments of analytical philosophy which encouraged its assimilation in English and comparative literature departments. The centrality structuralism assigned to language found a happy complement in the Anglo-Saxon practice of close reading. Theory's culture spilled over the academy's walls and influenced larger circles; two telling examples will have to suffice here. First, as Ryan shows, Theory provided conceptual *topoi* which inspired literary creation. Second, as Cousset illustrates, Theory quickly exerted a powerful influence in the American pop culture industry, exemplified in Woody Allen's "*Deconstructing Harry* (1997) which appeared in French under the title *Harry dans tous ses états*, because the verb 'to deconstruct' doesn't mean much [*dit rien qui vaille*] to the French audience" (119).[7] Furthermore, the culture of Theory in the Anglophone world became a means for conceptualizing one's group and identity. To the excitement of explaining the world was added the revelation of finding one's self and tribe, not to mention the liberating possibility of converting sex into an object of reflection and academic discussion. However, after becoming firmly rooted in the North American academic system, Theory was exported to the whole world, coalescing something close to a lingua franca, a set of common references that may even surpass literature's in its cohesion. This boomerang effect produced some uncanny returns in Europe as well, for instance when students read Spivak without knowing of Derrida. Even more fascinating is experiencing the mixture of both in a peripheral country like mine, Brazil, where, say, the French and the Anglophone Deleuze inhabit the same institutional space with sometimes very stimulating misunderstandings.

But a new genre does more than just convert a certain content, the experiential substratum mentioned above, into form, with the rules governing its functioning; it may also be viewed as expressing some underlying collective concern, in which case it can be approached as a symptom. One of Theory's most basic and crucial concepts is that of "text"; its initial structuralist formulation survived subsequent criticism and even today maintains wide currency in virtually all theoretical trends from deconstruction to postcolonial criticism and cultural studies. So let's revisit Barthes's seminal "De l'oeuvre au texte."[8] This quasi-manifesto is structured according to the binary opposition between the two nouns of the title. It is composed of seven "propositions" which deal with the following topics: method, genres, the sign, the plural, filiation, reading, and pleasure. The contradiction between the content of the concept of text and its *Darstellung* is striking, as has been generations of readers' blindness to it; however, even more revealing is the degree to which the text needs such binarism to stand on its own. The "work" is a "traditional notion ..., Newtonian" (1211), "a fragment of substance" (1212), "it is enclosed in a signified" [*se ferme sur un signifié*]" (1213), "is caught in a process of filiation" (1214), "is ... an object of consumption" (1215), the knowledge it yields is "quite sad" (1216), and so on. The exercise is worth trying: when one imagines the text without the counterweight of the work, the difficulty becomes apparent as the argument seems to float and acquire a dreamlike character. Hence, the intriguing reversal in the fact that the "text" is most productive when it is not taken on its own, but wrenched from the readerly work—which is not a bad definition of *S/Z*. There is something close to a performative paradox here in that the (great) interpretative insights take place in the backcloth of the work's limitations. However, no empirical object would be able to fulfill what is expected from the text, the libidinal energy invested in it, not even *Finnegans Wake*.[9] The fact that the text is not a real object allows us to posit that it fulfills a *compensatory role*, that it is supposed to offer something that existing culture is not capable of. From an Anglo-Saxon, anthropological sense of culture, the cohesion of a human group through a shared set of symbolic codes and practices, we move to the old-fashioned German one of *Kultur*, something that points beyond the sheer reproduction of existence. Barthes's case lets us glimpse how Theory can embody a yearning for something other, for a "more" that seems to be denied to existing culture. The leap is certainly a huge one, but even so I would like to argue that such a compensatory role is extensive to Theory as a whole: meaning here—together with the power of elucidation it performatively brings about—ends up fulfilling the role of expressing wonder in its own articulation.[10]

II

This discussion of the text as production can serve as a transition to the risks Theory poses to itself. Let's first investigate how Theory's contradictory transitivity generates its own temporal complications by going back again to the formative moment of structuralism: Gerard Genette's "Poetique et histoire," a lecture given at Cerisy-la-Salle in 1969, and published in *Figures III* in 1972. The text's main idea is that system and history can be reconciled once structures have been sufficiently studied so that they could be mapped out in time. Never mind the unfeasibility of the project—structures are too mobile, are too much embedded in time to be fixed—what is relevant to us here is this introductory observation:

> I remember answering Jacques Roger three years ago, in this same place, that concerning the so-called "formalist" criticism, this apparent refusal of history is just a provisory bracketing, a methodological suspension, and that this kind of criticism (which certainly will be called precisely *theory of literary forms*—or, in short, *poetics*) to me seemed destined, more than anything else, to meet history one day in its way. I would like now to try to say briefly why and how. (13)

The refusal of history is just a "provisional parenthesis," a "methodological suspension" that will be resolved by means of a new theory. This gesture is by no means particular, and can be found in countless other texts in the 1960s and 1970s, but it suffices to illustrate that figure typical to Theory, to use a term by the same Genette, of prolepsis: a projection to the future under the guise of a new name. Allusions to a completion in a foreseeable time abound in structuralism, which is perhaps natural given its ambition to unify the humanities in one single overarching scientific framework. This project was of course not realized nor, one is led to think, could it possibly be, but it is interesting to note how it legitimized concept formation. Proposing new terms and categories for literary analysis was justified in view of a coming fulfillment of the theory, which in turn was supported by the novel concept. In structuralism, presentism was a force not only of submitting the past to new reading codes, but also of conjuring the future in a dream of fulfillment.

The desire for an all-embracing general theory was soon criticized and abandoned (though it would be worthwhile to investigate its metamorphosed survival in the present), but the orientation toward the future persisted. Theoretical elaborations now point to their achievement as application, in what can be viewed as a promise: learn this new concept and your interpretative problems will be solved. Without a doubt, a number of theories, say Bloom's anxiety of influence or Moretti's distant reading, have been adopted and explored in different objects, but what is misleading about this promise is that it ignores that *the really productive (and exciting) moment is that of its formulation itself.* Applications are as rule derivative if not quite tedious.[11] No theory without the promise of a broader scope of validity than itself; no interesting theory when such extension is realized. Or to put it differently, the possibility of innovation is paid by forfeiting the future. Incidentally, this confers a new meaning, not deprived of irony, on that deconstructive conceptual suffix "to come."[12]

Theory's curious temporal structure leads us back again to the question of its relationship to production, now in relation to the neoliberal university, for whose modus operandi it seems to be strangely well suited.[13] In the first place, Theory speeds up the turnover of papers and books. Instead of having to master the historical sedimentation of a long-standing field, supported by old categories and the tradition of accumulated readings that give it unity, the critic can now confront a given corpus with a new concept, which as it were resets the whole debate. A more drastic case is that of ad hoc corpora that do not fit any preexisting disciplinary area; to be sure, new configurations of objects can be very interesting and exciting, but when the practice becomes an ethos in itself and the new is converted into an abstract value, something close to the logic of fashion is established. And let's remark in passing that the stricture against Theory regarding its often aggressive posture in debunking arguments, something defenders of post-critique are keen to point out, may at least in part be accounted for by the current competitive academic milieu. Theory's adaptation to university Darwinism in a context of the shrinking of tenured positions is not a fateful one, and it could very well vanish under different institutional conditions.[14]

Another aspect of Theory's elective affinity to production is the division of labor it helps establish. The other side of Theory's lightness and connection to the experience of the world is its association to use. It doesn't matter how abstract the Theory is—or better, the *more* abstract and general, the greater the possibility for application, however mediated and indirect, to the most varied realms of objects. The rise of Theory brought to the realm of culture (I was almost writing the sphere of Spirit) the semantic field of manufacture, which is composed of four levels. If cultural manifestations can be regarded as raw materials in need of explanation, criticism processes them as producing consumer goods; literary theory in a strict sense, concerned as it was with different ways to bring intelligibility to large group of artifacts, would fabricate durable goods; Theory, finally, corresponds to capital goods, since it produces interpretative machines.[15] Not surprisingly, these different levels are not just superposed by but end up erecting a hierarchy of their own, which then reconfigures the academic ladder, with the producers of reading machines now occupying the higher positions. Attempts at *overcoming* won't work precisely because of Theory's affinity to production: they can only reproduce Theory's logic, if less persuasively. "Post," "new," "after," "beyond" are conceptual particles which took shape together with the consolidation of Theory (note: pronouncing its death won't be effective either).

All this brings us to the problem of method, an exceedingly thorny one. I have never managed to think of a method for the study of literature except for a quite simple three-stage process of (1) inhabiting (to avoid "penetrating" or "immersing yourself") the object as much as you can; (2) having ideas; and (3) confronting these ideas with what has been written on the object (and repeating the cycle if need be). This may seem banal, which of course it is, but when compared to much of the usual practice it becomes strangely liberating. For very often Theory functions as ready-made methodology, furnishing preprepared conceptual tools and argumentative gestures for textual analyses. The exercise in theory classes of adopting a reading position (supported by a plethora of manuals and critical editions) at the same time that it transmits content restrains the critical imagination. To be sure, there are some movements of thought (the dialectic reversal, the deconstructive inversion of binary oppositions, the formation of constellations, etc.) that compose the backbone of reflection's actions, but these cannot be taught in a traditional way (imagine an exam: your categorical progression deserves a B+), but must rather be apprehended, as we'll see in a moment, mimetically.

The intelligent reader (yes, you) will have noticed that I have been trying to articulate a force field surrounding Theory, which comprises positive and negative elements in tension and which tries to mediate between Theory and processes outside it. To argue that Theory be considered a genre, rather than a field or a discursive formation, represents an attempt to solve the question of its complicated thrust for autonomization and the resulting problems of instrumentalization and neoliberal productivity. If a discursive formation is characterized by its capacity to generate language, whereas a field is unthinkable without a belief in its progression, the idea of genre eschews the representation of Theory as a machine, by converting its problematic semiautonomy into a formal trait.

This permits that we propose a twofold conclusion. In the first place, we can ask in what measure, if at all, the recent reformulations of reading and critique mentioned in the beginning will aspire to or unwittingly replicate the logic of (semi) autonomy. If the answer is in the negative, the risk will be of falling on a well-behaved but unexciting academicism. A positive reply, on the other hand, would have to show how all the negative aspects referred to might be avoided. Such a question is far from rhetorical, but here (at the end of the chapter!) is not the place to handle it. The more fitting task at this point is a different one, namely, assuming that Theory may still be recuperated, that it ought not be thrown in the trashcan of academic-critical history; how are we to still read it, acknowledging all the problems identified so far and even granting that more promising alternatives might be looming ahead?

III

What would it mean, then, to read Theory responsibly? Surrounding the adverb there is a subtle but emphatic distinction to be made, for when looking closely enough one can find in the word an ambiguity in transitivity. To be responsible in a good (I almost said responsible) sense is transitive: responsibility *toward* something, more precisely toward a kernel in that something that calls for responsibility. As this transitive impulse weakens and "to be responsible" begins to appear as a trait, and consequently a possession, responsibility acquires questionable moral shades. From what has been discussed so far, we can gather that a responsible reading of Theory would be one that would at the same time preserve Theory's creativity, at least provisionally evade the dilemma of its (semi) autonomy, and shun its crippling effects in fostering productivism and preformatting interpretation.

I would like to propose two reading strategies, which perhaps can be viewed as forming a dialectics of objectification: first, an *unproductive* reading of Theory from a utilitarian viewpoint, reading as an end in itself and for its own sake. Why does theory have to serve a purpose? Why can't it be just appreciated? Indeed, a noninstrumental approach allows us to imagine a fruitful relationship of Theory through its de-objectification in forgetfulness. Daniel Heller-Roazen's amazing *Echolalias* affords an instructive example in this regard. The book contains twenty-one small chapters in which forgetting in language is exposed as a highly active force, not the cause of loss but an agent of change. One of the work's merits lies in its refusal to provide a conclusion or a detached view of the cases it describes, which nevertheless beg for extrapolation. This silence becomes telling once we realize that there is progress in the unfolding of forgetting, which starts with phonemes, moves to literary and philosophical works, and the psyche, to reach theology in the end. Particularly instructive in our context is the chapter "A Tale of Abū Nuwās," which illustrates how the eighth-century Arabo-Persian Nuwās became a poet. The story deserves to be quoted in full:

> Abū Nuwās asked Khalaf for permission to compose poetry, and Khalaf said: "I refuse to let you make a poem until you memorize a thousand passages of ancient poetry, including chants, odes and occasional lines." So Abū Nuwās disappeared; and after a good long while, he came back and said, "I've done it."

"Recite them," said Khalaf.

So Abū Nuwās began and got through the bulk of the verses over a period of several days. Then he asked again for permission to compose poetry. Said Khalaf: "I refuse, unless you forget all one thousand lines as completely as if you had never learned them."

"That's too difficult," said Abū Nuwās. "I've memorized them quite thoroughly!"

"I refuse to let you compose until you forget them," said Khalaf.

So Abū Nuwās disappeared into a monastery and remained in solitude for a period of time until he forgot the lines. He went back to Khalaf and said, "I've forgotten them so thoroughly that it's as if I never memorized anything at all."

Khalaf then said, "Now go compose!" (191–2)

Certainly one does not learn theory as one memorizes lines, and without a doubt the process of forgetting is also dissimilar; nevertheless, in both cases there is a hard *work* to be performed. In Theory's case, this would probably entail erasing not only proper names, thus not respecting the authority and authorship over concepts, but also a solid terminology, for there is so much more going on in theory than just the names of concepts and categories. Be that as it may, the most important point is that both for poetry and for theory true forgetting can take place only after an intense period of immersion. I would say that achieving forgetfulness is a way of divesting Theory from the sphere of use, from the hand, to turn it into a form of comportment, inserting it in the blood stream, as it were. In other words, instead of parading concepts, it would involve absorbing their meaning and expression. Let us call this a mimetic or osmotic kind of reading and learning. Only after such learning is fully carried out can you yourself become Khalaf and tell yourself: "Now go interpret things!"

The other strategy points in the opposite direction, not a de- but a hyper-objectification of Theory—that is, not relying on the creative power of forgetting but exploring Theory's materiality. The days are long past when critics interpreted a literary text in order to recuperate the experience that animated the author to write it, or, later, the sense they were supposed to have inserted in it. In contradistinction, the current assumption is that criticism more discovers than retrieves meaning. This establishes performatively a structure that presupposes the text not to know everything about itself; the interpreter's function is to show it (of course, strong works seem to be aware not only of that which is revealed about them, but also of our own desire to do it). In this scheme, theory is the vehicle to bring intelligibility to the text, and, as such, it is conceived as present and transparent to itself. Theory speaks; its objects are spoken. It would then be refreshing to withdraw from Theory its claim to knowledge and suppose that it is more than its sheer propositional content: not a tool, but something quasi-intransitive. To express it in another way, how would one deal with assuming that Theory doesn't know everything about itself?

I suggested above that Theory as a genre could be viewed as a textual rearrangement of philosophy and literary criticism. Here, at the conclusion of this chapter, it is worthwhile to raise the question of its genetic relationship to literature. One of the jewels of Brazilian seventeenth-century literature is Padre Antônio Vieira's sermons. Reading them today we perceive an astounding political imagination, absolute command over the Portuguese language, and a dazzling theological erudition. And yet, such reading would be totally at odds with Vieira's conceptions of his own sermons, which were thought of as interventions, rhetorical pieces aimed at quite specific results. Might not Vieira's case be instructive for Theory? In view of it, the usual inclusion the adjective "literary" before "theory" may acquire a new emphasis, not literary *theory*, but instead *literary* theory. A few tentative examples, then: take Jameson's *The Political Unconscious*, singled out by recent critics as a privileged example of theory's vicissitudes (depth, suspiciousness, strong theory, etc.); one needs just a small gesture of detachment or estrangement (to use an old theoreteme) to view both in its overarching frame and sentence structure something of the epic, now unthinkable in literary terms. Or consider Barthes's already mentioned *texte*, perhaps in conjunction with Lacan's *objet petit a*: could they not be viewed as reconfigurations of the sublime? Or what to do with Derrida's question marks? Might they not, in their gesture to the reader, share something of the rhetorical essence of the sermon? Of course, these works may still be read for their propositional-conceptual content, just as one may read Vieira in search for the inspiration of God; one thing does not annul the other, although they can't happen at the same time. And this shouldn't be understood as simply matter of reading Theory as if it were literature either (though it would be entertaining to do it literally, imagining concepts as characters, arguments as plots, adverbs as setting, etc.)—for what is at stake here is turning the question into an answer, of striving to responsibly de-instrumentalize Theory and put to work everything that is sedimented in its complex and mixed constitution and which, to a great extent, has in its own way motivated this perhaps recalcitrant chapter.

Notes

1 Some of the relevant sources here include Latour, Best and Marcus, Bewes, Potts, Felski, Anker and Felski, Saint-Amour. In this volume, see especially Sugimori and Rothman.
2 Not to mention the fact that the introductions to each theorist seem to lose critical sharpness as we get closer to the present.
3 "Indeed, the arrogance of youth was their major asset. These rebellious *fils à papa* had nothing to lose and everything to gain. Sons of generals and industrialists, educated at home in prestigious *grandes écoles* and abroad at Oxford, they had acquired their haughtiness through an upper-class upbringing, elitist education, and entrepreneurial training." (Marx-Scouras 2)
4 All translations are my own, except when indicated otherwise. "Lifestyle accessoire" is in English in the original.
5 Focusing on the cultural aspect of Theory opens a new analytical perspective. Take conceptual neologisms, for instance: they not only try to designate unthought-of objects, but also provide the vehicle for the strengthening of collective ties and intersubjective identification.
6 It would be interesting to do a quantitative study with graduate students and professors to find out how much time is devoted to theoretical and literary works. At the very least it seems safe to say dividing one's energy into literature and theory has become a necessity and frequently a source of anxiety about how to dispose of one's time.
7 Meanwhile, here in Brazil "desconstrução" was adopted in political discourse to mean "prove the other wrong, showing their bad faith."
8 It is profitable to read this analysis together with Baines's chapter in this volume.
9 This is how Jonathan Culler puts it: "While opposing work and text, Barthes refuses to let text and work be concepts that operate at the same level or in the same way. One consequence of this is that while Barthes' account of the distinctions helps students find *du Texte* in older works, it does not help much dealing with avant-garde works, which always fall short of the radical ideal and which are not much illuminated by accounts showing them to fall short. His insistence that the move to *text* is not just a methodological shift but that there are indeed works (which sometimes contain *du texte*) makes the idea of the text seem something of a fetish, an ideal object so radical and disruptive that no actual discourse is adequate to the idea (while of course *works* really do exist)" (108–9).
10 It would be interesting to think Barthes's libidinal-aesthetic investment in theory together with his utter blindness, throughout his chameleonic career, vis-à-vis the concept of culture industry in Adorno and Horkheimer's sense.

11 Notice that this doesn't prevent them from being academically valid. What the university requires of research is that new knowledge be created, not necessarily interesting knowledge.

12 The future can also be found in theoretical discourse as an explicit preoccupation, sometimes not with the best results. In his book *Living with Theory*, Leitch starts with the metaphor of the futures market to ascertain Theory's posterity; the semantic field of capital, however, is infamously used in a totally neutral, descriptive fashion.

13 There is no space here to develop the argument, but the point would be that the privileging of research and its quantification at the expense of teaching is at the basis of the current erosion of an emphatic idea of university. Without the obsession with measurement, fierce competition would be impossible, as well as the penalties ensuing from losing. It is always sane to remember that some of the most important intellectual and academic practices are hardly countable.

14 See, for example, Ginsberg and Donoghue.

15 In my *Teoria (literária) americana*, I situate the Theory's productivism in the context of unequal international exchanges. In the same way that technology is conceived at the center of the world's capitalist system and then exported to the periphery, so new conceptual elaborations (the concept as the machine of thinking) are imported by marginal countries. In Brazil, theories are normally explained or applied, seldom evaluated through metatheory; moreover, concepts and theories as only rarely proposed (Roberto Schwarz is a happy exception here). This is particularly embarrassing in the case of elucidations of puns in foreign languages and the lack of daring to theorize what one's native tongue offers. Imagine the field day Lacan would have in Portuguese with the identity of "I speak" (*falo*) and "phallus" (*falo*), or Heidegger with two verbs for being (*ser* and *estar*).

References

Anker, Elizabeth S., and Rita Felski. *Critique and Post-Critique*. Duke UP, 2017.

Babich, Babette. *La fin de la pensée? Philosophie analytique contre philosophie continentale*. L'Harmattan, 2012.

Barthes, Roland. "De l'oeuvre au texte" (1971), *Oeuvres Complètes*, Éric Marty (ed.) Seuil, 1994.

Best, Stephen, and Sharon Marcus. "Surface Reading: An Introduction." *Representations*, vol. 108, 2009, pp. 1–21.

Bewes, Tim. "Reading with the Grain: A New World in Literary Criticism." *differences*, 21 no. 3, 2010, pp. 1–33.

Cousset, François. *French Theory. Foucault, Derrida, Deleuze & Cie et la mutation de la vie intellectuelle aux États Unis.* La Decouverte, 2003.
Culler, Jonathan. "Text: Its Vicissitudes." *The Literary in Theory.* Stanford UP, 2007. 99–116.
Cunningham, Valentine. *Reading After Theory.* Blackwell, 2002.
Donoghue, Frank. *The Last Professors. The Corporate University and the Fate of the Humanities.* Fordham UP, 2008.
Durão, Fabio A. "Do texto à obra," *Do texto à obra e outros ensaios.* Appris, 2019. 21–42.
Durão, Fabio A. *Teoria (literária) americana: uma introdução crítica.* Autores Associados, 2011.
Felsch, Philipp. *Der lange Sommer der Theorie. Geschichte einer Revolte: 1960–1990.* Fischer, 2016.
Felski, Rita. *The Limits of Critique.* U of Chicago P, 2015.
Genette, Gérard. "Poétique et histoire," *Figures III.* Seuil, 1972.
Ginsberg, Benjamin. *The Fall of the Faculty: The Rise of the All-Administrative University and Why It Matters.* Oxford UP, 2011.
Graff, Gerald. *Professing Literature: An Institutional History.* Chicago UP, 2007 [1987].
Heller-Roazen, Daniel. *Echolalias: On the Forgetting of Language.* Zone Books, 2005.
Herman, Peter C., editor. *Historicizing Theory.* State U of New York P, 2004.
Kauppi, Niilo. *French Intellectual Nobility: Institutional and Symbolic Transformations in the Post-Sartrean Era.* State U of New York P, 1996.
Latour, Bruno. "Why Has Critique Run Out of Steam? From Matters of Fact to Matters of Concern." *Critical Inquiry*, vol. 30, Winter 2004, pp. 224–48,
Leitch, Vincent. *Living with Theory.* Blackwell, 2008.
Leitch, Vincent. *Theory Matters.* Routledge, 2003.
Marx-Scouras, Danielle. *The Cultural Politics of Tel Quel. Literature and the Left in the Wake of Engagement.* Penn State UP, 1996.
McQuillan, Martin et al., editors. *Post-Theory. New Directions in Criticism.* Edinburgh UP, 1999.
North, Joseph. *Literary Criticism: A Concise Political History.* Harvard UP, 2007.
Patai, Daphne, and Will H. Corral. *Theory's Empire. An Anthology of Dissent.* Columbia UP, 2005.
Payne, Michael, and John Shad. *Life.After.Theory.* Continuum, 2003.
Potts, Jason, editor. "Dossier: Surface Reading." Special Issue, *Mediations*, vol. 29, no. 2, 2015.
Rabaté, Jean-Michel. *The Future of Theory.* Blackwell, 2002.
Rodowick, D. N. *Elegy for Theory.* Cambridge UP, 2014.

Ross, Stephen. *Theory and Modernism*. Routledge, 2009.

Ryan, Judith. *The Novel After Theory*. Columbia UP, 2012.

Saint-Amour, Paul. "Weak Theory, Weak Modernism." *Modernism/Modernity*, vol. 24, 2018, pp. 437–59.

Sedgwick, Eve Kosofsky. "Paranoid Reading and Reparative Reading, or, You're So Paranoid, You Probably Think This Essay Is about You." *Touching Feeling: Affect, Pedagogy, Performativity*. Duke UP, 2003.

4

Modernism, Critical Theory, and Affect Theory *Avant La Lettre*

Yan Tang

This essay presents a series of snapshots to index how two almost concomitant historical moments—those of modernism and Critical Theory (*Kritische Theorie*)[1]—anticipate, enable, or complicate the later transportation and mutation of affect theory into the humanities in the 1990s. As we continue to witness a definitional proliferation of "modernism" and "theory," my motivation for a loose periodization here is neither to reinscribe any sweeping generalization of "high modernism" nor to rebrand modernism by adding "new values" to it (i.e., "modernism is important because it now also contributes to affect theory"). The latter, in particular, might risk concealing modernism's ideological undercurrents behind its enticing affective affordance and theoretical valence. Looking at modernism and Critical Theory as both self-critical and historical moments, I trace how they morph into a generative genealogy that unsettles some conceptual and disciplinary boundaries without decontextualizing and depoliticizing their respective historical contributions and predicaments (Fabio Akcelrud Durão's essay in this volume has formulated Theory's (semi) autonomization and self-referentiality in great detail). What emerges from even the tip of this genealogy sketched out here is that modernism and Critical Theory orient us toward the knot of affect and ideology in their versions of "affect theory" *avant la lettre*. In other words: always historicize affect! Even though such an attempt never can or should entail a tight narrative about the historicity of affect—as affect always remains *avant la lettre* and precedes any "capture" in affect theory—it is not time to abandon history and ideology. At the end of the essay, I also bring together a group of contemporary theorists of affect whose work came out alongside and after affect's new nominalization in affect theory.[2] By doing so, I show that their theories of affect resonate with modernism's and Critical Theory's attention to the imbrication of affect and ideology, and they prompt us to seek more diverse citational practices in modernist studies' engagement with the question of affect. I consider this an urgent task, especially because variously political affects already permeate and mediate the feedback loop between aesthetic experience and critical pathos (see Rivky Mondal's intriguing discussion of aesthetic fidelity and attachment in her essay in this volume).

"How Perfectly Tomkins Understands *Us*"

Let's first return to 1995 when Eve Kosofsky Sedgwick and Adam Frank's "Shame in the Cybernetic Fold" and Brian Massumi's "The Autonomy of Affect" both came out.[3] The publication of these two essays marked a significant, if not inaugural, moment when the humanities disciplines transported and mutated post-Second World War scientific studies of emotion into an interdisciplinary realm of "affect theory." As I contend, this transportation is indispensable to modernist formal experimentation as a means to articulate the affinity between literary studies and affect theory (Sedgwick and Frank) and to mutate scientific studies of emotion into an excessive definitional proliferation of affect (Massumi).

In "Shame in the Cybernetic Fold," Sedgwick and Frank more than once compare Silvan Tomkins's writing style to modernist formal innovation. Describing themselves "becoming addicted to reading Tomkins" (498), they tune in closely to his syntactic rhythms that "remind one of Gertrude Stein's" (499): "Phrases, sentences, sometimes whole paragraphs repeat; pages are taken up with sentences syntactically resembling one another . . . sentences that don't exemplify a general principle but rather offer a sampling or listing of the possible. This rich claustral writing nurtures, pacifies, replenishes, then sets the idea in motion again" (498). Later in the essay, they highlight again the affinity between Tomkins's syntax and modernist style, this time Proust. "Tomkins's lists," they write, "probably resemble most the long sentences in Proust where a speculation about someone's motive is couched in a series of long parallel clauses" (509). They further describe this style as "[a] postmodern syntax that seems to vitiate the very possibility of understanding motive by pluralizing it as if mechanically, infinitely, seems with the same gesture to proffer semantic tools so irresistibly usable that they bind one ever more imaginatively and profoundly to the local possibilities of an individual psychology" (509). We might add that Tomkins's style described by Sedgwick and Frank also reminds one of Samuel Beckett's mathematical and combinatorial play of syntax in *Watt*.

Tomkins's style reinforces and *performs* his theory of affect which sees several key emotions as innate programs facilitating other physiological and psychological mechanisms without producing a teleological output. As Sianne Ngai has commented, "Tomkins writes in a way that might be said to mimetically amplify the basic principle behind his theory" (55). The synchronicity between *forming* and theorizing affect in Tomkins's writing allows Sedgwick and Frank to catalyze his "productive opacity" (510)—the fusion of human and machine, meaning and intensity, the qualitative and the quantitative—into a robust revivification of what they call "today's routines of theory" (512): namely, the persistent and self-perpetuating *habit* of thought that relies on structuralist binaries even when it outlives and critiques the historical moment of structuralism (497). Inspired by the mutually amplifying form and content of Tomkins's theoretical writing, Sedgwick and Frank's articulation of an imperative to break the habit of thought[4]—"make it new," as scholars of modernism will immediately recognize—exposes the centrality of modernist formal innovation to transporting and mutating Tomkins's affect theory into literary and cultural studies. Sedgwick and Frank are acutely aware of this correlation between form and affect in modernism and Tomkins's writing; toward the end of the essay, their statement of intent for introducing Tomkins into the humanities also describes our experience of reading and writing about modernism: "we want to propagate among our audience nodes of reception for what we take to be an unfamiliar and highly exciting set of moves and tonalities" (521). On this additional level of affinity, Sedgwick and Frank strike a chord with "us" as both humans and readers of modernism: "we've also longed to do something we haven't been able even to begin here: to show how perfectly Tomkins understands *us*" (521). Frank's project "Radio Free Stein" (2013–present) and Sedgwick's poems in *Bathroom Songs* are two recent examples of their continually fruitful "fold" of the analog and the digital, affect and form.

Writing "The Autonomy of Affect" partly against the backdrop of scientific studies of emotion contemporary with Tomkins's cybernetics-informed affect theory (1962–92), Brian Massumi theorizes affect by reinterpreting Hertha Sturm's work in *Emotional Effects of Media* (1987) and Benjamin Libet's experiment in "Unconscious Cerebral Initiative and the Role of Conscious Will in Voluntary Action" (1985). As Ruth Leys has already pointed out several places where Massumi misreads or appropriates the results of these studies in his essay,[5] I emphasize instead the centrality of modernist formal experiment and its logic of rupture to Massumi's essay. Not only does the modernist slogan of "make it new" reappear in his essay as "The stakes are the new" (87), but also the form of his writing operates as a mechanism of linguistic amplification similar to Tomkins's style, which proliferates language's desire to define and categorize into its affective excess. I read the form of Massumi's essay this way not so much to "salvage" his appropriations of these scientific experiments as to show the persistent shadow of modernism shared between his and Tomkins's aesthetic *forming* of affect theory.

Although Tomkins does not appear in "The Autonomy of Affect," Massumi's formulation of affect resonates with Sedgwick and Frank's description of Tomkins's repetitive style of listing. As Massumi writes, "The relationship between the levels of intensity and qualification is not one of conformity or correspondence, but of resonance or interference, amplification or dampening. Linguistic expression can resonate with and amplify intensity at the price of making itself functionally redundant" (86). His stylistic choice enables exactly this mode of amplification:

> Affect is this two-sidedness *as seen from the side of the actual thing*, as couched in its perceptions and cognitions. Affect is *the virtual as point of view*, provided the visual metaphor is used guardedly. For affect is synaesthetic, implying a participation of the senses in each other . . . Affects are *virtual synaesthetic perspectives* anchored in (functionally limited by) the actually existing, particular things that embody them. The *autonomy* of affect is its participation in the virtual. *Its autonomy is its openness*. Affect is autonomous to the degree to which it escapes confinement in the particular body whose vitality, or potential for interaction, it is. (96)

Affect's "two-sideness," "the virtual," "synaesthetic perspectives," "autonomy," and "openness"—we see this torrent of slippery concepts piling on to the extent of escaping language's effort to signify, define, and categorize. This process of definitional proliferation, thickened by the repetitive grammatical structure of "Subject + is/are," reminds us of Tomkins's lists. This style links with what Massumi calls "the new"—scholars of modernism again will immediately recognize this familiar rhetoric. "Could it be that it is through the expectant suspension of that suspense that the new emerges?" (87), Massumi asks. By "the expectant suspension of that suspense," Massumi refers to an infinite proliferation of "an echo of irreducible excess, of gratuitous amplification" (87). For Massumi, the forever irrecoverable gap between intensity (affect) and meaning making is the condition for the new. It is not hard to detect both Derrida and modernism haunting Massumi here. And like Sedgwick and

Frank, Massumi's formulation of affect and "the new" aims to break the habit of structuralist thought: "What they lose, precisely, is the expression *event*—in favour of structure. . . . For structure is the place where nothing ever happens, that explanatory heaven in which all eventual permutations are prefigured in a self-consistent set of invariant generative rules" (87). Massumi's rhetoric and style, which are so reminiscent of modernism, demonstrate an effort to create *mutations* of the meaning of "affect" instead of *permutations*. Mutations like this, of course, bear the risk of losing meaning and audience. Modernist artists are faced with the same challenge.

The theatre of linguistic proliferation continues in Massumi's essay, bringing us something that Sedgwick and Frank have not mentioned: American politics. Massumi applies his repetitive style to describe not just affect but also Reagan:

> Reagan politicized the power of mime. That power is in interruption. A mime decomposes movement, cuts its continuity into a potentially infinite series of submovements punctuated jerks. At each jerk, at each cut into the movement, the potential is there for the movement to veer off in another direction, to become a different movement. Each jerk suspends the continuity of the movement, for just a flash . . . each jerk is a critical point, a singular point, a bifurcation point . . . Reagan's gestural idiocy had a mime effect. As did his verbal incoherence, in the register of meaning. He was a communicative jerk. (102)

Massumi uses the repetitive description of "jerk" to capture—and at the same time to obscure and joke about—what he calls Reagan's "affective jingoism" (103). Interestingly, through the joke on "jerk" Massumi not only alludes to Reagan's first career as an actor but also more broadly synthesizes political performance with the aesthetic, especially the legacy of pantomime and silent films. What's also key here is that based on this analysis of political affect, Massumi moves away from ideology critique, arguing instead that ideology is no longer a sufficient concept to articulate "the global mode of functioning of power" (104). As I will discuss later, Lauren Berlant has offered a brilliant corrective to Massumi: "affect theory is another phase in the history of ideology theory" (53). For now, I turn to modernism's theorization of affect because it already warns us against another habit of thought: a post-ideological understanding of affect, as if affect and ideology were separable.

Modernist Theorists of Affect

Modernist formulations of affect theory *avant la lettre* show us that ideology is always embedded in aesthetic form's production of affect. Let's look at, for example, W. B. Yeats's conception of emotion in "The Symbolism of Poetry" (1900). Articulating key symbolist principles,[6] Yeats's essay treats emotions as "disembodied powers" that are not necessarily expressible: "All sounds, all colours, all forms, either because of their preordained energies or because of long association, evoke indefinable and yet precise emotions or, as I prefer to think, call down among us certain disembodied powers, whose footsteps over our hearts we call emotions" (156–7). For Yeats, what evokes such emotions is poetic rhythm, which "prolong[s] the moment of contemplation" and "keep[s] us in that state of perhaps real trance, in which the mind liberated from the pressure of the will is unfolded in symbols" (159). Yeats further theorizes that this indefinable state of emotion between the subjective and the objective allows a flow of emotion from the individual to the collective: emotion "flows out, with all it has gathered, among the blind instincts of daily life, where it moves a power within powers" (158). This correlation between poetic form and indefinable emotion not only anticipates affect's function of amplification emphasized by Tomkins, Sedgwick, Frank, and Massumi, but also crucially links with Yeats's belief in the politics of evoking emotion to "mak[e] and unmak[e] mankind" (157). One of the salient critiques of this politics can be found in George Orwell's essay "W. B. Yeats" (1943), in which Orwell traces the connection between Yeats's style and theory of occultism and his fascist tendency. "The very concept of occultism," Orwell writes, "carries with it the idea that knowledge must be a secret thing, limited to a small circle of initiates. But the same idea is integral to Fascism. Those who dread the prospect of universal suffrage, popular education, freedom of thought, emancipation of women, will start off with a predilection towards secret cults" ("W. B. Yeats"). The poet's desire to create a rhythm that hypnotizes and remakes "mankind" warns us of the possibility of an aristocratic fascist tendency mobilized by the creation and expansion of indefinable emotion.

In *Art*, Clive Bell's concept of "Significant Form" echoes Yeats's theory of indefinable emotion. Bell defines "Significant Form" this way: "In each, lines and colours combined in a particular way, certain forms and relations of forms, stir our aesthetic emotions. These relations and combination of lines and colours, these aesthetically moving forms, I call 'Significant Form'; and 'Significant Form' is the one quality common to all works of visual art" (23). The "aesthetic emotions" stirred in the viewer or reader, however, are not merely subjective reactions; for Bell, aesthetic emotions are able to absorb everything—including ourselves and our empirical world—and become the *only* base of our aesthetic judgment: "We have no other means of recognizing a work of art than our feeling for it" (23); "Art transports us from the world of man's activity to a world of aesthetic exaltation" (36); and "In this world the emotions of life find no place. It is a world with emotions of its own" (37). Thus, it makes sense that Bell is not greatly concerned with how exactly a work of art's Significant Form evokes our aesthetic emotions, since the nature of aesthetic judgment requires us to experience an extreme mode of subjective feeling that verges on its dissolving subjectivity in the work of art. Bell calls this world of a work of art its "ultimate reality" (60), and he eventually turns to religious experience to account for this aesthetic experience as "ultra-human emotions" (242). As another mode of "remaking" mankind and the world by losing oneself in it, Bell's theory of aesthetic emotion—let's call it the "immersion model"—also bears a (bio)politics not unrelated to his pacifism after the First World War (see Hussey).

Another way that modernist writers anticipate affect theory is to advance a historical and social understanding of emotion and feeling beyond mere subjectivism and relativism. Virginia Woolf and Ford Madox Ford are exemplary of this: they come at the question of emotion not with the intention to explicate how exactly form evokes the audience's emotion but with critical and aesthetic motivations to reactivate aesthetic experiences that are political, historical, and collective. In "Professions for Women," the angel looming between Woolf and her paper is a structure of oppressive moods as well as a conventional female character in Victorian literature. The affective quality of such moods is prominent in Woolf's description of "the shadow of her wing or the radiance of her halo" (151). To kill the angel, for Woolf, is not enough; to move past the angel, she has to "[tell] the truth about [her] own experiences as a body" (153), which manifests in how she uses aesthetic forms to produce a counter-mood to transgress the boundaries between the interior and the exterior, the metaphysical and the physical. Besides anticipating what Raymond Williams calls "the structures of feeling," Woolf also attempts to articulate the meaning of communal feelings through, for example, Mrs. Ramsay in *To the Lighthouse*:

> [A]nd she felt, with her hand on the nursery door, that community of feeling with other people which emotion gives as if the walls of partition had become so thin that practically (the feeling was one of relief and happiness) it was all one

stream, and chairs, tables, maps, were hers, were theirs, it did not matter whose, and Paul and Minta would carry it on when she was dead. (79–80)

Woolf's own style of the stream of consciousness, then, precisely cultivates a community of feeling when aesthetic experience transfers from the subjective to the collective (fictional characters and readers of fiction) beyond material differences. The wall between community-building and propaganda, of course, also becomes thin.

Ford Madox Ford also demonstrates a political and historical understanding of emotion, in particular a variable notion of sentimentality. In *The English Novel*, he considers sentimentality as both England's national sentiment and Anglo-Saxon aesthetic emotion. Attending to Samuel Richardson's "sentimentalizing" tendency as "his E string," Ford comments:

> Against that I have nothing to say. Anglo-Saxons are sentimentalists before everything and in all their arts, and it is probable that without sentimentality as an ingredient no Anglo-Saxon artist could work: certainly he could have no appeal. To produce national masterpieces in paint Turner must bathe his canvases deep in that gentle fluid; the English lyric is a marvel of sentimentality and so is English domestic architecture with its mellow—or mellowed!—red brick, its dove-cotes, its south walls for netted fruits. So the first of modern novelists must be one of the greatest sentimentalists. And on those lines his appeal is universal and everlasting. (72–3)

The nuance of Ford's notion of sentimentality is that it refers to refinement and mellowness instead of excessive indulgence; for him, sentimentality is integral to Englishness as both a national sentiment and a distinct aesthetic emotion, as long as one only has "a wholesome dose of sentimentality" (74). Ford further positions sentimentality in the intersection of political, historical, and aesthetic emotions that he traces back to the eighteenth century: "It had begun with Richardson. His vogue with the French would be incomprehensible if we were not able to consider that the French Revolution was, in the end, a sentimental movement, basing itself on civic, parental, filial, and rhetorical virtues" (114). Recognizing the felt resonance between the political emotion behind the French Revolution and the aesthetic emotion embedded in Richardson's work, Ford exemplifies, like Woolf, how to be a historian of historical feeling.

Critical Theory of/as Affect

If modernism reminds us that theories of affect cannot disregard affect's political and ideological components, the emergence of Critical Theory marked by Max Horkheimer's essay "Traditional and Critical Theory" among other Frankfurt School works foregrounds ideological mediation in the volatile sensory experience of the thinking and feeling subject. Sedgwick and Frank's interest in the irreducible errancy between the input of sensory data and the output of response to reality is already one of the key questions at the center of Horkheimer's call for critical theory. As he argues, in contrast to traditional theory which is "the sum-total of propositions about a subject" (188) based on logical deduction or induction within/controlled by social totality, critical theory "has society itself for its object" (206). Germane to affect in this distinction is that Horkheimer recognizes the inevitability of ideological mediation through the subject's sensory experience in any theory. Thus, he chooses to work within mediation/totality by turning to critical theory's own volitions, its "aggressive forces" that stimulate social transformation instead of conforming to "professional optimism" and "the happy feeling of being linked with an immense force" (214–15). Horkheimer's active cultivation of strong political emotions through Critical Theory resists a pessimistic social feeling of conformism that "the whole weight of the existing state of affairs is pushing mankind towards the surrender of all culture and relapse into darkest barbarism" (241).

If Horkheimer's vision of critical theory both conceptualizes and mobilizes strong affect, it also emphasizes disciplined uses of affect—"which incite while also requiring discipline" (215). The notion of "discipline" is particularly important; failing to impose political and ideological restraints on a theory/praxis that "incites" would potentially facilitate more extreme forms of inwardness and self-indulgence, either as political quietism or Fascism. On the other hand, discipline does not mean dogmatism, as Horkheimer acknowledges the open-endedness of Critical Theory driven by historical necessity: "There are no general criteria for judging the critical theory as a whole, for it is always based on the recurrence of events and thus on a self-reproducing reality" (242).

Horkheimer's emphasis on incitement and discipline as the double responsibility of Critical Theory is transferred into Herbert Marcuse's inquiry into the relationship between hedonism and the philosophy of reason. In his essay "On Hedonism," Marcuse examines the incompatibility between enjoyment and reason in a bourgeois capitalist society; while the philosophy of reason tends to fulfill universal interest by sacrificing individual happiness and gratification, hedonism preserves enjoyment as self-indulgence and further isolates the individual from engaging with antagonistic historical forces. Meanwhile, Marcuse proposes that the usefulness of hedonism is "in its falsehood insofar as it has preserved the demand for happiness against every idealization of unhappiness" (130), and "the truth of hedonism" lies in its potential to develop a "new principle of social organization, not in a different philosophical principle" (130). In hedonism, Marcuse also sees the value of sensuality's "receptivity" and openness that allows the immediacy between the individual's internal and external world without the mediation of labor process (128-9). Although we might push back against Marcuse's claim by arguing that immediacy itself is utopian in the current structures of capitalist societies, his theory ultimately tries to envision a mode of Critical Theory in which "the concept of happiness has been freed from any ties with bourgeois conformism and relativism" (142). If immediacy is indeed utopian, that is because Critical Theory itself is forever set in motion toward a utopian vision of society. Attending to various characteristics of sensuality in relation to reason, truth, and universality, Marcuse is able to theorize how different structures of society affect the empirical, collective political life. This is also why the aesthetic dimension plays such an important role in Marcuse's critical social theory. For Adorno, expressionism in particular strives for this immediacy: "To the extent that it aims at producing documents, transcripts—the surrealists later spoke of 'automatic writing'—of emotional states, expressionism strives for the ideal of a pure immediacy" (kindle location 2473). However, Adorno also points out the problem of immediacy: in expressionism it "transpires very quickly, very early on, that it is impossible to stay at the sheer point of expression" (kindle location 2488).

As a "critical mood" (Felski 6) rather than a cluster of specific arguments, Critical Theory's "aggressive forces" of critique become the object of contention in Rita Felski's *The Limits of Critique*. In the chapter entitled "Crrritique," Felski's brief sketch of "critique" in Horkheimer's "Traditional and Critical Theory" is accurate: "Critique is, in short, an openly committed form of scholarship that makes no pretense to neutrality, objectivity, or detachment" (141). Felski then turns to problematize this notion of critique and asks, "But who gets to claim the mantle of opposition?" (142). It is indeed a productive question to ask, as it touches upon the key problems of academic hierarchies of gender, race, class, geographical locations, and the like. (Both Masami Sugimori and Daniel Newman in this volume have touched upon the issues of academic hierarchies in thought-provoking ways.) Susan Stanford Friedman highlights this in her response to Felski, "What Felski implicitly suggests, however, is that we scholars and educators in the humanities should turn the spotlight (of critique) onto ourselves" (346). Yet Felski's satirical tone seems to risk undermining, instead of facilitating, her argument:

> *Crrritique*! The word flies off the tongue like a weapon, emitting a rapid guttural burst of machine-gun-fire. There is the ominous cawing staccato of the first and final consonants, the terse thud of the short repeated vowel, the throaty underground rumble of the accompanying *r*. "Critique" sounds unmistakably foreign, in a sexy, mysterious, pan-European kind of way, conjuring up tableaus of intellectuals gesturing wildly in smoke-wreathed Parisian cafés and solemn-faced discussions in seminar rooms in Frankfurt. (120)

Felski's rhetoric of exoticism embedded in her description of the mood of critique at its best performs exactly what Horkheimer calls "incitement" and at its worst appears susceptible to American nativism. Although much aligned with Sedgwick's reparative reading, Felski shows a more explicit departure from ideology critique while preserving her own ideology behind a seemingly playful rhetoric toward foreignness. In a less playful and more militant tone, Felski questions the use of ideology critique: "What is the use of demystifying ideology when many people no longer subscribe to coherent ideologies, when there is widespread disillusionment about the motives of politicians and public figures, when 'everyone knows' that hidden forces are at work making us think and behave in certain ways?" (46). Given the contemporary American political environment, it is not hard to counterargue that "everyone knows" is an overgeneralization (see Cristina Ionica's compelling discussion of truth in this volume), or that the incoherence of ideologies is itself a phenomenon needing further demystification. What particularly interests me, however, is that we begin to see a recurring rhetoric that urges us to move away from ideology critique through theories of affect; we have seen a similar rhetoric of ideology critique's insufficiency in Massumi's discussion of Reagan's postmodern politics.

This recurring attempt at departing from ideology critique in the humanities' use of affect theory sounds more interesting if we turn to Silvan Tomkins again, this time his concept of "ideo-affective." The humanities' importation of Tomkins's affect theory seems to have left out his discussion of the relationship between affect and ideology. In *Touching Feeling*, in the same passage where

Sedgwick discusses Tomkins's conceptualization of strong and weak theory, she quotes Tomkins: "It is the repeated and apparently uncontrollable spread of the experience of negative affect which prompts the increasing strength of the ideo-affective organization which we have called a strong affect theory" (135). While Sedgwick does not dwell on the phrase "ideo-affective organization," the term points directly at Tomkins's other major legacy in affect theory: his fraught theory of affect and ideology. As both Leys and Linda M. G. Zerilli point out, the highly reductive concept "ideo-affective resonance" is integral to Tomkins's affect theory. In "Left and Right: A Basic Dimension of Ideology and Personality," for example, Tomkins defines this concept as "the engagement of belief and feeling by ideology . . . when the ideo-affective postures are sufficiently similar to the ideological posture so that they reinforce and strengthen each other" (389). Based on this theory, Tomkins claims the *predictability* and *inevitability* of one's political leaning (ideological posture) amplified and perpetuated by their ideo-affective posture: "The right-wing ideologist urges the control of all the drives and the affects by reason . . . The left-wing ideologist stresses man's natural affective investment in himself as well as others" (403). It is likely that Sedgwick and Frank's importation of Tomkins's affect theory intentionally refuses to engage with his essentialization of an unbreakable tie and reciprocal intensification between affect and ideology; yet their reticence on this front also risks making room for more explicit quietism or disavowal whose symptoms have manifested in Massumi's and Felski's works.

"Another Phase in the History of Ideology Theory"

My reason to place Tomkins's flawed yet thought-provoking theory on affect and ideology under the spotlight is to introduce the following constellation of contemporary theories of affect that shares modernism's and Critical Theory's attention to the imbrication of affect and ideology, in particular through the concept of attachment. Conducting critiques of variously racial and sexual violence and heteronormative ideology, Wendy Brown, Lauren Berlant, Christina Sharpe, and Sara Ahmed, among others, extend and complicate the earlier importation of affect theory in the 1990s. This constellation of theorists offers theoretical frameworks not currently at the center of modernist studies' engagement with affect and calls for different citational practices in modernist studies.

The year 1995 witnessed the publication of not only "Shame in the Cybernetic Fold" and "The Autonomy of Affect" but also Brown's *States of Injury*. In chapter 3, "Wounded Attachment," Brown examines how liberalism incites *ressentiment* and perpetuates politicized identities' ironic resubscription to "a politics of recrimination and rancor" in seeking political recognition (55). Anchoring this *ressentiment* in the logic of pain, Brown asks, "what are the logics of pain in the subject-formation processes of late modern polities that might contain or subvert this aim?" (55). For politicized identities (gender, race, sexuality, etc.), this logic means that an individual with such identities "retains the real or imagined holdings of its reviled subjects as objects of desire" (60). Specifically, she describes *ressentiment* as a psychosocial mechanism that creates "affect (rage, righteousness) that overwhelms the hurt," "a culprit responsible for the hurt," and "a site of revenge to displace the hurt (a place to inflict hurt as the sufferer has been hurt)" (68). The ultimate culprit creating this logic, she argues, is liberalism, which "contains from its inception a generalized incitement to what Nietzsche terms *ressentiment*, the moralizing revenge of the powerless, 'the triumph of the weak as weak'" (66–7). Without further diving into Brown's analysis of how liberalism's incitement as such operates—a task this essay cannot do justice to—I want to highlight that Brown's formulation of *ressentiment* shows a problematic form of affective attachment bound up with the politicization of marginalized identities in ways that perpetuate liberalism's normative ideology. As I've argued elsewhere, and as modernism and Critical Theory also have shown us, affect is not innocent or politically neutral (see Tang). Brown's explication of "the moralizing revenge of the powerless" and the "triumph of the weak as weak" also extends to the implied political hierarchies that sanction the dichotomy of "the weak" (the subject marked with politicized identities) and "weakening" (the unmarked subject that *is able to* weaken themselves), a topic that also has sparked productive debates recently in modernist studies.

The notion of affective attachment recurs as different modes of felt relations and orientations in Berlant, Sharpe, and Ahmed. What Brown calls "wounded attachment" is pertinent to Berlant's concept of "cruel optimism": "a binding to fantasies that block the satisfactions they offer, and a binding to the promise of optimism as such that the fantasies have come to represent" (51). Situating such negative attachments in their historical and political conditions, Berlant insists that affective structures remain ideological. As she states, "affect theory is another phase in the history of ideology theory" (53), which pushes back against the recurring attempts to depart from ideology critique in affect theory. The specific context of Berlant's statement is her discussion of how intuition—a trained mind's habit of pattern recognition—becomes a site where affect and history converge "in all of its chaos, normative ideology, and embodied practices of discipline and invention" (52). Berlant's approach to intuition is anchored in a Marxist conceptualization of the historical present that pays sustained attention to affect's relationality. As she reminds us, "It [Marxism] has not claimed that subjects feel *accurately* or objectively historical—this is why the concept of ideology had to be invented—but this tradition has offered multiple ways to engage the affective aspects of class antagonism, labor practices, and a communally generated class feeling that emerges from inhabiting a zone of lived structure" (64). Critical Theory's function of incitement and inclusion of sensuality/enjoyment certainly belong to what Berlant references as Marxism's various ways to address the question of affect in relation to the operation of ideology.

Sharpe and Ahmed respectively propose two other modes of affective attachment, each anchored in specific historical and political situations. In Sharpe's *Monstrous Intimacies*, the black and blackened body from American slavery to post-slavery eras bears continual marks of forced intimacies, in particular sexual violence without consent. Attachment in Sharpe's work, then, is a reconfiguration of Wendy Brown's wounded attachment: attachment as an unhealed wound, not in the sense of *ressentiment*, but in the sense of black people's ongoing suffering and internalization of white people's violence. Through reading Gayl Jones's *Corregidora*, for example, Sharpe illustrates a forced attachment on racial, communal, and psychological levels, where

> the relationship among the four generations of the Corregidora women . . . are held together by their emphasis on reproduction, on passing on evidence, on making the horrors of slavery as "visible as the blood," and in reproducing for and reproducing the desires of the slave owner whoremonger old man Corregidora. Between them, among them, keeping them attached to each other, ingesting and reproducing this sexually violent history. (166)

Meanwhile, Ahmed examines how attachment can be a mode of feminist resistance. In *The Cultural Politics of Emotion*, Ahmed refers to feminist attachment as both "how one becomes attached to feminism" and "how feminism involves an emotional response to the world, where the form of that response involves a reorientation of one's bodily relation to social norms" (170–1). Particularly important in Ahmed's conception of feminist attachment is its unsettling not only of the hierarchy between thought and emotion but also of the stereotypical correlation between emotion and femininity. We might add that one of the most salient examples of the negative/reductive association of emotion with femininity in contemporary cultural products is Pete Docter's

Disney movie *Inside Out*, which portrays the turbulence of an 11-year-old girl's five personified emotions—joy, sadness, fear, disgust, and anger. If this sounds awfully familiar (hint: Silvan Tomkins), that is because Tomkins's student and colleague Paul Ekman in fact served as a consultant for the movie ("It's All in Your Head"). Through theorizing feminist attachment—pain, anger, wonder, and hope—Ahmed not only pushes back this reductive association but also problematizes Wendy Brown's formulation of *ressentiment*; as she contends, "a politics which acts without reaction is impossible" (174).

More or less informed by a historical materialist understanding of affect, all of the theorizations and reconfigurations of affective attachments outlined here provide modernist studies with numerous ways to think about (1) the ideological undercurrents of modernist representation, theorization, and formal production of affect and (2) the nature and implication of our attachment to the aesthetic affects of modernism and affect theory. Contemporary theories of affective attachment can help us investigate further into the theorization and aesthetic creation of affect: not necessarily benevolent, the communal, collective, or national feelings understood by Yeats, Woolf, and Ford are always charged with different political ideologies, power hierarchies, and positionalities. Kazuo Ishiguro, whose works bear many marks of modernist formal innovations, also portrays a cruel affective attachment or forced intimacy that glues together communities at the expense of ethics and love in *The Unconsoled*. In the current state of the new modernist studies, besides Sianne Ngai's brilliant book *Ugly Feelings*—which was published fifteen years ago—*Affective Materialities* (Watts et al.) is among the few works to pay full attention to the relationship between affect and ideology in modernist studies. By bringing together affect theory, eco-criticism, and new materialism, the volume attends to "bodies as relational, divergent, and affected, replete with urgent political and ethical implications" (2). The inclusion of Mel Chen, Judith Butler, Lauren Berlant, Ruth Leys, and other theorists of affect in *Affective Materialities* initiates and models for the modernist studies citational practices that create responsible and committed scholarship—or, to echo the title of our volume, various modes of "responsible reading." In his introduction to the recent cluster on Adorno's "Commitment" in *VLC*, Nathan Hensley envisions what such scholarship would look like:

> But if the humanities are to mean anything now, they should likely go beyond the merely descriptive or putatively disinterested investigations into fact and detail and historical context, and instead make inquiries into the domain of value. They should evaluate, hierarchize, and, in ways that exercise a faculty

beyond simple moralism, judge . . . And they might then ask, as we try to do here, what *care* is, anyway, and in what mechanisms—affective, cognitive, psychosocial, political—such primary concern might originate. (392–3)

Following up on Hensley's vision, I suggest that for us—readers who are amused, unsettled, entertained, provoked, confused, or repelled by modernist artworks—"care" means a mode of reading as both acknowledgment *and* critique, taking apart *and* building (see Moi; Kornbluh). Cultivating citational practices informed by historically anchored and more diverse theoretical accounts of political affect, I believe, helps modernist studies to not only "go beyond the merely descriptive" but also activates the self-awareness of one's complex attachment in encountering modernist aesthetic affects. The contemporary theories of affect indexed by my brief sketch here invite us to adopt vocabularies and conceptual frameworks to articulate how our critical pathos inevitably links with and interacts with what we read and study. "Responsible reading," then, means not only responsible scholarship but also an investigation into the privileges and limits in our *ability to respond* to modernist theories and aesthetics of affect (see Masami Sugimori's brilliant discussion of attachment, proximity, and positionality in the "Passing Responsibly" section of his essay in this volume). "Becoming addicted"—as Sedgwick and Frank put it—is only one part of our experience as readers of modernism; another part is sobriety.

Notes

1 Throughout this essay, "Critical Theory" (*Kritische Theorie*) refers to the concept coined by the Frankfurt School, in particular Max Horkheimer's "Critical Theory" contrasted with "traditional theory" in his essay "Traditional and Critical Theory."

2 "Affect" as a noun in Baruch Spinoza's *Ethics* is the result of the translation of "affectus." Brian Massumi's affect theory is largely informed by Spinoza and Henri Bergson. In scientific studies of emotion, such as in Silvan Tomkins's and Paul Ekman's works, "affect" as a noun has been used almost interchangeably with emotion. This line of affect theory inspires Sedgwick and Frank's writing. These two interrelated branches of affect theory further converge into the so-called affective turn in the humanities, and one of its landmarks is Melissa Gregg and Gregory J. Seigworth's edited volume *The Affect Theory Reader*. However, like Gregg and Seigworth, I am aware of the problems of the rhetoric of "turn": affect's in-between and ambivalent status always renders any neat narrative of "turn" impossible.

3 Gregg and Seigworth describe these two essays as "the watershed moment for the most recent resurgence of interest and intrigue regarding affect and theories of affect" (5).
4 Viktor Shklovsky observes a similarly modernist impulse to break a habitual thought pattern in his commentary on Tolstoy's works: "This method of seeing things outside their context led Tolstoy to the enstrangement of rites and dogmas in his late works, replacing the habitual religious terms with their usual meanings—the result was strange, monstrous" (167).
5 According to Leys, Massumi not only oversimplifies and erases the complexity of Hertha Sturm's research findings but crucially misunderstands "the lowered skin resistance in the viewers" as "a dampening of intensity" (321). Leys clarifies that "since lowered skin resistance is a sign of increased skin conductance associated with higher arousal, it is unclear from the data what if anything was dampened in this version" (321). Leys also harshly critiques Massumi's interpretation of Libet's experiment, arguing that he repeats Libet's "classical dualism of mind and body" (326).
6 As Arthur Symons also writes,

"Poetry," said Mallarmé, "is the language of a state of crisis"; and all his poems are the evocation of a passing ecstasy, arrested in mid-flight. This ecstasy is never the mere instinctive cry of the heart, the simple human joy or sorrow, which, like the Parnassians, but for not quite the same reason, he did not admit in poetry. It is a mental transposition of emotion or sensation, veiled with atmosphere, and becoming, as it becomes a poem, pure beauty. (120)

References

Adorno, Theodor W. *Aesthetic*, translated by Wieland Hoban, Kindle ed. Polity, 2018.
Ahmed, Sara. *The Cultural Politics of Emotion*. Edinburgh UP, 2004.
Bell, Clive. *Art*. Arrow Books, 1961.
Berlant, Lauren. *Cruel Optimism*. Duke UP, 2011.
Brown, Wendy. *States of Injury: Power and Freedom in Late Modernity*. Princeton UP, 1995.
Felski, Rita. *The Limits of Critique*. U of Chicago P, 2015.
Ford, Ford Madox. *The English Novel*. Constable, 1930.
Friedman, Susan Stanford. "Both/And: Critique and Discovery in the Humanities." *PMLA/Publications of the Modern Language Association of America*, vol. 132, no. 2, 2017, pp. 344–51, DOI: https://doi-org.ezproxy.library.uvic.ca/10.1632/pmla.2017.132.2.344. Accessed May 10, 2020.

Gregg, Melissa, and Gregory J. Seigworth. "An Inventory of Shimmers." *The Affect Theory Reader*. Duke UP, 2010, pp. 1–25.

Hensley, Nathan K. "Introduction." *Special Cluster: Commitment, Victorian Literature and Culture*, vol. 48, no. 2, pp. 391–405, DOI:10.1017/S1060150320000066. Accessed June 6, 2020.

Horkheimer, Max. "Traditional and Critical Theory." *Critical Theory: Selected Essays*, translated by Matthew J. O'Connell et al. Continuum, 2002.

Hussey, Mark. "Clive Bell, 'a Fathead and a Voluptuary': Conscientious Objection and British Masculinity." *Queer Bloomsbury*, edited by Brenda Helt and Madelyn Detloff. Edinburgh UP, 2016, pp. 651–98.

"It's All in Your Head: Director Pete Docter Gets Emotional in 'Inside Out.'" *NPR*, June 10, 2015, https://www.npr.org/2015/06/10/413273007/its-all-in-your-head-director-pete-docter-gets-emotional-in-inside-out.

Kornbluh, Anna. *The Order of Forms: Realism, Formalism, and Social Space*. U of Chicago P, 2019.

Leys, Ruth. *The Ascent of Affect: Genealogy and Critique*. U of Chicago P, 2017.

Marcuse, Herbert. "On Hedonism." *Negations: Essays in Critical Theory*, translated from German by Jeremy J. Shapiro. MayFly Books, 2009, pp. 119–50.

Massumi, Brian. "The Autonomy of Affect." *Cultural Critique*, no. 31, 1995, pp. 83–109, DOI: http://www.jstor.org/stable/1354446. Accessed May 10, 2020.

Moi, Toril. *Revolution of the Ordinary: Literary Studies After Wittgenstein, Austen, and Cavell*. U of Chicago P, 2017.

Ngai, Sianne. *Ugly Feelings*. Harvard UP, 2005.

Orwell, George. "W. B. Yeats." *Fifty Orwell Essays*. Project Gutenberg of Australia eBooks, http://gutenberg.net.au/ebooks03/0300011h.html#part20.

Radio Free Stein. https://radiofreestein.com/.

Sedgwick, Eve Kosofsky. *Bathroom Songs: Eve Kosofsky Sedgwick as a Poet*, edited by Jason Edwards, Punctum Books, 2017.

Sedgwick, Eve Kosofsky. *Touching Feeling: Affect, Pedagogy, Performativity*. Duke UP, 2003.

Sedgwick, Eve Kosofsky, and Adam Frank. "Shame in the Cybernetic Fold: Reading Silvan Tomkins." *Critical Inquiry*, vol. 21, no. 2, 1995, pp. 496–522, ProQuest, http://search.proquest.com.ezproxy.library.uvic.ca/docview/1297269679?accountid=14846. Accessed May 10, 2019.

Sharpe, Christina. *Monstrous Intimacies: Making Post-Slavery Subjects*. Duke UP, 2010.

Shklovsky, Viktor. "Art, as Device." Translated and introduced by Alexandra Berlina. *Poetics Today*, vol. 36, no. 3, 2015, pp. 151–74, DOI: 10.1215/03335372-3160709. Accessed May 10, 2019.

Spinoza, Baruch. *Ethics: Ethica Ordine Geometrico Demonstrata*. Floating Press, 2009. ProQuest Ebook Central, https://ebookcentral-proquest-com.ezproxy.library.uvic.ca/lib/uvic/detail.action?docID=413149. Accessed May 5, 2020.

Symons, Arthur. *The Symbolist Movement in Literature*. Archibald Constable, 1908.

Tang, Yan. "The Politics of Naming." *Modernism/modernity.* Print Plus, February 7, 2019, https://modernismmodernity.org/forums/posts/responses-special-issue-weak-theory-part-i.

Tomkins, Silvan. "Left and Right: A Basic Dimension of Ideology and Personality." *The Study of lives: Essays on Personality in Honor of Henry A. Murray.* Atherton Press, 1963, pp. 388–411.

Watts, Kara, Molly Volanth Hall, and Robin Hackett, editors. *Affective Materialities: Reorienting the Body in Modernist Literature.* UP of Florida, 2019.

Williams, Raymond. *Marxism and Literature.* Oxford UP, 1977.

Woolf, Virginia. "Professions for Women." *The Death of the Moth and Other Essays.* Hogarth Press, 1945, pp. 149–54.

Woolf, Virginia. *To the Lighthouse,* https://opentextbc.ca/englishliterature/wpcontent/uploads/sites/27/2014/10/To-the-Lighthouse-Etext-Edited.pdf.

Yeats, W. B. "The Symbolism of Poetry." *Essays and Introductions.* Macmillan, 1980, pp. 153–64.

Zerilli, Linda M. G. "The Turn to Affect and the Problem of Judgment." *New Literary History*, vol. 46, no. 2, 2005, pp. 261–86, DOI: https://doi.org/10.1353/nlh.2015.0019. Accessed May 10, 2020.

5

The Case for Prosthetic Thinking

Kathryn Carney

In this essay, I argue for the value of prosthetic theory and, subsequently, "prosthetic thinking" as a form of phenomenological, "reparative" thinking. Prosthetic thinking is reflected in a scholarship that doesn't take phenomenology as its object, but rather draws on its central tenets to inform a post-critical method. In doing so, I take up Paul Saint-Amour's invitation in "Weak Theory, Weak Modernism" and the *Modernism/modernity* volume on the same topic "to irritate a field into a state of self-scrutiny—or even a crisis of self-recognition—that generates fresh methods and collaborations, needed forms of humility and responsibility, unforeseen kinds of projects, and renewed or new reasons for undertaking them" (445). I commit to the theorization of prosthesis in hopes of producing a way of thinking that depends on bodily ecology and phenomenological experience as method, metaphor, and lived reality all at once.

Prosthesis remains underdeveloped as part of a critical interdisciplinary vocabulary despite its general conceptual ubiquity. While prosthesis has been at the center of posthuman thought from the interwar era (1918–33 by Germanist accounts, 1918–39 for many others) to the 1980s and beyond, both modernist studies and the post-humanities have largely overlooked it. My affinity for the concept of prosthesis comes from its unique importance in crip theory as well as its role in modernist history. In pursuit of theorizing prosthesis as an epistemological method, I blend salient aspects of Alia Al-Saji's concept of prosthesis with crip theory, critical disability studies, and phenomenology. I hope to demonstrate that this mode of thinking—*prosthetic thinking*—is self-reflexive and versatile. In a serendipitous language play, "prosthetic thinking" is a reparative and responsive method predicated on negativity itself.

Though prosthetic thinking is therefore a "weak" method, I prefer the language of *porosity* to break from the strong-weak binary that, even at its most effective and *détourn*'ed in Saint-Amour's hands, remains constraining. Though all things tend toward becoming their opposites, the pellicle of history accrued around "brittler binarisms" (Saint-Amour 440) like weak/strong needs more than inversion to be dissolved—a semantic sedimentation that Cristina Ionica astutely identifies in her essay here as "baggage" (xx). I suggest that *porosity*, not "weakness," is the condition of possibility, though one may understand porosity itself as a type of material "weakness" (as in a gap, lapse, or the more somatic "pore") that presupposes transmission, transition, and even transmutation. Ionica emphasizes the "derogation" instated by such binaries, to this end: "this aspect, more than any others, poses major problems for any attempt to mobilize 'nonnormative' meanings of 'weakness' at a theoretical level" (xx). Ionica's excavation of Christian meekness as an instrument of imperial-colonial organizations of bodily perception is also relevant here, though I remain concerned with her reliance on the language of pathologization in many ways normalized in the discussion of paranoid critique by Sedgwick. We would perhaps do well to think of the irreconcilable rhetorics of liberal society presented by Ionica by way of Melanie Klein as pathological *instead* as a double bind: an embodied impasse.

Though this distinction may appear arbitrary, it importantly entails moving away from the *moral* negativity and normativity of terms such as "others," "deviance," "disability," and so forth.[1] Prosthetic thinking, however, is not an experiment in exploring the positivist potentials of prostheses represented by the posthuman assemblage, for example. Instead, porosity here is strictly *negative*: it follows a formulation of philosophical prosthesis advocated for by Alia Al-Saji that hinges on lapse as a dialogic interruption ("interlocution") leading to hesitation and cultivating ethical engagement, not a writing- or speaking-over. Subsequently, I present a prosthetic reading of Djuna Barnes's *Nightwood* (originally published in 1937) to stage something like a "cripping" of (post-)critique.

Prosthetic Thinking

Al-Saji's philosophy as prosthesis depends on a phenomenological, and thus deeply embodied frame, to further her own conception of critical hesitation and develop what she calls a critical-ethical vision. This vision and the mode of embodied practice that wields it depend on disjuncture to resist objectifying and totalizing "visions" and the relationships they generate.

Prosthesis opens a dimension of being and thinking that organizes experience to create emergent relations. These new dimensions unfold such that the most possibility for novel thought and action develops in the spatially lived temporal interval, as well as in the physical "interval" of porous space between body and prosthesis. When established paradigms reach their limits, we encounter the opportunity to forge new ones through generative tension. This critical and creative act is predicated on lapse and absence rather than the presence one may associate with a prosthetic supplementation.

Al-Saji derives her understanding of prosthesis as both an embodied and theoretical process from her careful reading of Henri Bergson and Maurice Merleau-Ponty. For Al-Saji, to view philosophy as prosthesis is to open another dimension of experience, an epistemological fold:

> To say that philosophy is prosthetic is not to reduce it to an instrumental or utilitarian function but to show how it can become a *dimension* according to which we see and think. Indeed, such a description can serve to destabilize the dichotomy between practice and theory, nature and artifice, body and thought. *It renders thinking as bodily and material*—a speaking, gesturing, seeing, and moving philosophy. Not only does this mean that the living body is a ground for thinking and hence for philosophy, it also means that *ideas are bodily supplements or dimensions that dilate and structure the body as thinking body.* (355; emphasis added)

The dimension opened by prosthetic thinking (and, consequently, hesitation) is relational—or, said another way, transitive.[2] It constitutes everything in between the thinker and the thought, the body and the prosthesis. Merleau-Ponty calls this dimension of interstitiality and reciprocal imbrication "the chiasm" for its duality and reciprocity: it is both generated and generating, emerging from *durée* to organize subsequent experiential possibilities.[3] I must address, however, the apparently paradoxical relationship between the professed negativity of prosthesis and what would appear to be the positivist expansion embedded in "dilation:" I understand Al-Saji's use of "dilation" as conceptual and perceptual rather than material (see also Rothman's discussion of the dilational process of affirmative acts in this volume [xx]). The physical vector of the body remains unchanged through dilation, but the scope of its *experience* expands into the chiasm enveloping it. This sense of tension between positivity and negativity, oneness and twoness, is at the heart of a phenomenological epistemology: "The structure of the lived body as twoness (two eyes, two hands) and separation (*écart*) opens the possibility for diacritical difference and meaning, according to Merleau-Ponty" (Al-Saji 355). Perception's duality—to be at once in and of the chiasm, both perceiving and perceived—comprises the simultaneously discrete yet dual natures of our experience and knowledge. This also expresses the phenomenological notion of reciprocal relation, termed "reversibility" in Merleau-Ponty's work, that blurs the boundaries of *épistemē* and *technē*, body and prosthetic, and cause and effect.

To pursue a project of "critical-ethical" or "transformative vision" depends on the interval opened up by hesitation in the prosthetic act. Al-Saji uses "vision" in terms that are at once literal and figurative.[4] "Vision" refers to both embodied visual perception *and* figurative perspective (orientation, position) as a discursive stake. "Vision" is simply another word or metaphor for the paradigm by which things are made visible and legible to us—also termed episteme: through Al-Saji's articulation of prosthesis, we can understand the project I advocate for here as an epistemological method that prioritizes making such visions responsible.

The language of metaphor exposes yet another sense of ambiguous duality in the prosthetic act between actuality and virtuality. Prostheses expand the range of actions one is capable of performing in and through time by making alternative temporalities and their trajectories available to the hesitating body. The act of prosthesis is something of an inverse abjection whereby hesitation replaces horror; the prosthetic is neither fully conceptually nor physically incorporated into the body despite its role in the bodily schema. It remains both a part of and distinct from the body, as each aspect—the body and the prosthetic, the actual and the virtual, the spatial and the temporal—interpenetrates the other without altogether integrating.

Al-Saji's premise defamiliarizes (or, per Sara Ahmed's queer phenomenology, disorients) to forge a fresh perspective. Neither the act of prosthesis nor relationships to the world mediated by prosthetics are foreign to us. Conscious and critical engagement with them, however, is usually sequestered to the realm of the non-normate and relegated to the study of any subjectivity not considered "universal." This is a tendency of normativity or, as Paul Saint-Amour has it, perhaps another example of "dynamotropism": "our tendency to turn toward what is considered strong" (445). But strength, opacity, and seamlessness are not the goals of prosthetic thinking. The prosthesis is significant precisely because it *cannot* wholly accomplish the task for which we deploy it:

> This partial failure or "deficit" leaves an interval between need and action, between affect and response … instead we hesitate, becoming conscious of other possibilities of acting … the prosthesis … carries within it hesitation and the

potential for reflection. This openness is part of the creative power of prostheses. (Al-Saji 356)

As that which is "at once ... actual and virtual," the prosthetic renders the body, its action, and its thought porous and permeable (Al-Saji 360). It is a (dis)junction that creates possibility yet precedes action, multiplying and magnifying the sheer variety of potential operations or responses. The act of prosthesis is the simultaneous forgetting of one specific phenomenological epistemology to adopt and adapt to another—per Durão in this volume, the "hard work" is, in large part, *precisely* the forgetting of previous patterns of phenomenological knowledge *sans* prosthesis that makes this possible. For prosthesis to operate, Bergsonian *durée* must develop out of the gaps between the tool and its task; the joints—the cruces or seams of the prosthesis's operations—must remain visible. This is key, as generative synthesis and the deconstruction of dichotomies cannot happen without some degree of permeability—which is to say rupture, difference, and transparency. The act of prosthesis and its ensuing *durée* cultivates a spatiotemporal lapse to ultimately make space for the introduction of ethics into our "reading" of the text-as-world and world-as-text.

Prosthetic Thinking as Responsible Reading

Prostheses are unruly objects for unruly bodies. They represent a right to refusal, an acting up, and a "misfitting" resulting in a sort of methodological suspension (see also Durão xx).[5] This is where disability and queerness meet under the aegis of "crip": cripping is an intentional, embodied epistemological orientation *against* fixity that is only intensified in the act of prosthesis. Prosthesis as considered here ultimately represents a semiotic argument.

As a state of being and an operating principle for crip embodiment, prosthesis constitutes a modernist syntax of the body, a "formal experiment and ... logic of rupture" (Tang, this volume, xx). The porosity inherent to prosthesis is not a weakening but an active concession to rupture as perhaps one of the only "universal" existential conditions. By nature of its sheer unpredictability, then, a reparative, prosthetic thinking concedes to the partiality of perspectives and dispenses with the "perfecting" prerogative of paranoid critique. To borrow Tang's phrase from elsewhere in this volume, consider here the role of a prosthetic's affect as *avant la lettre*: the negative affect produced by its "failure" and *durée* are critically interrupting of action and motion. This affect constitutes the prosthesis's intervention into the habit-body.

Let's turn to reading responsibly with prosthetic thinking. *Nightwood* proves to be a prime candidate for practicing such a method due to its emphatic epistemological orientation toward rupture. The novel resists closure in every sense; the dualistic structure of subject and object is upended, with each person defined and narrated through the lens of another equally fallible figure. Each exists only as an approximation, an image drawn through opaque prose and an oscillatory narrative. In the sense that affect is regularly expressed as something sedimented into a character's bodily comportment, mind and body are reversible, syncretic, and inherently intertwined. Each character is represented as an ecology, a constellation of relations and affects, rather than any self-contained individual: apparently paradoxically, they are individualized *through* their relationality. As such, and like Robin herself, the text refuses its reader comfort, possession, and mastery. To this end, a "surface" reading and a "deep" reading would likely yield the same, inconclusive results.

Tension is the guiding convention of the novel; the plot is driven—generated, even—by the uneasy ecology of the characters. Their indeterminate relations are precisely what collect them together, with the winding narrative provided by the doctor only ever so loosely constituting an actual plot. *Nightwood* models both a prosthetic style of writing fiction and a parallel opportunity to engage with a text *epistemologically* prosthetically. If we approach the characters as embodied actants, there are plenty of prosthetic objects to be found—the "heirlooms" of Felix's confabulated heritage, the cabinet of curiosities representing Jenny's conquests, Matthew O'Connor's androgynous *accoutrements* or cane, among many others. However, such a superficial implementation of prosthetic theory is far too literal. Instead, I hope to demonstrate a prosthetic reading of a scene halfway through the novel in the chapter entitled "Watchman, What of the Night?"

With prosthesis as both metaphor and method in hand, so to speak, I can parse a particular passage—which appears to be a dense tapestry of absurdist non sequiturs and ambiguous aphorisms—as an epistemological claim. Our primary unreliable narrator of sorts, the self-identified "Dr. Matthew Mighty-grain-of-salt-Dante-O'Connor," leads us through a paean on "particular polarity." The night emerges as metonym for all things ineffable through this discussion of "how the day and night are related by their division" (Barnes 87). More than a story about difference, however, this "division" is articulated as a treatise on the treachery of binaries—especially that of subject and object.

To rupture the binary between subject and object is to ultimately rupture the foundations of Western representation based on semblance and analogic mimesis. Rhetorically, the characters of *Nightwood* constitute signifiers that resist successful signification—think of Robin's absence constituting her presence. Altogether, the plurality of each signifier's valences renders each iterative signification increasingly ineffectual. Nora emerges in this chapter as Red Riding Hood—notably hesitating in the presence of negativity: "Hearing his 'come in' she opened the door and for one second hesitated, so incredible was the disorder that met her eyes" (Barnes 84). Matthew becomes "the wolf in bed!" (85), a sign representing its own chiastic counterpart—its very inverse. Our cultural treatment of the body as master metaphor still presents a similar, particular signifying fallibility in the case of the face's simultaneous representation of likeness and difference. Matthew articulates this, saying,

> "Faces is it!" I screamed, "the face is for fools! If you fish by the face you fish out trouble, but there's always other fish when you deal with the sea. The face is what anglers catch in the daylight, but the sea is the night!"... "Ah, mighty uncertainty!" said the doctor. "Have you thought of all the doors that have shut at night and opened again?" (Barnes 99)

In positing faces and doors as portal analogs, O'Connor announces them as ontologically porous within his epistemological framework. Elsewhere, affect is expressed to not only exist between but also seep into bodies. The virtual is thereby made actual, in a strange alchemical, osmotic transubstantiation:[6]

> What an autopsy I'll make, with everything all which ways in my bowels! A kidney and a shoe cast of Roman races; a liver and a long-spent whisper ... and my heart that will be weeping still when they find my eyes cold ... and the lining of my belly, flocked with the locks cut off love in odd places that I've come on. (Barnes 107–8)

I have focused on Matthew here as a materialization synecdochal with many tendencies of the text. Characters, objects, and spaces alike are all described as being suspended in a stilted, unstable matrix of signification like that evidenced in Barthes's reading of Balzac's "Sarrasine" in *S/Z*: there is the early instance in which Hedvig plays the piano with "the masterly stroke of a man" (Barnes 10); the presence of the comically named Frau Mann, much less the descriptions of Robin's "masculinity" regarding relationships; and Matthew's room is described as "like the rooms in brothels ... yet ... also muscular, a cross between a *chamber à coucher* and a boxer's training camp" (85). This affect of instability not only exists between characters but also generates them *through* its tension ("It was more than a boy like me [who am the last woman left in this world, though I am the bearded lady] could bear" [107]). This is the affect of the prosthesis's negativity.

Like Barnes's use of language throughout *Nightwood*, prosthesis emphasizes the *remainder* of communication, of expression of all kinds: "Yes, we who are full to the gorge with misery should look well around doubting everything seen, done, spoken, precisely because we have a word for it, and *not* its alchemy" (90; emphasis added).

Cripping (Post-)Critique?

I hope that this discussion successfully shows the value of probing the depths of embodied experience for not only metaphors but also methods, as in the example of "prosthetic thinking." Prosthesis generates hesitation, which, in turn, generates new needs that themselves call for new acts of prosthesis. Hesitation is the moment of responsibility's emergence, whereas prosthesis is its actualization as care. Each is activated as an evolving, ever-shifting relation with the world. Though this may read as a simple formula—absence necessitates presence— the "presence" of prosthesis *proliferates absences* rather than precluding or "repairing" them. Prosthesis is nonetheless creative: all acts of prosthesis are porous, and, as such, reproduce opportunity ad infinitum. Consequently, I posit prosthesis as a cripping method of post-critique that promotes responsibility through an embodied ethics.

Prosthetic thinking is inherently responsive and thus responsible. Prosthetic thinking is dilational, expanding the experience available to us not in scale, but in scope. This dilation is also dialogic by nature: the expansion of scope occurs through contact with our others, be this contact spatially relational, as in the chiasm; verbal, as in communication; and so on. We denaturalize ourselves through the care of the other, the incorporation of our prostheses, and thereby give (our) body to objects artificially rendered discrete.

In "Weak Theory, Weak Modernism," Saint-Amour addresses anxieties around disciplinary "expansionism" buoyed by the (intentionally) spatial language of "territory." This word choice belies a larger problem at the intersection of humanistic practice with posthumanist methods: what is it, exactly, that "*belongs*" to us? Where do our bodies—of thought, inhabitance, or otherwise— end? Not coincidentally, these questions are the very same ones invoked by the prosthetic act. In this way, perhaps prosthetic thinking as a cripping method can expand the purview of modernist studies as a humanistic discipline *without* succumbing to the effacing tendencies of an assimilationist methodological model or the overly simplistic stringency of a purist one. Prosthetic thinking attempts to identify and engage with preexisting networks of heterogeneities, each narrating a unique dimension of experience and relationality, without sublating them. Prosthesis depends on syncretism, not hierarchy, to operate.

Conversely, what if we were to consider modernist studies prosthetic? As a field called into being by the emergent resonances of a broad constellation of interdisciplinary inquiries, modernist studies is surely appended to—an appendage of?—a broader academic historical project. And this project's sutures and dehiscences, too, remain visible. To actively cultivate this field as prosthetic would entail dismantling disciplinary hierarchies, which is a possible task if we harbor critical-ethical hesitation in our embodied and academic praxes alike. However, such a project at the level of a field of discourse rather than individual inquiries may be at odds with the nature of prosthetic lapse. Paraphrasing Merleau-Ponty to describe lapse as a variation on his "unthought," Al-Saji writes, "such an absence is not something of which we speak directly; rather, it is a dimension according to which we speak ... such a prosthesis has the structure of an interval rather than a thing" (361). As that which is unthought, as no[-]thing, the prosthetic lapse *cannot be institutionalized* though it *can* direct institutional tendencies. Instead, it lives on as an individual practice of responsibility among its practitioners, self-propagating and teaching by example.

Notes

1 Rosemarie Garland-Thomson's discussion of the "normate" is one example of a particularly effective exercise in "flipping the script" on normative language and discourses: "Naming the figure of the normate is one conceptual strategy that will allow us to press our analyses beyond the simple dichotomies of male/female, white/black, straight/gay, or able-bodied/disabled so that we can examine the subtle interrelations among social identities that are anchored to physical differences" (8). To this list, I would add "weak/strong."

2 This language comes from Fabio Akcelrud Durão's essay in this volume: "To be responsible in a good (I almost said 'responsible') sense is transitive" (xx). Keeping in mind theory's role as a novel, "ready-made" (xx) metanarrative emerging in postwar Europe, Durão goes on to explain that "there was a *cultural substratum* or

structure of feeling if you want in which theory thrived and which it also reinforced. Ideas were not just things one organized into arguments; instead, they invited ways of being and of interacting with other people" (xx; emphasis in original). Though "capital T" Theory simultaneously "seems often enough to be impatient with [its] objects" (xx), Durão's discussion demonstrates the utility in thinking of theory as a relational epistemological framework (in Durão's terms, a "genre") that can never truly be "intransitive" in the ways philosophy at times aspires to be.

3 The "chiasm" goes by many other names, including intercorporeity in other works of Merleau-Ponty. More recently, the phenomenology of porous intercorporeity has conceptually been taken up by Lee Edelman and Lauren Berlant in the use of "nonsovereignty" throughout *Sex, or the Unbearable* (2014) to describe the unsettling, uncanny vulnerability we experience when we become uniquely conscious of our body's fundamental porosity and precarity. This language picks up on the relational ontology of Emmanuel Levinas (and, after him, Judith Butler) while invoking and interrogating the strange metonymy between the states of our bodies and the bodies of our states.

4 While Al-Saji's article (and phenomenology at large) deploys latently ableist organizations and hierarchies of experience through its dependence on the visual, it nonetheless provides a useful interdisciplinary metaphor regarding the importance of perceptual perspective or positionality. Similarly, Donna Haraway in her article entitled "Situated Knowledges," writes that she "would like to insist on the embodied nature of all vision and so reclaim the sensory system that has been used to signify a leap out of the marked body and into a conquering gaze from nowhere" (581). Like Al-Saji's, Haraway's "vision" is and isn't literal: she uses this language to reassert the importance of knowledge's embodied quality. The "conquering gaze" in question is the retrospective gaze of history itself—"an illusion, a god trick" that "we have mistaken that for creativity and knowledge, omniscience, even" (Haraway 582, 587). Each thinker's project reaffirms the importance of dismantling a vision-centric hierarchy of perception to emancipate the knowledge embedded in other sensory modes and propel our practices of history (scientific, social, or otherwise) into self-reflexivity.

5 Rosemarie Garland-Thomson reminds us throughout her work that "misfitting" is itself an incredibly useful hermeneutic (see also note 1). That said, misfitting is perhaps at odds with Sedgwick's sense of weak theory as "making whole" (Cristina Ionica, this volume, xx).

6 In *Bíos* (Italian 2004/English 2008), Roberto Esposito briefly attends to prosthesis as a specifically modern rupture of both property and representation. He first discusses John Locke's conceptions of property and labor as themselves prosthetic and embedded within the subject's bodily schema: Just as work is an extension of the body, so is property an extension of work, a sort of *prosthesis* that through

the operation of the arm connects it to the body in the same vital segment; not only because property is necessary for the material support of life, but because its prolongation is directed to corporeal formation (65). As the national or institutional formulation of property, "territory" conceptually tethers space to the bodies that occupy it (albeit often unjustly). Understanding property as a psychic projection and extension of the bodily schema immediately moves this discussion into a realm of biopolitical critique. Further, Esposito marks the (omni)presence of the modern prosthetic in the early twentieth century as a turning point towards a secular mode of incarnation, the presence of one body (organic or inorganic) in another through surgical implants and transplants (168). He further insinuates that modern biotechnology unraveled the Western canon of mimesis itself insofar as the prosthetic challenges the role of Christ as God incarnate, a divine suturing of materiality and immateriality; the modern prosthetic contradicts the idea that the martyred body can never be physically and profanely "restored." Esposito, in turn, suggests that the prosthetic is but one of the many ways that modern technology and culture transcend the fetters of the system of representational conventions privileging semblance, essence, and the cohesion of the two that dominated the history of the Western iconographic tradition. Special thanks to Won Lee-Jeon for drawing my attention to this particular moment in the text and Esposito's explicit use of "prosthesis."

References

Al-Saji, Alia. "When Thinking Hesitates: Philosophy as Prosthesis and Transformative Vision." *Southern Journal of Philosophy*, vol. 50, no. 2, 2000, pp. 351–61.

Barnes, Djuna. *Nightwood*. New Directions, 2016.

Esposito, Robert. *Bíos: Biopolitics and Philosophy*, translated by Timothy Campbell. U of Minnesota P, 2008.

Garland-Thomson, Rosemarie. *Extraordinary Bodies: Figuring Physical Disability in American Culture and Literature*. Columbia UP, 1997.

Haraway, Donna. "Situated Knowledges: The Science Question in Feminism and the Privilege of Partial Perspective." *Feminist Studies*, vol. 14, no. 3, 1988, pp. 575–99.

Saint-Amour, Paul. "Weak Theory, Weak Modernism." *Modernism/modernity*, vol. 24, no. 3, 2018, pp. 437–59.

Part II

Method

6

Beyond the Search Image: Reading as (Re)search

Daniel Aureliano Newman

The proper way to read is to run on when anything isn't comprehensible.
—Ezra Pound, "Second Fytte" (qtd. in Rainey 152)

At the time of writing, you were preparing for your graduate seminar on experimental narratives. You were rattled by a reading you'd assigned for the first day, Beckett's "As the Story Was Told." Among the most affecting stories you'd ever read, it also proved beyond your grasp: you couldn't explain your response to the story, or even its basic facts. It gave you little interpretive foothold. It's uncomfortable being stumped by a one-page story, especially when students will expect guidance. But your discomfort was accompanied by an exhilarating curiosity, half bemusement, half piqued interest; in fact, the curiosity was produced *by* the discomfort. It reminded you of first reading *Ulysses* as an undergraduate, an experience you relive whenever you open your old Penguin copy and see the margins riddled with annotations including "WTF?"

* * *

The prospect of discussing Beckett's story reminds me of Gérard Genette's tongue-in-cheek statement that "the inconvenience of doing research is that by dint of searching you find—what you weren't seeking" (7–8). Is this a sneaky jab at a certain kind of reading, characterized less by enquiry than by confirmation bias? Had Genette said it in 2012 instead of 1982, we could easily read his quip as a contribution to post-critique, a loose coalition of approaches pursuing "alternatives to a suspicious hermeneutics" (Anker and Felski 1)—alternatives or at least additions to what Eve Sedgwick called "a paranoid critical stance" (126). For Sedgwick, "the first imperative of paranoia is *There must be no bad surprises*" (130), so everything must be anticipated and assimilated. Nothing in the text is without its assigned role in the system imagined by the paranoid reader, just as nothing in a dream can, according to Freud, be negated or dismissed by the dreamer. In this context, the possibility of finding something you weren't seeking is indeed an inconvenience, or worse. But isn't the point of research to find something new, unexpected? In this, research may be more like reading, or writing, than literary critics generally let on.

Paranoid reading is satisfying because it allots a role for every detail in the text, making it a meaningful part of a whole; thus, it denies the possibility of information in excess of the scope of the hypothesis. This is unfortunate, not because some details mean nothing (I don't believe that), but because it rewards readers armed with a *search image*, a term I borrow from biology that describes how some animals use a kind of targeted perception to detect hard-to-find prey. A search image is, in Reuven Dukas's definition, "a selective search for a particular cryptic prey type, which involves an increased probability of detecting that prey type and a reduced probability of detecting other distinct prey types" (qtd. in Punzalan *et al.* 306). The analogy with paranoid reading is irresistible: like predators equipped with a search image, readers are predisposed to find the clues that, once decrypted, will confirm their suspicions. That search images entail perceptual tradeoffs ("a reduced probability of detecting other distinct prey types") is also apt.

Behind post-critique lies the hope of reading for more than the self-fulfilling rewards of search images. Thus, Bruno Latour imagines a criticism that trades in "*multiplication*, not *subtraction*," "generating more ideas than we have received" (248). Relatedly, Rita Felski argues that "rather than looking behind the text—for its hidden causes, determining conditions, and noxious motives—we might place ourselves in front of the text, reflecting on what it unfurls, calls forth, makes possible" (12). Instead of "hypervigilance," Heather Love calls for more "attentiveness," for "acts of noticing" (237–8). Proponents of "nonfigurative reading" similarly call for "an overactive research imagination, a desire for … 'unnecessary information'" (Freedgood and Schmitt 3). Such approaches are not anti-critique; post-critique isn't about replacing or forgetting earlier modes. Post-critique is less troubled by "the categorical imperative to always problematize" (Friedman 348) than by how homogenous the modes of problematization have become: critique has become synonymous with just a few critical frameworks (notably Marxist and/or Freudian) that have, despite or indeed because of their hypervigilance, their own blind-spots. The Foucauldian framework of New Historicism, for example, ensures that its practitioners see data through a lens that, although illuminating, excludes cultural interpretations concerned with things other than the operations of power (Levine 116). In this light, I see the recent call for "weak theory" as post-critique's fellow traveler. The hope invested in weak theory lies, as Paul St. Amour (439) and Heather Love (237) have both noted, in alternatives to the "powerful reductions" of Theory.

The "weak" in weak theory raises concern, as both Cristina Ionica and Masami Sugimori argue with particular insight elsewhere in this volume. It may unwittingly participate in a rhetoric of exclusion whose consequences may be counterproductive; it may encourage quietism. It is also problematic because the nature of the weakness in question remains unclear. As I see it, weak theory has focused too much strength of claim on the rightness of our arguments and the assertiveness with which we make them. What if we understood the *weak* in weak theory differently? What if we saw weakness in terms of vulnerability, of theory's accountability to external checks? I am obviously influenced by the scientific training that preceded my move to literary studies. Scientists understand theory differently than humanists. I'm especially taken with the provisional standing of scientific theory, a form of weakness succinctly described by Stephen Hawking:

> No matter how many times the results of experiments agree with some theory, you can never be sure that the next time the result will not contradict the theory … Each time new experiments are observed to agree with the predictions the theory survives, and our confidence in it is increased; but if ever a new observation is found to disagree, we have to abandon or modify the theory. (10)

Scientists are of course not immune to the lures of over-strong theory, as Hawking indirectly goes on to suggest: "At least that is what is supposed to happen, but you can always question the competence of the person who carried out the observation" (10). Such questioning is necessary: the evidence often *is* questionable. But the danger of obstinate loyalty to theory is real, and questioning the observer's competence can become a way to dismiss inconvenient facts. Such realities notwithstanding, scientific theory's vulnerability is built into the scientific enterprise, into a dialectic of theory and observation; if science is liable to its own forms of paranoid reading, these are generally perceived as a problem, not standard procedure.

Without advocating a scientific model, I wonder what literary studies might gain from such a similar stance toward theory. As Latour writes in a not unrelated context, "every time a philosopher gets closer to an object of science that is at once historical and interesting, his or her philosophy changes" (234). I can't help quoting from "Why Has Critique Run out of Steam?," whose moral urgency has only grown clearer of late, and which so clearly demonstrates that post-critique is not just an academic exercise. "While we spent years trying to detect the real prejudices hidden behind the appearance of objective statements," wonders Latour, "do we now have to reveal the real objective and incontrovertible facts hidden behind the *illusion* of prejudices?" (227). Well, why not? Given the weaponization of doubt by climate-change deniers and conspiracy theorists, Latour's (qualified) rehabilitation of facts is bracing, politically as well as intellectually. It also reminds us that weak theory need not mean pulling punches, just accepting theory's status as a heuristic. Theory's power could lie not only in its ability to explain the facts but also in its readiness to capitulate when the facts don't cooperate. It occurs to me that modernism offers an ideal playground for testing out this possibility, given its notorious slipperiness, its polyvalence, and its tendency to anticipate and frustrate our interpretive frameworks.

So I return to my jitters about teaching Beckett's story and feel if not more in command of the text, then less upset about this powerlessness. The inaccessibility of the story's secrets, which my students may expect me to explain, makes me uncomfortable. But I'd like to treat my discomfort as an opportunity, a lesson for future researchers and teachers.

This chapter adumbrates—tentatively of course—a kind of responsible reading that reflects what I might call a hermeneutics of curiosity or "discovery" (the term favored by Susan Stanford Friedman [348]). It's an approach to research in which the search is foundational, and the question "why?" is always at the fore. The motivating questions are not "What's the code hidden behind the text?" or "What is the text *really* saying behind the veil of appearances?" but, rather, "Why is the text like *this*?" and, even more basically, "What is the text *doing*"? This approach is hardly original, nor is it anywhere close to meriting the name of Method; it is more a stance, an attitude toward the act of research. And it isn't incompatible with critique, though it may be said to defer critique while it does reconnaissance; nor does it defer *to* critique, which is only one of the significant ends toward which it might point. It accepts and embraces the fact that literature is often puzzling, finding in our puzzlement the seeds of interesting, potentially surprising findings.

This way of reading (at least provisionally) transforms theory from a framework we use as we read into a feature of the text for which we read. We read the text for its own immanent theorizations. Modernism, being resistant to singular readings and often at odds with readers' "experiential repertoires"

(Herman 1047), is ideally suited to the approach I present in this chapter.[1] What's more, modernist authors often appear to do what Virginia Woolf claimed she did in writing *Mrs. Dalloway*, that is, "to write the book first and to invent a theory afterwards" (*Essays* V: 549). If Woolf did "invent a theory" after the fact, however, she never shared it with us—and in this she resembles most of her modernist colleagues, including those who, like Henry James, T. S. Eliot, and E. M. Forster, theorized extensively about their craft. Still, most modernists simply wrote the book, and left it to us to invent the necessary theories. What's more, modernist experimentation often explicitly or apparently reflects a desire to theorize through the process of composition.

This chapter strives to model what this research approach might look like in practice, exploiting the fact that I am currently failing to make sense of a pattern of second-person narration in several modernist novels published between 1919 and 1935. The focus of my theoretical enquiry is narratology, partly because it reflects my own research interests and partly because some of modernism's most significant innovations were in the practice and theory of narrative. This part of the chapter is open-ended by design—not only because I remain unable to account for the pattern I have found, but also because the thrill of discovery resides in part in the unfinished nature of the search. I'm not proposing a move toward half-baked research writing! I'm simply suggesting that there ought to be, beyond conference presentations, a forum for sharing research at the productive edge of discovery and explanation—where readers might access *our* readings when they are still in the process of discovery. With apologies to Pater, we might need to share not only the fruit of our readings, but the experience of reading, which is inevitably the experience of being surprised, confused, beset not only by doubt but also by the thrill of curiosity. More than anything, it is crucial these records of the reading experience be accessible to our students. For it is in the classroom, as students, that we develop the attitudes and dispositions that will shape our research methodologies as researchers. My conclusion therefore turns to the crucial question of responsible reading as pedagogy.

Modernist Fiction and/as Narrative Theory

If paranoid reading finds its methodological foundations in Freud and Marx, the approach I seek to model here has a closer kinship to literary writers themselves, particularly those who performed narratological experiments apparently unmotivated by a specific goal or theoretical commitment. The "theories" we might find in their work would be to a great extent particular to the individual texts we read, and so they would only in the loosest sense be theories. Moreover, they are implicit in the texts that contain them, which might of course be read differently, for rather different, even opposite theories. Despite my apparent flirtation with pataphysics, Alfred Jarry's paradoxical "science of the particular" and "the excepted case" (Bök 9), I am thinking closer to the more traditional sciences, whose practitioners I have found to be, on the whole, much more receptive than are humanists to findings that overturned their theoretical commitments. In any case, the approach to responsible reading and theory I test out here is indebted less to Freud and Marx (though it is not incompatible with their systems) than to the OULIPO group, the New Novelists and their modernist precursors and contemporaries such as Michel Butor, who proposed, in "Le roman comme recherche" ("The novel as [re]search") that we see "the novel as a laboratory" (Butor 9).

Butor's notion of novels as experiments that can produce new worldviews recalls Virginia Woolf's advice to would-be critics in "How Should One Read a Book?": "Perhaps the quickest way to understand the elements of what a novelist is doing is not to read, but to write: to make your own experiment with the dangers and difficulties of words (*Essays* V: 574). This procedure is consistent with her account of writing *Mrs. Dalloway*; instead of "develop[ing] a theory and then apply it," she found it "necessary to write the book first and to invent a theory afterwards" (*Essays* V: 549). This practice may not be "philosophic," she admits, but it has the benefit of being consistent with what she calls, in "Modern Fiction," the writer's freedom (*Essays* IV: 160). The alternative is patent in "Freudian Fiction," Woolf's negative review of J. D. Beresford's *The Imperfect Mother* (1920), a novel she found to be cribbed on a single theory. Her dispute is not with the theory but with its assumption of supremacy: the problem is that a novelist armed with Freudian theory holds "a patent key that opens every door. It simplifies rather than complicates, detracts rather than enriches" (*Essays* III: 197). Yet Woolf was apparently uninterested in sharing the theories she invented while composing her books. Like most authors, she left the task to her readers, to us.

I wonder what Woolf would have made of Raymond Queneau's *Exercices de Style* (1947), which retells the same mundane anecdote in ninety-nine different styles and forms. Aside from the surprising richness Queneau extracts from his unpromising anecdote are the many cases in which the experiment fails. Some of the retellings, particularly those using arbitrary Oulipian permutations, are neither intelligible nor particularly interesting. How refreshing! Most radical about Queneau's novel is its implication that any text performs the same experiment in the interdependence of form and content. The difference is that we see only one version of *Mrs. Dalloway*, whereas Queneau gives us ninety-nine versions of his anecdote (and far more sonnets in his book of rearrangeable verse lines, *A Hundred Thousand Billion Poems*).

Narrative theory as we understand it today originates with the modernists, though they were not, of course, the first to theorize about narrative. From Henry James, E. M. Forster, and Virginia Woolf to Bakhtin and the Russian Formalists, the core concepts of narratology emerged in theoretical and critical works of the early twentieth century. I'm proposing here that modernists also contributed to narratology directly, through their narrative experiments. This is a corollary of Stephen Ross's argument in *Modernism and Theory*, which finds in modernism the roots of High Theory. Writing modernist narratives is a way of theorizing the nature, limits, and possibilities of storytelling. Proust's *Recherche* is, as Gérard Genette reveals, a narratological laboratory; but you could even say it is, in itself, a work of narratology-in-practice. We could thus better understand modernist fiction if we viewed its experimentalism not merely as a negative response to genre or stylistic conventions but as positive exploration of possible but untested "narrative" territory. Much work on modernism implies that it either passively reflects historical conditions or somewhat more actively embeds a critique of these conditions within its texts. Framing experimentalism as an effect—passive or active—to historical conditions does not sufficiently capture either the spurs or the mechanics of literary innovation. Though such a symptomatic approach to literature is necessary, it does not exhaust what literature offers to criticism. If that were so, we could skip the literary altogether and do sociology. Anyway, I favor a more agential response, such as Michael Levenson's argument that "one cannot alter the movement of history, but it is possible to change the form and style of one's response" (80).

Novelists like Joyce, Hurston, and Faulkner played narrative the way jazz musicians played their instruments, creating not just new music but a new musicology to boot. Experiments with narrative often reveal gaps in narratological models—gaps that might never otherwise gotten noticed. James theorized his own technique post hoc, finding such devices as the *"ficelle"* (55), which hasn't much influenced narratology, and the central consciousness, which has. Joyce used a form of free indirect discourse in *A Portrait of the Artist* that prevents readers from stabilizing ironic distance between the narrator and Stephen Dedalus; this was interpreted as sloppy technique—at least by Wyndham Lewis—until Hugh Kenner identified it as a new species of figural narration: "The Uncle Charles Principle" (18). (We still study this flagship modernist device, not using Kenner's term but speaking instead of a productive blurring of voices and sources of authority.) Innovative literature, of which modernist fiction is a significant species, is good at revealing the gaps in our theoretical and interpretive frameworks; it creates the need for new or expanded frameworks; you could even say its innovations *are* immanent theorizations just waiting to be taken up and formulated by the critic or theorist.

Such a view of modernist experimentation and narrative theory emphasizes the generative confusion we so often experience when we encounter difficult fiction, as I hope to demonstrate by turning, as I do now, to a remarkable yet unremarked phenomenon in modernist fiction, one crying out to be examined as Genette and Kenner examined Proust and Joyce. It has escaped notice, perhaps because it seems to be restricted to novels by women, most of which are little read. I call it *mixed-voice narration* because it combines figural narration in the third person with second-person narration, sometimes also with first person. It is messy and, as I know all too well, resistant to explanation.

The Polyvalence of Modernist You-Narration

The distinctive innovation in mixed-voice narration is the use of second-person narration, or you-narration. Typically linked to postmodern fiction (Fludernik 292), with male-authored canonical examples like Michel Butor's *La modification* (1957), Italo Calvino's *Se una notte d'inverno un viaggiatore* (1979), and Jay McInerney's *Bright Lights, Big City* (1984), second-person narration is in fact much older, going back to Hawthorne's "The Haunted Mind" (1835). You-narration in the recognizably modern sense emerged with May Sinclair's *Mary Olivier*, which contains what is, to my knowledge, the first instance of mixed-voice narration. What has received effectively no attention is the fact that Sinclair's novel is only the first of several cases of you-narration in modernist fiction by women. What struck me as I found more and more examples is that despite their formal similarities these cases of mixed-voice seemed to differ too much thematically to allow satisfactory taxonomies; these modernist narrative experiments simultaneously invited and rebuffed my attempts to incorporate them into the theoretical explanations I had invested in.

I became aware of this cluster of modernist novels while working on a paper on second-person narratives by Edna O'Brien and Jennifer Egan. My view was that second-person narration lends itself to feminist fiction seeking to represent, indeed enact, the problematics of inhabiting a female body in times of national crisis. The you-narration I found in contemporary women's writing (Jamaica Kincaid, Lorrie Moore, Nuala Ní Chonchúir, and others) convinced me of the aptness of Dennis Schofield's contention: "fluidity and undecidability" are "central to the value of second-person modality for much feminist and other oppositional and alternative writing" (105). My argument was that you-narration provides a powerful tool for reflecting the contradictions, frustrations, and possibilities of female agency and identity-formation when new forms of agency and identity are both tantalizingly more conceivable and still disappointingly unrealized. I was initially satisfied that my argument also held true for modernist cases of you-narration—at least those cases I encountered first, *Mary Olivier* as well as Rosamond Lehmann's *Dusty Answer*, Jean Rhys's *After Leaving Mr. Mackenzie*, and *Voyage in the Dark*. Then I discovered more cases of modernist mixed voice, and even as their variety began to create difficulties for my argument, my search image enabled me to overread the patterns that confirmed it.

I knew that narrative techniques, including second-person narration, cannot be assigned in one-to-one correspondences with a specific politics or ideology; there is, in Jan Alber's review of current narrative studies, "no inherent or stable link between narrative techniques and ideological implications" (3). But it was only when I became overwhelmed by the evident diversity of uses of you-narration that I had to admit that my argument was, if not incorrect, then too restrictive. Some of the characters referred to as "you," for instance, are male; beyond this fact, inconvenient as it was to my argument, was the sheer variety of those to whom the "you" was addressed: characters young and old, straight and queer, native and immigrant, upper class and working class. The novels in question, moreover, vary hugely in style, theme, and genre. Was there some underlying similarity connecting all these novels—an ideological consistency made visible by the remarkable similarity of their use of mixed-voice narration? I wanted there to be something and to a great extent I believe there is; yet its nature remains tantalizingly and bracingly beyond my comprehension.

My aim here is not to address the problem of modernist mixed-voice narration. But the problem has put me into an interpretive predicament I'd like to use as a case study, a demonstration of reading beyond the search image, or reading *for* the theories created by the text's nexus of form, content, and context. By creating this new and defamiliarizing narrative situation, the authors quoted below are not only expanding the scope of what narrative means, what it is, and what it can do: because form is a kind of content, they are also in fact performing theoretical and critical explorations at the limits of representation. What are the results of these explorations? I'm still working on it. If mixed narration offers me an ideal example of modernist narratives "doing" theoretical work, the nature of that theory remains inaccessible to me.

But this is something you, reader, and I can do together. As you read on, then, consider modernist mixed-voice narration, and ask yourself: what is *up* with these shifts between first-, third-, and second-person narration?

Let's begin with a short chapter from *Mary Olivier*, an excellent representative of mixed-voice narration in general. Here Mary has passed the age at which she thought she would, following a hereditary pattern, become mad:

> Forty-five. Yesterday **she** was forty-five, and to-day. To-morrow **she** would be forty-six. **She** had come through the dreadful, dangerous year without thinking of it, and nothing had happened. Nothing at all. **She** couldn't imagine why **she** had ever been afraid of it; **she** could hardly remember what being afraid of it had felt like.
>
> Aunt Charlotte—Uncle Victor—
>
> If **I** were going to be mad **I** should have gone mad long ago: when Roddy came back; when Mark died; when **I** sent Richard away. **I** should be mad now.
>
> It was getting worse.
>
> In the cramped room where the big bed stuck out from the wall to within a yard of the window, Mamma went about, small and weak, in her wadded lavender Japanese dressing-gown, like a child that can't sit still, looking for something it wants that nobody can find. **You** couldn't think because of the soft pad-pad of the dreaming, sleep-walking feet in the lamb's-wool slippers.
>
> When **you** weren't looking she would slip out of the room on to the landing to the head of the stairs, and stand there, vexed and bewildered when **you** caught her. (Sinclair 425)

Clearly the shifts between third, first and second person are nonrandom; yet I can see no clear or consistent pattern or logic to explain them. Perhaps the fact of the shifts itself is significant, rather than the etiology of individual shifts. Still, that's not an explanation. In any case, Sinclair was not done with mixed-voice narrative. Her description of the small upper-class child in *Life and Death of Harriet Frean* is a case in point:

> Suddenly a thought came rushing at **her**. There was God and there was Jesus. But even God and Jesus were not more beautiful than Mamma. They couldn't be …
>
> Saying things like that made **you** feel good and at the same time naughty, which was more exciting than only being one or the other. (16–17)

Jean Rhys's use of mixed-voice narration is occasionally less mystifying. In *After Leaving Mr. Mackenzie*, for example, it often serves to distinguish between narrative past and present:

> She [Julia] wondered why the maid had looked at **her** with such unfriendly eyes. But hadn't **she** always suspected, ever since **she** knew anything, that human beings were—for not reason or for any reason—unfriendly?
>
> When **you** were a child, **you** put **your** hand on the trunk of a tree and **you** were comforted, because **you** knew that the tree was alive—**you** felt its life when you touched it—and **you** knew that it was friendly to **you**, or, at least, not hostile. But of people **you** were always a little afraid. (115)

This apparently simple distinction, which in this case suggests that adult Julia views her childhood self as a different person, is not consistently upheld in Rhys's fiction. In *Voyage in the Dark*, primarily narrated by Anna Morgan in the first person, the switch to you-narration suggests a more complicated kind of dissociation, more troubling than mere temporal distance:

> He said, "Why do you ask me the one thing you know perfectly well I won't do?"
>
> **I** didn't answer. **I** was thinking, "You don't know anything about me. I don't care anymore." And **I** didn't care any more.
>
> It was like letting go and falling back into water and seeing yourself grinning up through the water, **your** face like a mask, and seeing the bubbles coming up as if **you** were trying to speak from under the water. And how do **you** know what it's like to try to speak from under water when **you**'re drowned? (84)

As mentioned above, I initially approached mixed voice convinced that the device was deployed to capture experiential aspects of being a girl or woman in the late nineteenth and early twentieth century. Yet in *Adam's Breed*, Radclyffe Hall uses a narrational mode much like that of *Harriet Frean* to recount the experiences of Gian-Luca, son of Italian immigrants in England:

> **Gian-Luca** having no one to talk to, and having no language wherewith to talk in any case, found himself, as all infants must be, at a great disadvantage in relation to life ... [His wet-nurse] Rosa Varese ... had lost her own baby of croup in the very nick of time to provide **you** with dinners, but all this of course **you** did not know, nor would you have cared if **you** had. **Your** emotions were entirely concerned with **yourself**, not through any wish of **yours**, but by order of that something that commanded **you, Gian-Luca**, to live. (18–19)

Perhaps shifts between third and second person reflect an attempt to narrate the experience of non-belonging, the fragmentating effects of otherness. This seemed like a workable hypothesis for the texts above, and even more so for Lehmann's *Dusty Answer*. Its protagonist, Judith, is a young woman who, with intriguingly minimal fuss from either her fellow character or the narrator, has passionate affairs with lovers of both sexes, notably Jennifer.

> Beside Jennifer **she** felt herself too slim, too flexible, almost attenuated ... **Judith** crept closer, warming the part of **you** which **you** never had been able to untie and set free, the part that wanted to dance and run and sing ... **You** could not do without Jennifer now. (137)

This is truly very strange; it would seem accidental, sloppy, if such rapid shifts from third to second person were not so consistently part of the narrative. It is tempting to read shifts to you-narration as a reflection of heightened emotion, particularly of an erotic nature:

> There was Jennifer ... bending down final to kiss **you** a tender good night. **Judith** tried to think of [her male lover] Roddy. A little while ago he had been stooping over **her** as Jennifer stooped now, with eyes that were different and yet the same. (Lehmann 152)

But such explanations are frustrated by similar shifts that seem largely devoid of troubled identity, eroticism, or drama. For example, in a passage describing Judith at Cambridge:

> This week there was nothing in **your** mind save the machine which obeyed **you** smoothly, turning out dates and biographies, contrasting, discussing, theorizing.
>
> **Judith** walked in a dream among the pale examination faces that flowed to their doom. (Lehmann 182)

It was when I read Bowen's *The House in Paris* that my certainties abandoned me. Here the "you" is polyvalent and apparently without a consistent logic. It is sometimes a generalized "you" (equivalent to the third-person "one"):

> The weight of being **herself** [Karen] fell on her like a clock striking. **She** saw the clothes **she** would put on to go home in hanging over a chair. While it is still Before, Afterwards has no power, but afterwards, but afterwards it is the kingdom, the power and the glory. **You** do not ask yourself, what am **I** doing? **You** know. What **you** do ask yourself, what have **I** done? **you** will never know. (166)

But it also includes a more individuated, specific "you" that sometimes clearly indicates Karen:

> For **Karen**, she was the afterdark Naomi who used to slip into **your** room after lights were out to put mended stockings back in **your** drawer. She was not

supposed, of course, to mend **Karen**'s things. Thinking **you** were asleep, she would creep softly past the bed. (119)

Elsewhere the "you" refers specifically to Karen's unborn son Leopold, which seems to make Karen the narrator—though this doesn't add up, since the narrator refers to Karen in the third person:

Having done as **she** knew **she** must **she** did not think there would be a child: all the same, the idea of **you, Leopold**, began to be present in her. (165)

So ... what is to be made of the maddeningly diverse uses of mixed-voice narration in modernist fiction? It is such a distinct and unusual form that it begs to be accounted for; yet despite its remarkable consistencies across authors, it is too variable for such an account. I'm aware the foregoing paragraph has done little more than string together quotations, exactly the kind of writing I discourage in my students. I have indeed come closer to replicating Jessie Redmon Fauset's modernist treatment of racial passing in "The Sleeper Wakes," as identified by Masami Sugimori in his contribution to this volume: it "just shows ... and never explains." But my goal here hasn't been interpretation; it is to make you curious. To this end, and consistent with the "descriptive" thrust of weak theory (St. Amour 444), I might suggest that some showing may sometimes serve us better than telling, espective decryptive telling! In short, I want you to wonder, *Why this pattern? What are these authors, differ as they do biographically and aesthetically, seeking to theorize exploring through this—to my knowledge—unprecedented narrative situation? Is it related to the burst of second-person narration in feminist and postcolonial fiction since the 1980s? Big questions. You ponder them, wondering.*

Responsible Reading for a Responsible Pedagogy

You had the jitters: what if your students had nothing to say about Beckett's "As the Story Was Told." What if they wanted *your* interpretation? You wanted to be able to admit your own lack of coherent interpretation, but would that embolden them, as you hoped, to wade into the text open-minded, curious to see what they could find? Or would it simply create an awkward silence? It felt risky. What you hoped to present as responsible reading might strike the students as their professor's abdication of interpretive duty—or worse, your interpretive incompetence! Still, you'd give it a shot, sustained by what one of the strongest of Strong Theorists had to say about "what Beckett refuses to deal with, interpretation. He shrugs his shoulders about the possibility of philosophy today, or theory in general" (Adorno 121–2).

* * *

Before even learning its name, I knew paranoid reading's success in literary studies had to do with its appeal in the classroom. I remember from my student days the thrill of adopting "a perpetual stance of systematic suspicion that ennobles the scholar-critic and diminishes what is studied" (Friedman 344). It was a competitive performance: me versus the text, me versus my peers' readings, my theory versus a naïve or insidious product of ideology. Mastering the interpretive and rhetorical practices of critique did more than guarantee good grades and professorial approval; it was the ticket into an exclusive circle.

But this mode of reading is attractive to just a fraction of those who take literature classes, including those who plan to major in the subject. With dropping enrollment in the humanities, we can't afford to repel those who love books but don't recognize that love in strong theory and the hermeneutics of suspicion. Know this: I was exactly that kind of undergrad. I stuck to it, partly out of stubbornness, partly out of righteous certainty that my interests were interesting, and largely out of luck: I had many great professors who were more than accepting of my approach. I could easily have been like Katie Armstrong, a minor character in Zadie Smith's *On Beauty*. A shy but enthusiastic midwestern freshman attending "a fancy East Coast school" (249), Katie "comes to class very excited …, determined this time, *determined* to be one of the three or four people who dare to speak" (252). She's been "moved" by what she's seen in Rembrandt's *Seated Nude* (251); she's eager to share her ideas. She never had a chance: her professor is determined to read the painting suspiciously: "'What we're trying to … *interrogate* here,' he says, 'is the mytheme of artist as autonomous individual with privileged insight into the human … Is this nude not a *confirmation* of the ideality of the vulgar? As it is already inscribed in the idea of a specifically gendered, class debasement?'" (252). Unlike the painting whose particularities Katie finds so significant, according to the professor *Seated Nude* is just another manifestation of ideology. And so "the class escapes Katie; it streams through her toes as the sea and sand when she stands by the edge of the ocean and dozily, *stupidly*, allows the tide to draw out and the world to pull away from her so rapidly as to make her dizzy" (253). And here Katie, who had "lost her [Christian] faith slowly and painfully two years earlier" (251), vanishes from the narrative; it appears that she's lost her faith in the arts much faster—fast enough to make us dizzy.

I *was* Katie when I started to study literature. If I didn't quit as she does, it was because I wasn't 16 but pushing 30, confident enough and less afraid of disapproval. But many others surely get discouraged, feeling there is no place for them in the club. When I say we can't afford to lose them, I don't mean financially (though flagging enrollment is a real threat). Teaching that reading doesn't mean *only* paranoid reading wouldn't amount to selling out the arts; it would be a recognition of the *liberal* foundations of our field, liberal not as in liberalist or neoliberal but as in broad and generous.

What would this look like? More importantly, how might we teach it? The last thing I'd advocate is a free-for-all, every-reading-is-equally-valid approach to literature. Going back to modernist mixed-voice narration, I know it would be counterproductive to unleash untrained students on such a complex cultural product. Teaching responsible reading might require more emphasis, during early university years, on analysis than on interpretation, on close reading and its attendant tools: prosody, rhetoric, stylistics, genre analysis, and so on. It might, relatedly, emphasize literal reading, teaching students to pay "attention to textual details that are significant in their own right rather than in what they omit or repress" (Schmitt 14)—if not as an end in itself, then as groundwork for figurative, allegorical, paranoid, or other forms of second-order reading. It might include the use of more creative assignments, and perhaps more attention to the process of writing: how authors generate and think about their work. It would almost certainly involve looking beyond disciplinary boundaries, opening its claims to external scrutiny. In other words, it might strive more for the breadth that Stephen Jay Gould didn't hesitate to call "wisdom" (52). One incontestably wise contemporary thinker, Marilynne Robinson, admits that her admiration for universities coexists with her knowledge "that varieties of nonsense that would not last ten minutes if history or experience were consulted can flourish there" (43). Reading more broadly is a way to consult history, or experience.

Most of all, though, I think the key to teaching responsible reading lies in reconceiving our attitude toward the objects of our study. There are many ways of envisioning this reconception—see, for example, elsewhere in this volume, Fabio Akcelrud Durão's definition of Theory as a semiautonomous literary genre, Kathryn Carney's argument for theory-as-prosthesis, or Matthew Gannon's Adornian view of the reading subject recreating or co-enacting the text (xx)—but its practice appears to be inextricable from more tightly linking the use of Theory to the experience of reading. To share with our students our experience of being baffled, frustrated, curious, and surprised by our reading—indeed demonstrate *live* that reading is "an act of composition—of creative remaking that binds text and reader in ongoing struggles, translations, and negotiations" (Felski 182)—may be the easiest way of imparting that the point of research is to find what you weren't seeking.

Note

1 That said, difficulty is obviously not a uniquely modernist quality, and my approach could be applied to any form of literary difficulty: texts rendered difficult through historical or cultural distance, even texts rendered difficult through their apparent simplicity.

References

Adorno, Theodor. "Trying to Understand *Endgame*," translated by Michael T. Jones. *New German Critique*, vol. 26, 1982, pp. 116–50.

Alber, Jan. "The Ideological Ramifications of Narrative Strategies." *Storyworlds: A Journal of Narrative Studies*, vol. 9, nos. ½, 2017, pp. 3–25.

Anker, Elizabeth S., and Rita Felski. "Introduction." *Critique and Postcritique*, edited by Elizabeth S. Anker and Rita Felski, Duke UP, 2017, pp. 1–28.

Bök, Christian. *Pataphysics: The Poetics of an Imaginary Science*. Northwestern UP, 2002.

Bowen, Elizabeth. *The House in Paris*. Anchor, 2002 [1935].

Butor, Michel. *Essais sur le roman*. Gallimard, 1992.

Felski, Rita. *The Limits of Critique*. U of Chicago P, 2015.

Freedgood, Elaine, and Cannon Schmitt. "Denotatively, Technically, Literally." *Representations*, vol. 125, no. 1, 2014, pp. 1–14.

Genette, Gérard. *Palimpsestes: La littérature au second degré*, Taurus, 1982.

Gould, Stephen Jay. *I Have Landed: The End of a Beginning in Natural History*. Harmony, 2002.

Hall, Radclyffe. *Adam's Breed*. Penguin, 1986 [1926].

Hawking, Stephen. *A Brief History of Time*. Bantam Books, 1988.

Herman, David. "Scripts, Sequences, and Stories: Elements of a Postclassical Narratology," *PMLA/Publications of the Modern Language Association of America*, vol. 112, no. 5, 1997, pp. 1046–59.

James, Henry. *The Art of Fiction: Critical Prefaces*. U of Chicago P, 2011.

Kenner, Hugh. *Joyce's Voices*. U of California P, 1979.

Latour, Bruno. "Has Critique Run Out of Steam? From Matters of Fact to Matters of Concern." *Critical Enquiry*, vol. 30, 2004, pp. 225–48.

Lehmann, Rosamond. *Dusty Answer*. Virago, 2006 [1927].

Levenson, Michael. *Modernism and the Fate of Individuality: Character and Novelistic Form from Conrad to Woolf*. Cambridge UP, 1991.

Levine, Caroline. *Forms: Whole, Rhythm, Hierarchy, Network*. U of Chicago P, 2015.

Love, Heather. "Truth and Consequences: On Paranoid Reading and Reparative Reading." *Criticism*, vol. 52, no. 2, 2010, pp. 235–41.

Punzalan, David, HelenRodd, and Kimberley A.Hughes. "Perceptual Processes and the Maintenance of Polymorphism through Frequency-dependent Predation." *Evolutionary Ecology*, vol. 19, 2005, pp. 303–20.

Queneau, Raymond. *Exercices de Style*. Gallimard, 2012.

Rainey, Lawrence. *A Poem Containing History: Textual Studies in The Cantos*. U of Michigan P, 1997.

Rhys, Jean. *After Leaving Mr Mackenzie*. Penguin, 1977 [1931].

Rhys, Jean. *Voyage in the Dark*. Penguin, 2000 [1934].

Robinson, Marilynne. "What Kind of Country Do We Want?" *The New York Review of Books,* vol. 67, no. 10, 2020, pp. 43–6.

Ross, Stephen. "Introduction: The Missing Link." *Modernism and Theory: A Critical Debate*, edited by Stephen Ross, Routledge, 2009, pp. 1–17.

Schmitt, Cannon. "Tidal Conrad (Literally)." *Victorian Studies*, vol. 55, no. 1, 2012, pp. 7–29.

Schofield, Dennis. "Beyond 'The Brain of Katherine Mansfield': The Radical Potentials and Recuperations of Second-Person Narration." *Style*, vol. 31, no. 1, 1997, pp. 96–117.

Sedgwick, Eve Kosofsky. *Touching Feeling: Affect, Pedagogy, Performativity*. Duke UP, 2003.

Sinclair, May. *Life and Death of Harriet Frean*. Virago, 1986 [1922].

Sinclair, May. *Mary Olivier: A Life*. NYRB Classics, 2002 [1919].

Smith, Zadie. *On Beauty*. Penguin, 2005 [2000].

St. Amour, Paul. "Weak Modernism, Weak Theory." *Modernism/Modernity*, vol. 25, no. 3, 2018, pp. 437–59.

Stanford Friedman, Susan. "Both/And: Critique and Discovery in the Humanities." *PMLA/Publications of the Modern Language Association of America*, vol. 132, no. 2, 2017, pp. 344–51.

Woolf, Virginia. *The Essays of Virginia Woolf*, vol. III: 1919–1924, edited by Andrew McNeillie. Hogarth Press, 1988.

Woolf, Virginia. *The Essays of Virginia Woolf*, vol. IV: 1925–1928, edited by Andrew McNeillie. Hogarth Press, 1994.

Woolf, Virginia. *The Essays of Virginia Woolf*, vol. V: 1929–1932, edited by Stuart N. Clark. Hogarth Press, 2009.

7

On the Advantages of Saying "No" (to Binaries, Totalizations, "Weakness," "Modesty," "Humility")

Cristina Ionica

The notions of "weakness," "modesty," and "humility" currently circulating in theory and modernist studies are problematic for several reasons, although some of their underlying principles are commendable and their advocates' work on specific literary authors/texts can be inspiring. Paul Saint-Amour identifies, as a common thread in contemporary theorizations of weakness (including Eve Kosofsky Sedgwick's), "not a vehement, dialectical negation of either strength or critique but an interest in the work accomplished by the proximate, the provisional, and the probabilistic" (440). In this reading, "weak" seems to mean *inclusive* and *wary of absolutes*, and the essays included in Saint-Amour's 2018 *Modernism/modernity* issue on "weak theory" and "weak modernism" operate in this mode. However, the semantic-ideological baggage of "weakness" cannot be so easily dismissed (especially since much of it clashes with weak theory's promise of decenteredness and inclusivity), and at least some advocates of weak theory do aggressively dismiss "critique." My essay starts and ends with some considerations on names/categories, and, in between, questions several tenets of weak theory as articulated by prominent proponents—with the aim of reaffirming the cognitive relevance and political import of critique today.

"Baggage"

Semantically and historically, "weakness," "modesty," "humility," and the binaries within which they acquire meaning and value uncomfortably evoke patriarchal psychosexual and socioeconomic conditioning. This connection has also been made by Saint-Amour (438), Holly Laird, and others, but I would insist on the additional complications caused by these terms' resoundingly *Christian* undertones. Saint-Amour warns of a "tendency of descriptive and dismissive senses of weakness to interfere with one another," stressing that "in taking up non-normative forms of weakness we are also reclaiming a term of derogation—even as no theoretical embrace of weakness is reducible to such a reclamation" (438). What I would stress instead is that the weak/strong binary and its associated semantic domain have been used, historically, to devalue and demonize marginalized groups in ways more complex and duplicitous than the mere acknowledgment of "weakness" as a term of derogation may suggest—and that this aspect, more than any other, poses major problems for any attempt to mobilize nonnormative meanings of "weakness" at a theoretical level.[1]

For millennia and across cultures, women and sexual minorities have not just been proclaimed physically, intellectually, and morally weak but *also* condemned as "unnatural" if they exhibited unsanctioned types of strength. (*Sacrificial* forms of strength have, unsurprisingly, always been applauded.) In terms of race and class, the same binary was mobilized to deny victims' intellectual abilities *and* overstate their physicality to justify their continual subjection to exhausting physical labor. (For instance, reading knowledge notoriously equaled a death sentence for American slaves. Today, assumptions of intellectual inferiority continue to bar access to certain professions and domains of knowledge for persons of color, and myths such as their higher tolerance for pain persist even within the medical system.) In short, marginalized groups have not simply been dismissed, historically, as weak but have been consistently—duplicitously and fraudulently—*anchored, within the weak/strong binary, to whichever pole best fit the needs of those in power*.

Furthermore, "weakness" and its semantic domain have already been "reclaimed" (positively recast) by Christianity in deeply problematic ways. While "the meek shall inherit the earth" (Matthew 5.5) may have been initially meant to function as an empowering reclamation of a term of derogation, institutionalized Christianity has consistently used words from this domain—for centuries, always within a logic of perpetual deferral of benefits—to safeguard the patriarchal production of obedient subjects. In other words, historically, "weak" and its semantic domain have systematically been mobilized to maintain the underprivileged ("the weak") in perpetual subordination *whether the "weakness" in question was assigned positive or negative connotations.*

This is a toxic load too all-encompassing to allow for meaningful reclaiming today. Saint-Amour insightfully notes that "baggage" can "unbalance" and "productively decenter" concepts and contexts (438), but baggage can also painfully and unproductively weigh one down.[2] I am not aware of any attempt, from advocates of weak theory, to account for the toxic Christian contribution to the "baggage" of weakness. It is equally problematic that, in exploring other potential terminological options, theorists of "weakness" seem to keep stumbling on terms from the same semantic domain, such as "modesty" and "humility" (Jeffrey Williams, Saint-Amour, and others note this semantic clustering but do not comment on its Christian undertones and view it as a mere renunciation of big claims in criticism/theory). In my view, the patriarchal-Christian imposition of weakness, modesty, and humility as *attributes to be cherished* by the oppressed (an imposition endlessly beneficial to those in power) has irredeemably compromised the very notion of *reclaiming* such terms—and institutionalized Christianity is not the only culprit. Traditionalist and extremist regimes of any religious/political orientation systematically use the same strategy to the same ends. Perhaps we should not hurry to reclaim words reminiscent of impositions still used to justify rape, femicide, and other hate crimes in so many parts of the world today. (The word "modesty" will always make my skin crawl.) We should also be, more generally, wary of words embedded into binaries implicitly supportive of hierarchical structures, in a world of—to quote Thomas Piketty—medieval-era levels of wealth inequality. As a believer in social justice, I fear that embracing such notions would leave us unarmed in the context of increasingly aggressive initiatives and impositions from corporate power, "alt-right" political movements, and male heads of state with totalitarian inclinations.

"Weak" vs. "Strong": Categories and Contents

My most recent academic research makes extensive use of Gilles Deleuze and Félix Guattari's theorization of "machines" and of some recent theories of revolution partly derived from their works (Michael Hardt and Antonio Negri, Thomas Nail, etc.)—which are all "leaky," "rhizomatic," "relational," and "centrifugal," working through a kind of "cross-stitching" (Wai Chee Dimock's definition of weak theory, 736–40), and concerned with "the proximal, the provisional, and the probabilistic" (Saint-Amour's already cited definition, 440). But can such theories' *weakening* of what they identify as *dogma* in earlier theoretical iterations be properly defined as *weakness*? Doesn't *weakening* a stronger and rigid adversary require *strength*? Given my preferred theoretical approaches' far-reaching sociopolitical implications, I would not describe them as "weak." (Gianni Vattimo's *pensiero debole*, which partly inspired the current uses of "weakness," has always struck me as a misnomer, given its critical function and its associated ethical and political commitments.) Are my preferred theoretical approaches "strong," then? Not in the sense in which weak theory has redefined the word—as masculinist, exclusionary, obsessively accusatory, and dogmatically totalizing (arguably a rather *strong* indictment).

This is not an exaggeration. Many theorizations of "weakness" do not simply carve a space for different analytical modes within the continuum of theoretical discourse but posit "weak" approaches as a necessary replacement of whatever they designate as "strong." Some scholars locate this aggressive disjunction in the work of some of Sedgwick's followers, but it is already present in Sedgwick's essay on "paranoid reading." Sedgwick claims to have "no wish to return to the use of 'paranoid' as a pathologizing diagnosis" and to object merely to "paranoid inquiry" having become a dominant critical protocol in academia (*Touching Feeling* 126). She also grants that the suspicions expressed in "paranoid inquiry" are not necessarily "delusional or simply wrong," and that paranoid strategies represent "*a* way, among other ways, of seeking, finding, and organizing knowledge" (130). However, such comments amount to a few sentences in a thirty-page essay that systematically associates theories hurriedly classified as "paranoid" with forms of affect of obvious pathological (aggressively delusional) and unproductive quality.

Sedgwick borrows her notions of strong and weak theory from a peculiar conceptual framework advanced by Silvan Tomkins, wherein *theory* means *affect theory* in the precise sense of a *meaning or interpretation mobilized by a certain affect*. Paranoia is Tomkins's example of a "strong theory" *par excellence*—and psychoanalysts, *analysands*, and critical theorists are said to "theorize" their experiences and observations on affect in equivalent ways. In this framework, a "theory" becomes increasingly strong (extends its reach to cover additional experiences of a certain type) as it fails to mitigate negative affect. This perhaps insightful way to explicate the functioning of affect is not an ideal way to explicate the workings of critical theory. *Strong affect* tends to be associated with pathological states in psychology and psychiatry, so it makes sense for "strong" to translate as undesirable in that context—but how successfully can such assumptions apply to critical practice? Is *any* attempt on the part of a theory to increase its explanatory efficiency and reach (to account for additional negative experiences/aspects) paranoid? Surely a theory becomes problematic in that sense if it makes illogical or overreaching moves—not if it makes *any expansion move whatsoever*. (Is intersectionality paranoid?) While acknowledging the influence of "early cybernetics' interest in feedback processes" in Tomkins's theorization, Sedgwick insists that Tomkins does not negate the presence of a "metalevel of reflection" in the works of, say, Sigmund Freud (compared to the "theorizations" of his analysands) but merely asserts that there is "no ontological difference" involved (*Touching Feeling* 133). Again, even if we accept this as an accurate description of the functioning of affect, to what extent does it cogently explicate critique? Tomkins focuses on finding *commonalities* in the functioning of affect within a wide category of human experiences. However, in any fair discussion of the specificity of critique, we ought instead to focus on *points of differentiation* from other types of activities/experiences.

My reservations concerning Sedgwick's discussion of weak/strong theory extend to her core objections to "paranoid inquiry." First, in her section titles, Sedgwick presents *paranoia* as "anticipatory," "reflexive and mimetic," "a strong theory," a theory of "negative affects," and one that "places its faith in *exposure*" (*Touching Feeling* 130–43). However, in the body text of those sections, she systematically discusses these aspects as faults of "paranoid inquiry." Apparently barely distinguishable from clinical paranoia, the forms of critical theory Sedgwick designates as "paranoid inquiry" (1) are so keen on never experiencing "bad surprises" that they continually project the bad outcomes they then validate; (2) attempt to swallow the entire field of textual/cultural interpretation; (3) quickly become tautological, failing to produce any "real conceptual work" (136) in encountering additional negative social aspects; (4) have no use for positive experiences, focusing strictly on negativity; and (5) continue to focus on *unveiling truths* in a world where the truth is generally known but has become banal/has been instrumentalized by establishment forces.

Sedgwick's observation that many violent acts committed today are not hidden but flaunted, in an attempt to entrench arch-conservative values, is perhaps even more relevant now than at the time she wrote this essay. Still, I am not convinced that *most* consequential truths have generally been revealed already, that an interest in (or even an obsession with) unveiling truths is necessarily a paranoid symptom, or that a focus on exposing truths implicitly makes a theory unable to address forms of violence exerted in the open. As for the first four traits—I would have found it difficult to figure out who, among the theorists we continue to find relevant today, might fit that profile if Sedgwick hadn't named names. This brings me to my second main objection to Sedgwick's theorization of "paranoid inquiry": she relegates a number of major theorists to the "paranoid" category *summarily*, to say the least, and the counterexamples she offers are rather odd choices (not just Tomkins, but also Melanie Klein, as we will see).

Sedgwick mentions, in *strictly negative* contexts, Karl Marx, Friedrich Nietzsche, and Freud (via a detour through Paul Ricoeur's "hermeneutics of suspicion"—a notion on which her own "paranoid inquiry" is partly predicated); Fredric Jameson, Michel Foucault, and Jacques Lacan; and, specifically, Judith Butler's *Gender Trouble*. In the subsections on "paranoia," she engages at some length with Butler's book and with D. A. Miller's *The Novel and the Police*, but Miller is credited with self-awareness and nuance in applying paranoid strategies—an honor none of the others is granted. With the exception of Butler and Miller, the critics/theorists listed above are referenced, briefly, once or twice—and while valid objections have been brought against specific aspects of their works within their respective theoretical fields, Sedgwick barely acknowledges that. Thus, Marx, Nietzsche, and Freud (who, for Saint-Amour, actually constitute an "early strand" of weak theory, 442) are summarily dismissed as being universally, abusively imposed on academic writers by the critical establishment—as "mandatory injunctions" in a "hermeneutics of suspicion" (Sedgwick, *Touching Feeling* 125). So is Lacan, but not Klein, whose approach repeatedly receives praise (128, 132)—although Lacan's attempt to define the workings of patriarchy through a "phallic function" (whose effect or "value," since it is a *function*, implicitly *varies* with the input) is arguably less restrictive than Klein's inescapable "aggression" and binary set of "positions."[3] In one passage, Foucault is dismissed, via Miller, through the following disjunction:

> Writing in 1988—that is, after two full terms of Reaganism in the United States—D. A. Miller proposes to follow Foucault in demystifying "the intensive and continuous 'pastoral' care the liberal society proposes to take of each and every one of its charges" (viii). As if! I'm a lot less worried about being pathologized by my therapist than about my vanishing mental health coverage—and that's given the great luck of having health insurance at all. (Sedgwick, *Touching Feeling* 141)

It is, however, not clear how Tomkins's or Klein's theories might better address the latter than Marxist or Foucauldian theory, or why the two types of problems could not be addressed *in tandem* as symptomatic of an increasingly conservative and exploitative socioeconomic system that *both* exerts control under the guise of "care" *and* "divests itself of responsibility" (Sedgwick's phrase, *Touching Feeling* 141) under the guise of offering "freedom." Finally, one of Sedgwick's major imputations is that strong theorists obsessively focus on just one/two affects, whether positive or negative (she lists "ecstasy, sublimity, self-shattering, jouissance, suspicion, abjection, knowingness, horror, grim satisfaction, or righteous indignation"), always to "reifying and, indeed, coercive" effects (146)—but, instead of supporting this charge through detailed examples, she merely doubles down on her accusatory rhetoric through an anti-totalitarian joke:

> It's like the old joke: "Comes the revolution, Comrade, everyone gets to eat roast beef every day." "But Comrade, I don't like roast beef." "Comes the revolution, Comrade, you'll like roast beef." … Comes the revolution, Comrade … you'll faint from ennui every minute you're not smashing the state apparatus; you'll definitely want hot sex twenty to thirty times a day. You'll be mournful *and* militant. You'll never want to tell Deleuze and Guattari, "Not tonight, dears, I have a headache." (146)

None of the affects listed earlier by Sedgwick connects specifically to Deleuze and Guattari's theories, and their rejection of Maoism and notorious subjection to attacks and harassment by Maoist theorists/activists makes them an odd choice as the endpoint of this emphatically extended punch line. The sex-related comments may allude to Guattari's tumultuous sex life and related convictions, but not so much to his collaborative theoretical work with Deleuze. No other theorist is mentioned by name in the passage, though "jouissance" can be traced to Lacan, "sublimity" to Jean-François Lyotard, "self-shattering" to Leo Bersani, "abjection" to Julia Kristeva, and so on. These theorists' body of work can, however, hardly be reduced to a mere fixation on one or two affects or central concepts, and their political positioning makes some of them questionable choices in association with an anti-totalitarian joke (Kristeva prominently supported Maoism but Lyotard, for instance, criticized Stalinism, Maoism, as well as, generally speaking, any totalizing tendencies he saw as potentially supportive of rigid sociopolitical structures in Marxist thought). At best, the passage reads like a loosely focused diatribe rather than a targeted critical objection—a strange rhetorical choice in a text supposedly critical of totalizing and aggressive theoretical moves. At worst, the point of the joke might simply be to associate the centrality of those concepts within contemporary theory to the crushing impositions of a totalitarian state—an ethically questionable rhetorical move for obvious reasons.

In short, the part of Sedgwick's essay dedicated to "strong theory"/"paranoid inquiry" pathologizes large areas of critical theory through quick and often problematic examples while embracing theories (Tomkins, Klein) that, on examination, seem more totalizing than the ones she rejects. At the level of diction, a strong polarization is built: "paranoid inquiry" is (as the phrase indicates) delusional, aggressive, and "academic," while "reparative practice" promises healing and is more akin to everyday experience. The much shorter part of the essay dedicated to reparative reading attempts to soften this opposition, but the excessively negative tenor of the previous sections clashes with its conciliatory claims rather than allowing for a more complex argument to emerge. Sedgwick summarily connects the reparative attitude to positive experiences of surprise (*Touching Feeling* 147) and of love (149) occasioned even by texts, situations, and practices otherwise still embedded in a heteronormative and in other ways limiting culture (151), and she locates this attitude in some queer practices and especially in camp (147–50). She comments, in her conclusion, that reparative practices can sometimes be displayed by "the most paranoid-tending people" (a curious conciliatory claim that seems to pathologize *theorists* rather than refer to textual features), and she redefines the reparative and the paranoid as "mutable positions" both at the level of individual personalities and in the larger arena of "shared histories, emergent communities, and the weaving of intertextual discourse" (150). These more or less positive claims, however, seem at odds with her very definition of "paranoid inquiry" as perpetually negative, perpetually in expansion, and essentially *closed* to whatever forms of reading and experience the reparative brings. They also raise additional questions concerning Sedgwick's previous dismissal of a large number of theorists/theories as "strong" and "paranoid." Are we to understand that Marx, Freud, Lacan, Foucault, or Butler could be used as a theoretical basis for reparative practices after all? Which parts, and to what extent? And if we find that much of what they say can be used in that manner, would their theoretical systems stop being "strong" and "paranoid"?

Ultimately, the question is both whether or not divisions like strong *vs.* weak or paranoid *vs.* reparatory truly hold and whether or not they are necessary. In a later essay on Klein, where Sedgwick discusses in more detail her derivation of "reparative practice" from Klein's definition of a reparative impulse characterizing the depressive position, the reparative is further unpacked as follows: our encounter with a situation/text (our "reading") can be reparative in relation to the object itself (in the way the depressive position may generate altruistic feelings for the well-being of an outside object), and/or to our internalized part-objects related in whatever ways to that situation/text ("Melanie Klein" 636–7).

Let us consider again, via this definition, the strands of critical theory Sedgwick singles out as "strong" and "paranoid" in her earlier essay. Do they truly lack the traits Sedgwick associates with the reparative? After all, critical theory does engage in positive gestures toward *some* outside objects (situations deemed positive; promising developments; texts the theorists, for lack of a better word, *love*); aggressively criticizing damaging outside objects (situations or texts) can arguably support the well-being of *other* outside objects (individuals subjected to injustice and oppression, for instance); and negative critical gestures can serve a reparative function in relation to our internalized part-objects, too. Perhaps Klein's paranoid/schizoid and depressive positions are, then, *not* ideal concepts from which to derive firm distinctions in the field of theory and critique—and perhaps "strong" and "weak" are not the best descriptors, either. "Paranoid" and "strong" tendencies in critical theory tend to be noticed, unpacked, criticized, and corrected, as *faulty* argumentation practices, *within the very field of critical theory* all the time—this is simply the form commonly taken by critical and theoretical practice in diachrony.

Unfortunately, as far as problematic definitions and rejections of "strong theory" and/or "critique" go, prominent later advocates of "weak theory" and of "weak" modes of "reading" (not *critique*) can be even more dismissive. Some define "weak" and "strong" approaches as mutually exclusive (which Sedgwick doesn't fully do) and go to extremes in attempting to neutralize any critical mode as strictly destructive, unappreciative, narcissistic, and/or a dead end—all in the name of a new "modesty," "humility," and love of reading variously designated as "thin description" (Heather Love), "surface reading" (Stephen Best and Sharon Marcus), "just reading" (Marcus), and so on. Rita Felski proposes "postcritique," offers a more sophisticated thesis in support of her proposal, and explicitly rejects some of the more extreme claims made by others, but even her approach imputes to "critique" as a whole a series of procedures difficult to identify as omnipresent in the forms of cultural theory and critique practiced today or in the works of the theorists who inspired them.

Best, Marcus, and Love view socially critical modes of textual inquiry as a conceited and self-righteous misuse of literary texts—"critics" supposedly use literary texts as props in a discussion of whatever social observations they wish to advance, while the texts themselves are less concerned with social criticism and more with aesthetic pleasure and the affective transmission of human experience. This implies that social criticism is a mere afterthought in the literature we value (demonstrably not true of many literary texts) and that a focus on social criticism is always to the detriment of other aspects of the text (an odd and difficult to justify disjunction that posits "weak" modes of "reading" as not just different but *better*). Best and Marcus define their preferred mode of "surface reading" in opposition to "symptomatic reading" (as practiced, for instance, by Jameson)—the latter, described as a "heroic" attempt at "wresting meaning from a resisting text or inserting it into a lifeless one" (5), given to "suspicious and aggressive attacks" (11), and preoccupied with uncovering latent meanings in texts to the point of dismissing more manifest meanings. "Surface reading" focuses, instead, on what is "evident, perceptible, apprehensible" in texts, "neither hidden nor hiding"—and is, as such, a "practice of critical description" (11). However, as Ellen Rooney notes, this definition questionably assumes—against a history of evidence to the contrary—that unmediated forms of "description" are possible, as well as that whatever the text is "saying about itself" (Best and Marcus 11) would be "more visible on its surface than at some depth" (Rooney 124). After all, as Elizabeth Weed reminds us, the relation between "manifest" and "latent" content, under whatever name—in Althusser, Lacan, Freud, or Marx—is not a mere matter of occultation but of *distortion* and *dislocation* (169), so an approach programmatically limited to "surface" and "manifest" matters would not necessarily be more objective or legitimate. Best and Marcus present their focus on more readily manifest aspects of texts as a matter of *political realism* concerning the revolutionary potential of both literary texts and critical/theoretical work, and they define their "less glamorous" project as follows: "Instead of turning to literature for models of how to overcome constraint, or for a right way to live under capital, or to register the difference between our critical freedom and the limits placed on others, we are interested in how to register the ways that constraints structure existence as much as breaking free of them does" (17, 18). However, considering this definition, it is difficult to see in what ways their mode of reading might be *fundamentally different* from the "strong"/"symptomatic" mode they reject. Marxist, psychoanalytic, and gender theory, for instance, have always been concerned with "the ways that constraints structure existence." Should interpretations of literary texts be more solidly and extensively anchored in close readings of the literary texts in question—both in terms of manifest and latent meanings? They should, and not all are. However, Best and Marcus do not seem interested in criticizing specific overreaching moves in theory/critique but in rejecting wholesale all approaches that move beyond the "surface" of the text. On the other hand, Best and Marcus themselves produced wonderful readings of specific texts that reveal their "surface" to be rather deep, as did most of the contributors to the special issue of *Representations* prefaced by their essay.

Should it still be called "surface," then, and do we really need to elevate this binary to methodological status?

For Love, while Sedgwick may have described "paranoid reading" in excessively negative terms (237), her essay both argues and performs "the impossibility of choosing" between the paranoid and the reparative (239). As also illustrated through my earlier reading, Sedgwick does perform "paranoid" criticism herself in her essay and does briefly argue, in her conclusion, for the possibility of combining the two. However, her discussion is more than a little lopsided—and it is, in fact, this aspect of Sedgwick's argument that ultimately informs Love's own approach. Love proclaims reparative modes of reading to be "*better* at the level of ethics and affect," as well as "epistemology and knowledge" (237; emphasis added). She adds, "Even though paranoid or, in terms borrowed from Silvan Tomkins, strong theory can organize vast amounts of territory and tell big truths, it misses the descriptive richness of weak theory. Weak theory stays local, gives up on hypervigilance for attentiveness; instead of powerful reductions, it prefers acts of noticing, being affected, taking joy, and making whole" (337–8). Thus, like Sedgwick, Love uses tendentious diction to pathologize and disparage "strong" forms of inquiry ("hypervigilance," "reductions") and defines the pursuits of weak theory through terms suggestive of maximal unobtrusiveness and solicitude. However, no proof is provided that whatever Love considers "strong theory" could not and, indeed, does not pursue *both* "big truths" and "joy"—or that limiting oneself to "acts of noticing" and focusing on "taking joy and making whole" is preferable as a social and aesthetic practice *under any circumstance.*

Felski explicitly rejects other scholars' "language of textual surfaces over depths" (190) and acknowledges both that negativity may be justified/required in some instances and that some critical approaches operate with predominantly positive categories. Despite that, she ultimately defines socially oriented modes of critical inquiry as a "thought style" (2) or "mood" (20)—and corresponding "language game" (29)—predicated on a "hermeneutic of suspicion," negative, fixated on power, and generally blind to issues of love/attachment: "Perhaps it is time to start asking different questions: 'But what about love?' Or: 'Where is your theory of attachment?'" (17–18). Love and attachment are obviously not synonyms—attachment can be secure or insecure, healthy or unhealthy, and so on; theories of attachment *do* circulate within critical theory; any discussion of attachment would unavoidably entail some focus on power; and, finally, insofar as issues of power relate to social justice, at the core of any discussion of power there is love—in the specific forms of *solidarity* and *care*. Felski is, in fact, fully aware of these aspects, as her later discussion shows, but she continues to indulge, throughout the book, in "playful" rhetorical excesses that detract from her more subtle points and make her position seem more extreme than it is.[4] In chapter 3, where she compares socially oriented modes of critical inquiry to the police inquest, she provides descriptions such as this: "the present-day inspectors of literary studies ... stomp their muddy boots through the drawing rooms of culture while laying bare its complicity in a history of wrongdoing" (90). The striking diction used relates to a previously discussed British crime drama scenario wherein a police officer "descends on the home of a prosperous Edwardian family" to solve a murder and, in the process, foregrounds substantial class-based conflicts (90)—so the "muddy boots" comment is, supposedly, *not* a dismissal. However, its rhetorical excess generates an image of critique as always inconsiderately, inelegantly, aggressively in pursuit of a guilty party, and subsequent generalizations endorse that charge: "The plot line of suspicion takes on a life of its own, priming readers to approach a text in a spirit of heightened mistrust and to search for signs of reprehensible activity"; "We may gain a temporary upper hand over the texts we interrogate, but at the cost of ever being surprised, stirred, reoriented, replenished, or called to account by the words we encounter" (91, 114). In chapter 4, Felski claims that, as a rhetorical mode, critique posits itself as a neutral "response" (defines itself as "secondary") but is in fact perpetually negative, opposes itself (as "intellectual") to everyday life while also claiming to speak "from below" (from a position of lower authority), and "does not tolerate rivals" (105, 121, 127, 134, 140, 147)— while ceaselessly offering thoughtful counterexamples along the way. Chapter 5 uses, as a title, Latour's phrase "Context stinks!"—but Felski's argument is not that "historical knowledge is to be discarded or brushed aside" but that one should avoid "sociohistorical generalities and critical condemnations that, in seeking to explain everything, explain very little," as well as attempts "to glue a text fast to the moment of its first appearance" (183). Why, then, does Felski insist on defining, in her conclusion, *critique* (and not a limited set of critical practices) as blind to aesthetic value and to affect, negative and power obsessed, and closed to critical self-examination, and why does she propose "postcritique," her preferred mode of reading, as a matter of *description* rather than interpretation (188–90)? Most contributors to this volume and many academic writers in general share Felski's interest in affect, in readings equally concerned with aesthetic and political aspects, in the literary as a source of joy, and so on but seem to have always been able to locate all these aspects *within* critique. To quote Diana Fuss, we "may be reading very different books"

(353–4)—or, rather, we may be reading the same books very differently. We are—all of us, in our different ways—engaging in critique.

My point is not that the supporters of "description" and opponents of "critique" quoted above engage in erroneous or illegitimate reading practices in their interactions with literary texts but that their positing of their reading practices as fundamentally different/at the opposite pole from critique operates with tenuous definitions of critique and carries problematic unacknowledged implications. In my concluding section, I will discuss two such core problems: the underlying assumption that negativity and positivity cannot coexist, and that—if one must choose—positivity and affirmation are always preferable; and a more general tendency toward binarisms in situating both their own cultural practices and those of others. Both these aspects conflict with major values supporters of "description" and opponents of "critique" claim to uphold, and both comport serious political risks today.

Disjunction vs. Symbiosis

Several respondents to the 2018 *Modernism/modernity* issue on weak modernism and weak theory raise major concerns with "weakness" as a theoretical positioning. Julian Murphet and Stephen Ross worry that "modest" and "minimally critical" approaches may limit the humanities' impact on contemporary debates concerning class, gender, racial, and environmental problems. Ross advocates for an understanding of the role of criticism "along Foucault's terms instead of those of the proponents of the new weakness: as a mode of resistance to totalization rather than its embrace." Ross, Laird, David Ayers, Omri Moses, and Susan Stanford Friedman object to weak theory's self-positioning as a polar opposite to whatever it defines as "strong," insistence on operating within such binaries, and overlooking of the totalizing/universalist implications of that positioning. Friedman proposes as the ultimate "test" for a theory its *usefulness* or *generative qualities*, advocating for theoretical work that is "provisional, open-ended, and reparative" but still *political* and, as such, "not weak." Several contributors to the *Responsible Reading* volume raise additional issues with the "weak/strong" binary—for instance, Kathryn Carney draws attention to its ableist implications.

My own reservations toward the terminology and conceptual framework of "weak theory" and its associated forms of "reading" or "description" also concern their underlying universalism and binarism—from a slightly different but convergent perspective. Let us start with the unacknowledged universalism of these orientations—an odd enough trait considering their constant charge that "strong theory" is totalizing. "I am so paranoid I think Sedgwick's essay is about me," of course, but what of a theory that preemptively and categorically *locks* me in a paranoid position? And is the mere act of asking *whom it is about* paranoid, too? Supporters of "weakness" and "description" appear to be arguing against an ill-defined adversary. Jameson, Lacan, Foucault, and many others have been interpreted in widely different ways and used for widely different critical and theoretical purposes during the last decades. Are some of those uses "strong" and "paranoid" to the point of caricature? Perhaps, but does that justify declaring Jameson, Lacan, or Foucault entirely ill-suited for our approach of contemporary sociocultural phenomena? I should perhaps mention that I find several aspects of Lacanian theory "generative," in Friedman's definition, but I have not used Foucault or Jameson substantially in any of my published research so far. This is really not about theoretical attachments but about responsibility and rigor. We all seek joy and mobilize creativity in our academic work—"critique" is not a ceaseless exercise in negation—and there is, in fact, joy and creativity in negation, too. (Felski acknowledges the latter but ultimately classifies it as additional proof of the negativity of "critique"—see, for instance, her discussion of "suspicious reading" in chapter 3, esp. 108–11.) Joy and responsibility, creativity and rigor, positivity and negativity are, in short, not mutually exclusive—they are, arguably, necessary and symbiotic ingredients in any relevant critical and theoretical practice.

This brings us to the issue of binarisms and of their tendentious clustering in theorizations of "weakness." At the "weak" pole, we have provisionality, openness, flexibility, positivity, attachment, and reparative ends; at the "strong" pole, rigidity, totalizing tendencies, fixed categories, negativity, aggressive rejection, and pathological suspicion. First, these binaries are simply inconsistent, especially when applied to *entire theoretical frameworks* rather than to specific examples of theory/critique (once again, even Felski's sophisticated concessions ultimately do not seem to make a difference for her conclusion, so her work cannot serve as a counterexample here)—so much so that their relevance and necessity come into question. Can we rigorously and coherently group *theories* (rather than specific aspects or ideas) into categories such as *flexible* vs. *rigid*, and what is the *generative* quality of doing so? Second, these binaries are obviously not descriptive but evaluative—both in themselves and through the way they cluster. Sedgwick's or Felski's claims to the contrary notwithstanding, opposing "paranoid inquiry" to "reparative practice" (Sedgwick) *is* an evaluative move, as is claiming the term "description"—ostentatiously denotative of objectivity—for one's practice while professing to have "no quarrel with interpretation" (Felski 190). Finally, these binaries' evaluative clustering problematically proclaims positivity as generally preferable and beneficial, and negativity as generally undesirable and destructive. It may seem like a low blow to cite, in this context, the phrase "No means no" or former US President Donald Trump's systematically positive comments on white supremacists' human qualities. I am not suggesting that supporters of "weak theory" and "description" would advise us to embrace positivity in *such* contexts. I am, however, saying that the problem with "preferring" an element in a binary structure is not that we might sometimes run into intractable exceptions but that we would *endlessly* find ourselves in reductive positions difficult to reconcile with *countless* salient examples of social practice. Saying "no" is still a luxury for so many of us who supposedly live in democratic countries—and, in many parts of the world, for women, low-income individuals, and sexual/racial/religious minorities, this minimal freedom remains a distant dream. Perhaps what we should start "preferring" is a move away from rigid definitions and disjunctions.

Let me end by symbiotically employing positivity and negativity in some final remarks on "truth" and "exposure." For billions of people today, "truths" continue to be hidden and to have substantial meaning—and the fact that we sometimes feel *overwhelmed* by truths does not make them banal or our acting on them inconsequential. Totalitarian regimes (many still in existence) and their occultation and disinformation practices are obvious examples. But, more generally, the "information age," with its explosion of available data, requires *more* critical work (not less) in distinguishing between relevant data and "noise," in breaking through massive waves of misinformation, and in finding ways to use relevant information in ethical and socially beneficial ways. From this perspective, the "negativity" of critique is a prerequisite of any constructive move. Fortunately, despite the reservations expressed by some advocates of "weak theory" and "description" concerning the political potential of critical theory or "critique," there is evidence that the work of critique has, in fact, been positively consequential in the last decades. Generations X, Y ("millennials"), and Z—more likely to have pursued higher education and, by implication, more exposed to forms of cultural critique in colleges and universities—hold significantly more egalitarian and inclusive values than the generations before them.[5] "Critical thinking" courses have been a requirement for college and university students in all programs for many years. These courses typically familiarize students with social justice issues and attempt to prompt socially aware and inclusive responses—that is, they mobilize "suspicion" and "negation" within processes of social analysis but also display "positive" or constructive components in prompting students to imagine solutions, experience solidarity, build citizenship values, and so on. From a cognitive perspective, acquiring a "suspicious" mind frame is *desirable* and *difficult to achieve* rather than pathological and/or dull. As David Perkins, Tim van Gelder, and others note, critical thinking is a highly *contrived* activity that does not come naturally to humans, being typically hindered by a "make-sense epistemology" based on intuitions that certain propositions "sound right" and by strong tendencies toward "belief preservation" (Perkins et al. 186; van Gelder 42, 45). Our students' increasing lack of tolerance for discrimination and oppression—arguably developed through exposure to critical thinking practices in school and through interactions with others of a similar mindset—is a salient instance of the symbiotic relation between "negativity" and "positivity" within any relevant and desirable social development/practice. It is, I suggest, by preserving this symbiotic relation that we can maximize the humanities' impact on contemporary social justice debates.

Notes

1 My objections against the semantic and theoretical construct "weak theory" in this essay focus mostly on the "weak" designation. For an insightful discussion of the unacknowledged assumptions involved in using the word "theory" in the construct "weak theory," see Masami Sugimori's essay in this volume.
2 "Queer theory" could serve as an example in support of Saint-Amour's claim, but "weak theory" would be a false analogue. "Queer" is a narrow-scope, deconstructive term (not the opposite of "heterosexual" but a rejection of binarism and normativity in all matters of gender and sexuality), whereas "weak" has an enormous semantic reach, has always been part of binary structures, and continues to be used as such by advocates of "weak theory" today. In addition, "queer" has never been used to encourage anyone to embrace oppression, whereas "weak" has a history of such use too long and damaging to ignore.
3 Gila Ashtor notes that "the aggressive attribution of unambiguous unconscious intent that is a hallmark of Kleinian technique ought to register as wildly at odds with the enlarged interpretive freedom that Sedgwick invokes Klein to represent" (191). That seems equally true of Sedgwick's crediting of Klein's paranoid/schizoid and depressive "positions" with flexibility. Their placement in a binary relation and positing as apt to cover the entire spectrum of infantile *as well as adult* object relations render them more totalizing and reductive than some of the models Sedgwick rejects.
4 See Yan Tang's essay in this volume for additional observations on the ways in which Felski's "militant tone" and "playful rhetoric" (69) risk undermining her argumentation.
5 See, for instance, Anthony Cilluffo and D'Vera Cohn; Kim Parker et al.; or any recent political polls broken down by age group.

References

Ashtor, Gila. "The *Mis*diagnosis of Critique." *Criticism*, vol. 61, no. 2, 2019, pp. 191–217, DOI:10.13110/criticism.61.2.0191.

Ayers, David. "Weak Theory or Bad Ideas?" *Modernism/modernity*. Responses to the Special Issue on Weak Theory, Part II, March 10, 2019, https://modernismmodernity.org/forums/posts/responses-special-issue-weak-theory-part-ii.

Bersani, Leo. *The Freudian Body: Psychoanalysis and Art*. Columbia UP, 1986.

Best, Stephen, and Sharon Marcus. "Surface Reading: An Introduction." *The Way We Read Now*. Special issue of *Representations*, vol. 108, no. 1, 2009, pp. 1–21.

Butler, Judith. *Gender Trouble: Feminism and the Subversion of Identity*. Routledge, 1990.

Cilluffo, Anthony, and D'Vera Cohn. "6 Demographic Trends Shaping the U.S. and the World in 2019." *The PEW Research Center*, April 11, 2019, https://www.pewresearch.org/fact-tank/2019/04/11/6-demographic-trends-shaping-the-u-s-and-the-world-in-2019/.

Deleuze, Gilles, and Félix Guattari. *Anti-Oedipus: Capitalism and Schizophrenia*, translated by Robert Hurley, Mark Seem, and Helen R. Lane. Minnesota UP, 1983.

Dimock, Wai Chee. "Weak Theory: Henry James, Com Tólbín, and W. B. Yeats." *Critical Inquiry*, vol. 39, no. 4, 2013, pp. 732–53.

Felski, Rita. *The Limits of Critique*. Chicago UP, 2015.

Foucault, Michel. *Histoire de la sexualité*. Gallimard, 1976.

Foucault, Michel. *Surveiller et punir: naissance de la prison*. Gallimard, 1975.

Friedman, Susan Stanford. "Provisionally Persistent." *Modernism/modernity*. Responses to the Special Issue on Weak Theory, Part III, April 2, 2019, https://modernismmodernity.org/forums/posts/responses-special-issue-weak-theory-part-iii.

Fuss, Diana. "But What about Love?" *PMLA/Publications of the Modern Language Association of America*, vol. 132, no. 2, 2017, pp. 352–5.

Hardt, Michael, and Antonio Negri. *Commonwealth*. Harvard UP, 2009.

Jameson, Fredric. *The Political Unconscious: Narrative as Socially Symbolic Act*. Cornell UP, 1981.

Kristeva, Julia. *Pouvoirs de l'horreur: essai sur l'abjection*. Seuil, 1980.

Lacan, Jacques. *L'éthique de la psychanalyse, 1959–1960*, edited by Jacques-Alain Miller. Seuil, 1986.

Laird, Holly A. "Notes Toward a Feminist Politics of 'Weak Theory.'" *Modernism/modernity*. Responses to the Special Issue on Weak Theory, Part II, March 10, 2019, https://modernismmodernity.org/forums/posts/responses-special-issue-weak-theory-part-ii.

Love, Heather. "Truth and Consequences: On Paranoid Reading and Reparative Reading." *Criticism*, vol. 52, no. 2, 2010, pp. 235–41.

Lyotard, Jean-François. *Leçons sur l'analytique du sublime*. Galilée, 1991.

Lyotard, Jean-François. *Political Writings*, translated by Bill Readings and Kevin Paul Geiman. U of Minnesota P, 1993.

Marx, Karl. *Capital: A Critique of Political Economy*, vol. 1, translated by Ben Fowkes. Vintage, 1977.

Miller, D. A. *The Novel and the Police*. U of California P, 1988.

Moses, Omri. "Weak Affect, Weak Theory, Dynamic Systems." *Modernism/modernity*. Responses to the Special Issue on Weak Theory, Part IV, May 16, 2019, https://modernismmodernity.org/forums/posts/responses-special-issue-weak-theory-part-iv.

Murphet, Julian. "Decadence." *Modernism/modernity*. Responses to the Special Issue on Weak Theory, Part II, March 10, 2019, https://modernismmodernity.org/forums/posts/responses-special-issue-weak-theory-part-ii.

Nail, Thomas. *Returning to Revolution: Deleuze, Guattari, and Zapatismo*. Edinburgh UP, 2012.

Parker, Kim, Nikki Graf, and Ruth Igielnik. "Generation Z Looks a Lot Like Millennials on Key Social and Political Issues." *The PEW Research Centre*, January 17, 2019, https://www.pewsocialtrends.org/2019/01/17/generation-z-looks-a-lot-like-millennials-on-key-social-and-political-issues/.

Perkins, David N., R. Allen, and J. Hafner. "Difficulties in Everyday Reasoning." *Thinking: The Expanding Frontier*, edited by W. Maxwell and J. Bruner. Franklin Institute P, 1983, pp. 177–89.

Piketty, Thomas. *Capital in the Twenty-First Century*, translated by Arthur Goldhammer. Belknap, 2014.

Ricoeur, Paul. *Freud and Philosophy: An Essay on Interpretation*, translated by Denis Savage. Yale UP, 1970.

Rooney, Ellen. "Live Free or Describe: The Reading Effect and the Persistence of Form." *Differences*, 21, no. 3, 2010, 112–39.

Ross, Stephen. "Provocations on the Philosophy of Weakness." *Modernism/modernity*. Responses to the Special Issue on Weak Theory, Part IV, May 16, 2019, https://modernismmodernity.org/forums/posts/responses-special-issue-weak-theory-part-iv.

Saint-Amour, Paul K. "Weak Theory, Weak Modernism." *Modernism/modernity*, vol. 25, no. 3, 2018, pp. 437–59.

Sedgwick, Eve Kosofsky. "Melanie Klein and the Difference Affect Makes." *South Atlantic Quarterly*, vol. 106, no. 3, 2007, pp. 625–42, DOI:10.1215/00382876-2007-020.

Sedgwick, Eve Kosofsky. *Touching Feeling: Affect, Pedagogy, Performativity*. Duke UP, 2003.

Tomkins, Silvan. *Affect, Imagery, Consciousness*, 4 vols. Springer, 1962–92.

van Gelder, Tim. "Teaching Critical Thinking." *College Teaching*, vol. 53, no. 1, 2005, pp. 41–6. *EBSCOhost*, DOI:10.3200/CTCH.53.1.41-48.

Vattimo, Gianni. "Dialettica, differenza, pensiero debole." *Il pensiero debole*, edited by Gianni Vattimo and Pier Aldo Rovatti. Feltrinelli, 1985, pp. 12–28.

Weed, Elizabeth. "Gender and the Lure of the Postcritical." *Differences*, vol. 27, no. 2, 2016, 154–77, DOI:10.1215/10407391-3621757.

Williams, Jeffrey J. "The New Modesty in Literary Studies." *Chronicle of Higher Education*, 61, no. 17, 2015, pp. B6–B9, chronicle.com/article/The-New-Modesty-in-Literary/150993/.

8

Weak Theory, "Responsible" Reading, and Literary Criticism

Masami Sugimori

In "Weak Theory, Weak Modernism," Paul K. Saint-Amour perceptively integrates insights from philosophy, psychology, sociology, and modernist studies to argue not only that weakness constitutes a significant portion of allegedly strong modernism but also that weakness-informed reading practice would enhance literary studies. In an equally perceptive fashion, Saint-Amour acknowledges a variety of challenges surrounding such an approach. They include the danger of becoming *too* weak, that is, "unrigorous, quietist, anti-theory, anti-intellectual" (445) or prone to reduce modernism to "a semantically empty trademark" (455). Inversely, weak theory also risks reverting to "implication in, even ... predication on, forms of strength" (442) through totalitarian application of weakness as a "centripetal power" as well as through leaning "toward doctrine, coherentism, triumphalism, and sovereign self-understanding" (455). To avoid these pitfalls, Saint-Amour seems to suggest, requires a careful and scrupulous application of the theory.

A variety of responses came up, some of them specifically to these difficulties, in the *Modernism/modernity* Print Plus issues that followed. While most responses primarily assess the term "weak," my focus on practical application equally attends to its "theory" status—configured as at once separate from and superordinate to literary "criticism"—a status that bears its own distinct problematics particularly when coupled with "weak." I will make the case that the current construction of "weak" plus "theory" contains issues that obstruct the fulfillment of its goals. As a way to address these issues, I propose a "responsible reading" practice—drawing on Saint-Amour's own use of the adjective—an approach featuring "responsible" as a less binary-oriented alternative to "weak," and "reading" as a less metanarrativistic alternative to "theory." The final sections apply such reading, starting by adding to Wai Chee Dimock's weak-theoretical reading of William Faulkner's visit to Japan and ending with an exploration of Jessie Redmon Fauset's 1920 short story, "The Sleeper Wakes."

Problems: Methodological and Theoretical

Does weak theory offer a valid interpretive methodology applicable to specific literary works? Does that methodology effectively distinguish itself from those of other theories? For instance, does the application of weak theory not end up close reading for the weak in a supposedly strong subject matter, and thus merely combining a familiar analytical method with the *topic* of weakness?

Saint-Amour's essay itself offers a case study for these questions, as it consists of a survey of weak theory (drawing upon Rita Felski's "post-critique," Gianni Vattimo's "weak thought," Silvan Tomkins's "weak affect theory," Eve Kosofsky Sedgwick's "reparative reading," etc.) and a revaluation of modernism as a movement generally associated with strength, masterfulness, and normativity. This revaluation, which also demonstrates a weak-theoretical method of interpretation, is nonetheless impeded by the theory's own premises. For example, informed by Jeffrey Williams's "new modesty" and, more tacitly, by post-critique's skepticism of critique's "diagnostic" and "allegorical" attitude to the object of study (Anker and Felski 4–8), weak theory attempts to overcome "'symptomatic reading'—that is, ... interpretive modes whose primary aim is to expose the ruses of ideology, decode the encryptions wrought by the unconscious, or otherwise penetrate the surfaces of texts to get at their truer, occulted depths" (Saint-Amour 439). However, Saint-Amour's rereading of modernism reveals how Mark Granovetter's concept of "weak ties" helps address a formerly neglected parameter of modernists' interpersonal network. In so doing, it conducts the same kind of ideological exposure, concerning the emphasis modernist scholarship has put on the notion of strength. Such emphasis indeed derives from the ideological construction of academia, as the valorization of "strength" in various academic discourses, such as the recommendation letter and evaluation of student work (446–7), has facilitated the institution's productive and reproductive functions. This problem reflects a predicament on the level of theoretical formulation. For, given that dominant ideology facilitates its operation by normalizing its exertion of power, attending to the suppressed weakness of an allegedly strong subject matter inevitably entails ideological exposure.

Weak theory's reliance upon the strong/weak dichotomy, as well as its actual power play—both investigated by Cristina Ionica's essay in this volume (Chapter 7)—also invites reductive reading and thus prevents the theory from fulfilling its mission in literary-analytical application. For instance, Dimock's "Weak Network: Faulkner's Transpacific Reparations," itself an insightful examination of Faulkner's post–Second World War attempt at "reparative narratives," nevertheless betrays the difficulty of applying weak theory without forceful, if tacitly, argumentative maneuvers. One can find an example in her analysis of Faulkner's following remark at the August 1955 Seminar in Nagano, Japan:

> My side, the South, lost that war, the battles of which were fought not on neutral ground in the waste of the ocean, but in our own homes, our gardens, our farms, as if Okinawa and Guadalcanal had been not islands in the distant Pacific but the precincts of Honshu and Hokkaido. ("To the Youth" 185)

To frame her discussion in terms of weakness, Dimock has to impose the strong/weak binary upon this statement. To her, accordingly, the reference to Okinawa, Guadalcanal, Honshu, and Hokkaido shows Faulkner's way of addressing "the steady-state, weakly but persistently gnawing sense of having been brought low" (592).

Yet, even if one accepts Dimock's measurement of such a "gnawing sense" in terms of strong or weak, reading weakness in Faulkner's place choice, let alone in contrast with what Dimock implies is a stronger alternative of Hiroshima and Nagasaki, seems itself an interpretive power play suppressing a relevant dimension of his consideration of Japan's geography and war experience. It is true that one could make a contrast between these atomic-bombed cities ("the best-known names" for "spectacular destruction," according to Dimock [592]) and less famous locations. However, the semantic context of his reference, that is, extension in the form of battlegrounds' proximity or distance, would make it a category problem, rather than a matter of Faulkner's weakness-conscious choice, for these cities—not islands like Okinawa, Guadalcanal, Honshu, and Hokkaido—to make their way into the sentence, particularly if, as Dimock rightly conjectures, he scrupulously phrased it. Indeed, to the Nagano audience he addressed only a decade after its firsthand experiences, the Second World War mayhem is no less about Okinawa and Guadalcanal (locations of major, devastating ground battles), or about Honshu—the island on which Nagano is located—and Hokkaido (those of repeated airstrikes, on both military and civilian targets), than Hiroshima and Nagasaki. The somewhat roundabout phrase, "brought low," also exemplifies Dimock's repeated and often awkward use of metaphorical "low"-ness to evoke weakness, the concept to be demonstrated. Dimock calls Faulkner's view of "[d]efeat as a spur to experimentation" a "low-bar starting point" (594) in accordance with her equally loaded designation of "losing" as "low-bar experience known to many" earlier in the essay (590).[1]

Dimock's essay itself is a cogent literary study informed by close textual, intertextual, and contextual examination. And significant potential lies in the project of weak theory, whose deliberately "weak" formulation, based on "a loose parcel of concepts and heuristics" (Saint-Amour 440) both in and outside of humanities fields, could "productively decenter what [it] encounter[s]" by attending to "the subjunctive, the speculative, and the counterfactual" (438). Yet the combination of the terms "weak" (which functions in opposition to "strong") and "theory" (which evokes a metanarrative status as opposed to critical practice where it is applied) seems to put weak theory against itself. In other words, in literary-analytical application weak theory attempts to decenter the object of study but has to stop short of decentering its own metanarrative role, as exemplified by the actually recentering methodology—whether it be argumentatively loaded close reading or binary-oriented naming—used to identify weakness in the object.[2] This also problematizes weak theory's distinctiveness as a literary theory, particularly if it virtually operates through finding, and then constructing an argument around, a formerly unrecognized weakness and thus only combines traditional examination with a *topical* focus on weakness.

Responsible Reading

On a disciplinary level, too, weak theory bears a metanarrative tint, as Saint-Amour's description of its enterprise couples "theorizing and field-construction" together (438). Yet, given what weak theory aspires, particularly its radical attempt to reach out for "the subjunctive, the speculative, and the counterfactual," I think that a bottom-up, non-definitive, and non-teleological approach would best carry it out.[3] With that in mind, I propose "responsible reading"—not as an alternative to weak theory but rather as a practical catalyst designed to facilitate its actualization in literary inquiry. Indeed, the adjective "responsible" comes from Saint-Amour's own usage when he warns of executing "field expansion" abusively:

> It [an appropriate vigil against abusive expansion of modernism] would also mean attending to the complex interactions between two kinds of field

expansion: one motivated by a sense of *responsibility* to reach beyond what historically has been a small, Eurocentric, predominantly white male canon; the other exercised as an *entitlement* to claim expertise in anything, anywhere, at any time. In what cases, we would want to ask ourselves, does the claim of responsibility function as a warrant for the exercise of entitlement? What role might weak theory play in vitiating such warrants? And how might an ethics of humility help us to responsibly weak ways of engaging works, persons, subjects, and areas that we aren't entitled to engage strongly? (454)

This passage indicates that, unlike "weak," "responsible" can carry multiple binary relationships—including an uncommon one, with "entitled," evoked here—leading to potentially productive multivalence. Indeed, each of the multiple meanings activated (such as dutiful, ethical, and humble) fits well with weak theory's goal of attending to formerly neglected, suppressed, or unimagined dimensions of the object of study.

First of all, the common meaning, "Of a practice or activity: carried out in a morally principled or ethical way" ("Responsible"), informs weak theory's project of ameliorating various forms of neglect that have kept marginal subjects marginal. And, specifically, this definition warns us of weak theory's pitfall as regards the arbitrariness over what is weak or strong. Second, an obsolete meaning—"corresponding or answering (to something)," derived from French origin *responsable*—illuminates a promising aspect of weak theory's project and the challenges that accompany it.[4] Corresponding to, and thus pursuing congruity with, the object of study, instead of selecting or rejecting portions to achieve a forced consistency in one's reading, accords with Saint-Amour's incorporation of weak affect theory, particularly in that "[w]eak theory is *descriptive*, seeking to know but not necessarily to know better than its object" (444). At the same time, the fact that all three sample sentences in *Oxford English Dictionary* adopt the word in a negative or conditional clause (such as, "The Mouth large, but not responsible to so large a Body," in John Fryer's 1698 travel writing, *A New Account of East-India and Persia*) may indicate the difficulty of fully executing such responsibility—a difficulty that obstructs weak theory's attempt at holistic and attentive inquiry. Fryer's example, concerning a body part's failure to correspond with the size of "so large a Body," may also turn our attention to the dilemma that a critic has to work on the impossible mission of fully capturing the infinitely multifaceted object.

This difficulty in developing effective correspondence also challenges weak theory's undertaking of addressing the formerly unaddressed aspects of the object as well as formerly marginalized perspectives on it. Here, Richard Rorty's liberalist pragmatism, with its cultural relativism properly modified, would provide a useful model.[5] The assumption of "a God's-eye point of view," Rorty argues, does not help our truth-seeking efforts because "[o]ur acculturation is what makes certain options live, or momentous, or forced, while leaving others dead, or trivial, or optional" (13). Instead, he calls for "solidarity," characterized by open-minded, democratic dialogue through which to pursue consensus. (Such openness to dialogic feedback exchange is "responsible" in yet another obsolete meaning of the word, namely, "capable of being answered.") Yet, for Rorty, the attempt to "reduce objectivity to solidarity"—which he calls a "realist"-ic, as opposed to "pragmatist," inclination—is futile, given the absence of universal rationality capable of resolving the conflict between varying cultural frameworks (22). In the spirit of responsiveness, however, I propose that responsible reading reintroduces the sense of objectivity—not as a teleologically defined final product but as a subjunctively posited goal toward which its execution aims—with the model that treats conflicts over objectivity not as a dead-end but as yet another object of exploration.

A Revisit to Faulkner's Nagano

Such an open-minded, endless pursuit of better understanding resonates productively with Emmanuel Levinas's formulation of responsibility in the form of *mauvaise conscience*. Here, as Stephen Ross's introduction to this volume shows, "the indeterminacy ... has nothing to do with an ultimately untouchable otherness of the cultural object so much as with the perpetual work of interpretation" (12). As *mauvaise conscience* posits the subject's responsible attitude not only to a text or artifact but also to human otherness, it is worth revisiting and rereading Faulkner's Nagano in 1955, filled with faces and English inflections foreign to him. The following attempt at a responsible reading of this encounter aims to contribute to what Dimock calls a "reparative reading as additive in this crowdsourced sense" (588) as regards the network-reparative efforts made at the seminar. It also involves attending to the foreign other's subjectivity, and even to what has been lost in translation and miscommunication and thus missed by the inevitably Anglophonic logocentrism of English studies.

Japan did, and continued to, present an exotic otherness to Faulkner, and his mission under the State Department's Exchange of Persons Program, designed as a charm offensive to check Communism's Asian influence, inevitably involved strategic geopolitics, if highly sugar-coated, predicated upon the self/

other dichotomy. Indeed, his short essay "Impressions of Japan" makes casually reductive observations typical of Orientalism: "So kind the people that with three words the guest can go anywhere and live: Gohan; Sake: Arrigato [sic]... And one more word: ... Sayonara" (184). Indeed, such reduction of Japanese language to just four words, the last of which suggests the speaker's unwillingness to engage, results from its frustrating difference from "western memory": "But then no more, because there is nothing for western memory to measure it against; so not the mind to listen but only the ear to hear that chirrup and skitter of syllables like the cries of birds in the mouths of children, like music in the mouths of women and young girls" (179).

Thus, it is remarkable that Robert A. Jelliffe's record of "Meeting with Nagano Citizens"—put together from seven Q&A sessions held in the Gomeikan hotel where Faulkner stayed—opens with his active foregrounding and problematization of such othering. Faulkner introduces himself "only incidentally as an American" but "as one man, a stranger who has been made welcome in your country" (Jelliffe 137). Though he and the audience undeniably make a hierarchical relationship between the giver and the recipient of a lecture—and, more broadly, of the world power's loaded goodwill—Faulkner tries to translate it into that "between simple human beings" (137). Accordingly, he proposes "not to make speeches, lecture to one another, but to talk to one another" so that later he could also convey to Americans "what Japanese men and women told me about Japan, about what the Japanese people think about Americans, and what the Japanese people think we should do, that conditions that we have known in the last ten years will never happen again" (137-8). Here, even the language barrier leads to a thoughtful response suggestive of Levinasian *mauvaise conscience*, as exemplified by the first exchange:

Q.: Which one of your works do you advise us to read first, and which next, and so on?
F.: Thank you, that was very good English. I'm ashamed when I hear the Japanese people speak my language, and I can't speak theirs. (138)

To the questioner's presumably unfluent utterance, Faulkner's initial praise of "very good English" is rather paternalistic. However, he immediately follows up with an acknowledgment of the barrier, himself taking responsibility for it and seeking for an affective connection through sharing the feeling of "shame" the questioner may have felt.

One could call this just a lip service on Faulkner's part. Indeed, the interaction that follows undeniably indicates a master-student relationship with the awestruck audience eager to learn from the great author—a relationship also manifest in the footage by the US Information Agency's film documentary *Impressions of Japan* (1955). Yet one listener chimes in and ventures a question with a personal anecdote. This question, closely examined by Dimock, is worth a full quotation, particularly because a reading responsive to the Japanese audience's subjectivity may help us to recognize a formerly unaddressed, bilateral aspect of the ongoing network-reparative effort:

> Q.: The scene of soldiers drinking liquor which appears in the beginning of the book *Soldier's* [sic] *Pay* made me recall an occurrence which arose just after the end of the Pacific war. When I was standing on one of the platforms at Nagoya, some American soldiers came along and forcibly held my neck, making me drink whisky. They then passed the bottle among themselves, drinking from the same bottle that I had drunk from. Since considerable time has elapsed since the time that *Soldier's* [sic] *Pay* was written of, and since things are quite peaceful now, I don't imagine that such things happen nowadays. Could you tell me whether such scenes can be seen? (Jelliffe 141)

Faulkner's answer, that the soldier himself was "really not accountable for what he might do," given young American soldiers' psychological disorientation after the abrupt end of traumatizing wartime violence (141–2), might sound ethically insensitive. Yet, as Dimock points out, it nevertheless indicates Faulkner's effort to illuminate the winners' vulnerability where "[n]o one wins [in war], since winning is never an option" and, accordingly, explore "the possibility of a further common ground, something like a non-tragic sequel to World War II" (594).

Dimock strives to capture a holistic picture of the scene and, if implicitly, rightly acknowledges its impossibility, by announcing that she offers "at least three reasons" there are for the Q&A exchange's noteworthiness (593) and thus leaving the room for additional input from the "crowdsource." And, indeed, there may be more to it. The "reasons" she names take Japanese people's subjectivity into account, noting a "basis for emotional connection between postbellum South and Japan in 1955" (593). However, when Dimock attributes this connection to a "shared sense of humiliation" which, she assumes, the "Japanese interlocutor would pick up on and respond to" (593), this reading does not correspond fully with the affective context for his question. On the most literal level, curiosity in the man's question is hard to miss. The term "forcibly" and the phrase "things are quite peaceful now" may have struck Dimock as indicative of his "sense of humiliation." But the possibility remains that he used the adjective "peaceful" as opposed to "wild," just like the opening scene of *Soldiers' Pay*, instead of "violent" or "humiliating." Given the common Japanese phrase *kubi wo tsukanda* falls into translational lacuna (i.e., more aggressive than "put his arm around my neck" but less so than "forcibly held my neck"), could it not be that the "humiliating" power hierarchy came more from the English language and its second-language translation than from the Japanese man's affective response to the episode?

I suspect these possibilities because of the man's repeated projection of his experience onto the opening scene of *Soldiers' Pay*, Faulkner's first novel published in 1926. Right after the First World War Armistice, deprived of an opportunity for martial glory, Joe Gilligan, a demobilized Private, and Julian Lowe, a young air cadet, find themselves to be what Joe calls "unworthy strangers in a foreign land" though they are in their native America (6). Here, Joe makes Julian drink his bad whisky, "pushing the bottle suddenly in his mouth and tilting it," but in this very sentence Faulkner makes Joe's earlier utterance, "You are among friends," performative and has his third-person narrator refer to them as "new friend[s]" (6). Possibly comparing his encounter with American soldiers to that between metaphorical and literal "strangers in a foreign land," the Japanese man may even have found in it a boisterous display of brotherhood, with the existing power relations challenged by the soldiers themselves. Indeed, the order of drinking—himself first and then the soldiers—inverses the tradition of *sakazuki goto* sake-cup sharing, where even brotherhood pledge proceeds according to a strictly hierarchical, rank-based protocol. The Japanese man's nonjudgmental interpretation and representation of the soldiers' action show the possibility that a reparative network may have begun forming—in the direct aftermath of the national devastation and destruction—a decade before Faulkner's effort unwittingly let it show.

Close reading of textual evidence has helped my attempt at responsible reading, but speculative exploration of the object's probabilistic dimensions, especially concerning miscommunications due to language barriers, has informed my undertaking none the less. Significantly, the episodes of reparative US-Japan exchange, not only between the Japanese man and American soldiers but also between Faulkner and the Nagano audience, themselves indicate how such bilingual miscommunication can paradoxically open up the space for a reading of the other outside of the subject's existing frame of reference, which in turn performatively promotes an open-minded, nonjudgmental interaction. As Fumiko Fujita documents, not only Japanese people's limited English proficiency but also Faulkner's own reticence, accent, fast speech, and low-pitched, monotonous voice repeatedly hindered their communication (103–4, 113–18, 120–1). And seminar participants' accounts suggest that their nonjudgmentally speculative filling of the informational void—exemplified by Naotaro Tatsunokuchi's interpretation of Faulkner's aloof taciturnity not as "arrogant self-importance" but as "resulting from humility" (qtd. in Fujita 114, my translation)—may even have drawn out formerly unrecognized sides of the novelist.

Indeed, an account by Shozo Kajima, then early-career scholar and translator of Faulkner's work, unwittingly reveals how Faulkner's and the Nagano audience's reparative reading of each other actually developed only slowly, over the course of his stay, and how this process benefited from the language barrier and resulting failure of communication. At the first Gomeikan panel, Kajima volunteered the Q&A's first question.

> I simply wanted to save the moment [from a long nervous silence following Faulkner's listener-unfriendly talk]. Permitted to ask a question, I stood up and asked, "If it is so difficult to communicate, if the environment is so hard to overcome, how can we communicate between Japan and America?"
>
> Faulkner replied, "That's why I am here."
>
> Laughter went up from the participants; I felt that at least I had broken the ice, but was he making fun of my question? (3)

Curiously, Robert A. Jelliffe, the Q&A's facilitator and the editor of *Faulkner at Nagano*, did not include this exchange in the book. It is not clear why he began his record instead with the above-discussed, later exchange featuring Faulkner's kind response to an unfluently made request for book recommendation. Jelliffe may not have found Faulkner's cavalier answer and the audience's laughing response—and even Kajima's question itself, foregrounding the ongoing failure of US-Japan communication on both ends—to fit well with the program's goals. Indeed, given that Faulkner's talk, on the very topic of US-Japan communication, was itself hard to follow, Kajima's question may have struck the novelist, as well as other Japanese attendees, as insinuatory to the awkwardness. Hence Faulkner's rather defensive claim to the authoritative position "here" in the linguistic contact zone—from which to bridge the gap with his own words—and the audience's "laughter" downplaying the question's disruptive potential.

This first encounter thus left all parties filling the failed communication with judgmentally reductive interpretations. A change, however, comes with

Faulkner's growing awareness of most listeners' limited knowledge not only of the English language but also of his works. "We hadn't overcome the difficulty of reading his works, which were so unfamiliar to our traditional concept of the novel," Kajima recalls, which "disappointed" but also "relieved" Faulkner (3):

> This combination of our naiveness and his honesty, of our innocence and his sincerity, made the Seminar dialogue quite interesting and revealing. If we had been American professors in the early years of Faulkner studies, we would have been far more cautious and timid in throwing such innocent questions at him. We would have been more prying and sharp to get inside him, which would have made Faulkner nervous, closed or sarcastic. (4)

This perspective provides an additional context in which the question about "forcibl[e]" liquor sharing, though it does indicate the interlocutor's familiarity with *Soldiers' Pay*, may have been asked—and perceived by other Japanese listeners—as the expression of nonjudgmental curiosity rather than a sense of humiliation. Though Faulkner may simply have acted according to his recognition of an easy audience, such a reaction made him all the more responsive and responsible, "trying to perform his duty with kindness" (4). Indeed, while the lack of preexisting frame of reference led the audience to ask apparently "silly, inconsequential questions," Kajima noticed that "Faulkner answered these questions with honesty and sincerity, taking the silliness out of them and making them significant," thus "revealing" himself beyond the usual "nervous, closed or sarcastic" self (4). Tellingly, with all its actual presence and influence, this aspect of the seminar was excluded from *Faulkner at Nagano*'s record of more directly meaningful exchanges. And it was also suppressed in Kajima's own memory—as it represented "his immature ghost of the green days" (3)—though he knew that, regardless of the lack of linguistic or psychological reference, it was part of Faulkner's, and his own, Nagano. "I knew I would be embarrassed to read the book again," he writes of *Faulkner at Nagano*, "because in some sense I was everywhere in it" (3).

"The Sleeper Wakes"

How would responsible reading help to enhance our understanding of a literary work? I attempt to answer this question using a fictional narrative of racial passing, "The Sleeper Wakes," by Jessie Redmon Fauset. As a term meaning a light-skinned African American's permanently or temporarily living as white, "passing" dates back to the time of slavery, with the oldest example considered to derive from public notices concerning fugitive slaves (Sollors 255). Nineteenth-century America saw both nonfictional slave narratives and fictional works that feature racial passing, but it was in the early twentieth century—propelled partly by the debate over black self-identification and racial pride during the New Negro Renaissance—that the passing fiction had a remarkable boost in African American literary production: James Weldon Johnson's *The Autobiography of an Ex-Colored Man* (1912), Walter Francis White's *Flight* (1926), Nella Larsen's *Passing* (1929), Jessie Redmon Fauset's *Plum Bun* (1929) and *Comedy, American Style* (1933), and George Schuyler's *Black No More* (1931), to name just a few book-length works.

Early-twentieth-century African American literature itself bears a notable relevance to weak theory's project of addressing modernism in its "laterally associative instead of vertically definitional" dimensions (Saint-Amour 453). As Mark A. Sanders suggests, top-down formation of modernism, such as "high modernism" characterized by definitive parameters like "epistemological crisis, fragmentation, alienation, and cultural exhaustion" has only a limited capacity to represent literary works of the New Negro Renaissance (129). Instead, Sanders finds what he calls "heterodox modernism" in their attempt to address "the stalled projects of democratic development and nation building" (130), where disordered representation comes not top-down from the zeitgeist of epistemological crisis but bottom-up from New Negro writers' lived experiences of "the harrowing dissonance between constitutional guarantees and systematic political oppression" (137).

The motif of racial passing also entails issues pertinent to weak theory's focus of inquiry. In tandem with pseudoscientific racialism based on physiognomy, the idea of detecting racial passing involved what post-critique scholars call critique's "diagnostic" approach. In particular, such detection draws upon "a speech act and a stance or orientation: one that is predicated on the revelatory force of an examining gaze" as well as "the belief that such scrutiny will bring problems to light that can be deciphered by an authoritative interpreter" (Anker and Felski 4). Most passing novels question such authority. The protagonist of Larsen's *Passing*, for example, debunks whites' self-claimed ability to decipher bodily clues as "the most ridiculous ... silly rot" (11). Paradoxically, however, problematizing racial passing necessitates presupposing the presence of racial passing, thus forcing those novels to operate under the assumption of the white-looking character's *actual blackness*. This leads to the problem of what Tomkins calls strong affect theory, which Saint-Amour summarizes as "*decryptive*, bent on decoding or unmasking a vast array of phenomena in order to avoid bad surprises" (444). In other words, the narratively troubling indeterminacy of a white-looking person's race is translated into the "good," narratively useful surprise of his/her actual blackness, which facilitates characterization, plot development, and denouement. (This surprise is "good" to the racial ideology of early-twentieth-century America, too, for it turns the unknown into black and thus helps reinforce the hegemonic discourse of binary racial classification.)

Fauset's "The Sleeper Wakes," published in the NAACP's *Crisis* magazine for which she was the literary editor, features beautiful, innocent, and naïve Amy Kildare. Though her skin has "pearl and pink whiteness," no one knows her race except that, when she was five, a "tall, proud, white woman" dropped her at the Boldins, a middle-class black family in Trenton, New Jersey (168). Projecting herself onto the heroines of "pretty girl pictures" (169), Amy runs away to New York at the age of 17 and begins to live as white. Two years later, a white artist helps her to rise in New York society and marry Stuart James Wynne, a wealthy retired broker in his fifties. On his Virginia estate, Stuart, a Georgia native with "race-pride" and "huge intolerant carelessness characteristic of occidental civilization" (226–7), harshly treats his black servants, particularly Stephen, a rebellious young valet who reminds Amy of Cornelius Boldin, the boy she grew up with. One day, Amy comes across Stephen fighting back against Stuart and, in an impulsive attempt to protect him from possible lynching, she tells the husband that she is black. Stuart divorces her, while still providing her with a small house in New York and three servants. Through four years of hard work, however, Amy develops a successful career as a fashion designer and earns her way out of financial dependence. With this newly gained freedom, Amy realizes that "her mind was busy with little intimate pictures of that happy, wholesome, unpretentious life" at the Boldins (273). The story ends as she decides and arranges to return to the still welcoming Boldins.

The easily accessible, straightforward prose of Fauset's fictional works has struck most readers as traditional and uninnovative. Reference, if any, to her connection to the modernist avant-garde has most often concerned her role as a "midwife," discovering and supporting young black writers such as Jean Toomer. Indeed, "The Sleeper Wakes" appears a typical sentimental story with the titular theme of developmental "awakening"—from morally and racially insensible to mindful and, as regards racial identity, from white to black. Accordingly, whether they acknowledge Amy's racial indeterminacy or not, critics have focused on African American issues in or around the story, such as anti-lynching aesthetics and attitudes toward immigration,[6] rather than attend to that very indeterminacy.

Such approaches do stand valid, but there is more to "The Sleeper Wakes." Curiously, a 1995 reviewer calls the piece "an uplifting but sentimental story of moral and racial awakening" (Curb 140) but also notes that the overflow of sentimentality pushes the limit of credibility: "Amy's innocence and unconsciousness seem barely credible, as she drifts into adulthood on the wings of pale beauty and no moral convictions until, unaware of racial struggles, she rises to defend her husband's servants" (141). Indeed, through her third-person narrator, Fauset takes pains not to let simplistic binaries frame the story vertically or monovalently. On the contrary, she pays a highly responsible/responsive attention to the protagonist's simple but often inexplicable mind, and the story subtly invites a similar reading practice for the reader to capture its complex and even self-contradictory world more fully. Not only Amy's racial identity but also the *mode* of her racial identification is indeterminate, multiple, and variable, as the third-person narrator conveys contradicting parameters as they are, with little intervention to fit them into coherent characterization.

For example, as the story progresses, it presents Amy's race as an environmentally determined variable ("Am I going to be colored now [that I am part of a black family]?" [Fauset 168]), an attribute defined in binary terms ("am I white or colored?" [168]), a pragmatic value, defined behaviorally rather than cognitively (the narrator tells that "[s]he went immediately to a white Y.W.C.A" on arriving in New York, followed by sentences that explain the action only inconclusively [170]), an affective and intuitive interpersonal bond ("I *am* colored, … I feel it inside of me. I must be or I couldn't care so about Stephen" [228]), an invariable given, which one can only "want" or "hope" to choose ("She wanted to be colored, she hoped she was colored" [273]) and, right before the ending, an irrelevant overclassification: "She would never make any attempt to find out who or what she was … 'Citizen of the world, that's what I'll be'" (274). Though some of these formulations do contribute to the story's plot development, Fauset's narrator does not connect them as a developmental transition of Amy's racial attitude or of her character.

The story's treatment of elements in their chaotically unorganized and even contradictory coexistence also has to do with its approach to modernism. While fragmentary language, as in the stream-of-consciousness technique, enables a modernist writer to represent a character's disordered inner reality more directly, the story's traditional third-person narrator and sentimental framework complicate its incorporation of such an enterprise. Specifically, Fauset occasionally applies free indirect style. This technique, while still sustaining a third-person narration, reflects the diction, syntax, and content of a character's own inner psychology and thus can convey his/her subjective thoughts and feelings in a form closer to their original flow. In the story, free indirect narration mostly represents Amy's interior, such as the ejaculation "She was free, free!" when she pays off her debt to Stuart (Fauset 273). Yet, while objective third-person narration and subjective free indirect narration play separate roles for the most part, they occasionally overlap with each other as if to decenter the story's representational authority through individually flawed but interactively additive contributions from Amy and the narrator. As the story moves to New York, for instance, free indirect narration shows Amy's motive for leaving the Boldin family in her simple diction and colloquial syntax: "Not that she was the least bit unhappy but because she must get out in the world,—she felt caged, imprisoned" (170). Another colloquially structured passage, discussing the same question, follows in the next paragraph: "Perhaps it was because of her early experience . . ., perhaps it was some fault in her own disposition, concentrated and egotistic as she was, but certainly she felt no pangs of separation, no fear of her future. She was cold too,—unfired though so to speak rather than icy,—and fastidious" (170). The sophisticated diction suggests its origin in the third-person narrator but, as indicated by the repeated use of "perhaps," the narrator's explanation is no more authoritative or validated than Amy's.

As in many passing narratives, Fauset's narrator notes the protagonist's careless self-absorption and lack of group loyalty in terms of "irresponsib[ility]" (169). However, the story's repeated complication of normative interpretive frameworks predicated upon the white/black, subject/object, and even modernist/non-modernist binaries invites the reader to reach for the aspects of the character and her world unattended by such frameworks. The narrator-character merging occurs also in the scene where Amy confronts Stuart over Stephen:

> How, *how* could she keep him [Stuart] back! She hated her weak arms with their futile beauty! She sprang toward him. "Stuart, wait," she was breathless and sobbing. She said the first thing that came into her head. "Wait, Stuart, you cannot do this thing [lynching Stephen]." She thought of Cornelius—suppose it had been he—"Stephen,—that boy,—he is my brother." (229)

The first sentence activates free indirect narration to represent Amy's first-person thought ("How, *how* can I keep him back!") in third person. The second sentence, while its exclamation point appears to continue the same narrative mode, derives actually from the third-person narrator's own utterance, as indicated by a reference to the "futile beauty" of Amy's arms. Not only is the narrator agitated here, but her description also turns out to be not entirely true. For, though Stuart's confident assumption of the detectability of passing ("Don't you suppose I know a white girl when I see one?") immediately dismisses Amy's claim, when she "caught his arm again" her arm manages to stop Stuart to listen (229). Indeed, when Amy tells him Stephen is really not her brother, "[t]he light of relief that crept into his eyes did not escape her, it only nerved her" enough to tell him she is black (229), thus indicating that the scenario of Amy as Stephen's sister was not utterly unthinkable to him. Deep down, even Stuart, a powerful instrument of dominant racial ideology (characterized by "insatiable desire for power; keenness, mentality; a vast and cruel pride" [273]), suspects a limitation of clear-cut binary classification. There is indeed room for Amy's illogically associative formulation of her racial identity, predicated upon the subjunctively evoked ("suppose it had been he") identification of Stephen, Cornelius and herself.

Passing Responsibly

In the humanities, an object of study always involves a network of subject positions different from that of the reader. So, in its utmost effort to attend to the object, responsible reading requires a kind of passing in one way or another. Then, can responsible reading genuinely achieve its goal, particularly the task of reaching for the provisional, probabilistic, and subjunctive? Did my Japanese extraction make me *close enough* to hypothesize the affective formation of the Japanese audience in 1955? What about my self-proclaimed responsible reading of African American literature? Would one of the key takeaways from that reading—that straightforward identification, or even a composite of relevant identificatory parameters, cannot fully capture one's existence—doom or redeem the cause?

Pamela L. Caughie's post-structuralist pedagogy of passing offers some helpful input, though her main focus is on racial or ethnic passing as necessitated in the multiethnic (literature) classroom:

> The point of passing is not simply to say there is no origin, no presence, no ground, no body but rather to continually pose the question of the limit. Thus, the question of responsibility is linked to one's practice rather than one's position,

to the *practice* of writing in the poststructuralist sense of that term: not writing as communication or expression but as dissemination. Dissemination opens a gap between the writing and the meaning, between the performance and the reception, between the critical practice and its intended effects. In the endless return of that gap lies the ethical significance of passing. (46)

This "gap" points to the ultimate impossibility of authentic performance as well as of full signification of the object. Yet it also points to the importance—and "responsibility"—of continuing to perform and signify, with a constant awareness of the gap itself. While post-structuralist linguistics often sidelines historicized, corporeal, and interacting human subjects, Caughie does not exclude the validity of collectively making this "endless return," which, along with her consideration of "reception" and "effects," might open up a possible compatibility with continued, cumulative, lateral, and interactive dialogue. Indeed, with all the problematics of and challenges to weak theory, such productive debates continue to develop around it, making the formerly neglected a little more visible at each and every step.

Notes

1 Responsible reading, as I envisage it, shares the emphasis Madelyn Detloff's response to weak theory places on hermeneutic openness that allows for "an ongoing engagement with culture as it evolves in ways we can't always predict" (n.p.). As regards the limitations of weak theory and Dimock's essay, however, my take differs from that of Detloff, who considers them to be "not categorical or methodological, but contingent, local, and temporal" (n.p.).

2 In their analysis of Virginia Woolf's and Kate Zambreno's amateuristic, "obliterary" critical productions, Melanie Micir and Aarthi Vadde adopt careful wording to indicate the same predicament that accompanies weak theory. Indeed, they refer to their essay's relationship with weak theory in notably provisional and subjunctive terms: "we see in obliterature an opportunity to reanimate the modernist memory project under a weakly theoretical umbrella" (520). Accordingly, the contrast between amateurism and professionalism does not fall into a simplistic binary, much less that between strength and weakness: "Canonical and obliterary works orbit around one another, calling the canon's power and obliterature's powerlessness into question precisely through their proximity" (521).

3 Susan Stanford Friedman takes issue with weak theory's self-designation as "weak" but proposes an adjustment that still sustains its "theory" status. At the same time, her configuration of "theory" focuses on its practically hermeneutic dimension

and, with its flexibility and engaged responsiveness to the object, coheres well with my take on "responsible reading": "I do not regard theory as a more or less closed system (a totality), but rather as a set of interrelated generalizations that allow for a new understanding of a group of specific instances. In this sense, all theories are provisional, probalistic [sic], and open to being replaced by other theories, especially by significant shifts in basic paradigms" (n.p.).

4 While acknowledging the multivalence of "responsibility," Paul Ricoeur finds the term's juridical and philosophical significance around the meaning of "imputation," figured as separate from that of "responsiveness," and thus develops his discussion "outside the semantic field of the verb 'to respond'" (13). Similarly, Garrath Williams focuses on the moral dimension in his survey of the term's philosophical history. The meaning of "to respond" turns out to be a key parameter, nevertheless, in both Kantian (emphasizing individuals' rational choice) and Humean (emphasizing humans' affective tendencies) approaches. For, as Williams points out, responsibility as configured in either fashion draws upon intra- and interpersonal feedback in the forms of "general responsiveness to others … a sense of responsibility for our actions … and tendencies to regard others as responsible" (n.p.).

5 Kate Stanley also finds a pragmatist undertone in the aspect of weak theory that derives from Tomkins's and Sedgwick's affect theories. Specifically, Stanley points to an echo of William James's "pragmatist method" characterized by improvisation, pluralism, and consequence-oriented approach. At the same time, she suggests that the pragmatist project of bridging oppositional values draws less upon a binary model than weak theory does: "for pragmatists the 'middle way' more reliably emerges out of interactions that confuse and confound the very categories of tender and tough" (n.p.). As regards Rorty's cultural relativism, my reservation goes along with Rita Felski's, as she expresses, though conditionally, her appreciation of "a fair or responsible reading" and thus disagrees with Rorty's interpretive approach which blurs "the differences between finding things out and making them up, between imposing our ideas on a text and learning something from a text" (Felski 115).

6 See Castronovo and Ammons, respectively.

References

Ammons, Elizabeth. "Black Anxiety about Immigration and Jessie Fauset's *The Sleeper Wakes*." *African American Review*, vol. 42, nos. 3–4, 2008, pp. 461–76.

Anker, Elizabeth S., and Rita Felski. *Critique and Postcritique*. Duke UP, 2017.

Castronovo, Russ. "Beauty along the Color Line: Lynching, Aesthetics, and the *Crisis*." *PMLA/Publications of the Modern Language Association of America*, vol. 121, no. 5, 2006, pp. 1443–59.

Caughie, Pamela L. *Passing and Pedagogy: The Dynamics of Responsibility*. U of Illinois P, 1999.

Curb, Rosemary Keefe. Review of *The Sleeper Wakes: Harlem Renaissance Stories by Women*, edited by Marcy Knopf. *MELUS*, vol. 20, no. 3, 1995, pp. 140–3.

Detloff, Madelyn. "On Going ... Ongoing ... Going On." *Modernism/modernity Print Plus*. Responses to the Special Issue on Weak Theory, Part I, vol. 3, cycle 4, February 7, 2019, modernismmodernity.org/forums/posts/responses-special-issue-weak-theory-part-i.

Dimock, Wai Chee. "Weak Network: Faulkner's Transpacific Reparations." *Modernism/modernity*, vol. 24, no. 3, 2018, pp. 587–602.

Faulkner, William. "Impressions of Japan." *Faulkner at Nagano*, edited by Robert A. Jelliffe. Kenkyusha, 1956, pp. 178–84.

Faulkner, William. *Soldiers' Pay*. Liveright, 2011 [1926].

Faulkner, William. "To the Youth of Japan." *Faulkner at Nagano*, edited by Robert A. Jelliffe. Kenkyusha, 1956, pp. 185–8.

Fauset, Jessie Redmon. "The Sleeper Wakes." *Crisis*, vol. 20, nos. 4–6, August 1920, pp. 168–73; September 1920, pp. 226–9; October 1920, pp. 267–74.

Felski, Rita. *The Limits of Critique*. U of Chicago P, 2015.

Friedman, Susan Stanford. "Provisionally Persistent." *Modernism/modernity Print Plus*. Responses to the Special Issue on Weak Theory, Part I, vol. 4, cycle 1, April 2, 2019, modernismmodernity.org/forums/posts/responses-special-issue-weak-theory-part-iii.

Fujita, Fumiko. 藤田文子. *U.S. Cultural Diplomacy and Japan in the Cold War Era*. アメリカ文化外交と日本: 冷戦期の文化と人の交流. U of Tokyo P 東京大学出版会, 2015.

Jelliffe, Robert A., editor. *Faulkner at Nagano*. Kenkyusha, 1956.

Kajima, Shozo. "Remembering Faulkner: Warmness, Sincerity, Openness at Nagano Impressed Everyone." *The Faulkner Newsletter & Yoknapatawpha Review*, vol. 9, no. 2, 1989, pp. 1, 3–4.

Larsen, Nella. *Passing*, edited by Carla Kaplan. W. W. Norton, 2007 [1929].

Micir, Melanie, and Aarthi Vadde. "Obliterature: Toward an Amateur Criticism." *Modernism/modernity*, vol. 24, no. 3, 2018, pp. 517–49.

"Responsible." *OED Online*, 3rd ed. Oxford UP, 2010, www-oed-com.ezproxy.fgcu.edu/view/Entry/163862?redirectedFrom=responsibility#eid. Accessed July 21, 2020.

Ricoeur, Paul. "The Concept of Responsibility: An Essay in Semantic Analysis." *The Just*, translated by David Pellauer, U of Chicago P, 2000 [1995], pp. 11–35.

Rorty, Richard. *Objectivity, Relativism, and Truth: Philosophical Papers*, vol. 1, Cambridge UP, 1991.

Saint-Amour, Paul K. "Weak Theory, Weak Modernism." *Modernism/modernity*, vol. 24, no. 3, 2018, pp. 437–59.

Sanders, Mark A. "American Modernism and the New Negro Renaissance." *The Cambridge Companion to American Modernism*, edited by Walter Kalaidjian. Cambridge UP, 2005, pp. 129–56.

Sollors, Werner. *Neither Black nor White yet Both: Thematic Explorations of Interracial Literature*. Harvard UP, 1999.

Stanley, Kate. "Tough and Tender." *Modernism/modernity Print Plus*. Responses to the Special Issue on Weak Theory, Part I, vol. 3, cycle 4, February 7, 2019.

Williams, Garrath. "Responsibility." *Internet Encyclopedia of Philosophy*, iep.utm.edu/responsi/.

Part III

Practice

9

Absolutely Small: Sketch of an Anarchist Aesthetic

Roger Rothman

Beyond Critique

A specter is haunting Theory—the specter of affirmation. All the powers of Old Theory have entered into a holy alliance to exorcise this specter: the masters of suspicion and their acolytes hold fast to the work of unmasking hidden forces of oppression, but the ghost shows no sign of departing. Though Bruno Latour's 2004 essay "Why Has Critique Run Out of Steam?" has drawn the lion's share of attention and seems to pinpoint the haunting to the early years of the new century,[1] in reality, the ghost of affirmation first appeared in 1997 in Eve Kosofsky Sedgwick's deliciously titled essay, "Paranoid Reading and Reparative Reading; or, You're So Paranoid, You Probably Think This Introduction Is About You."[2] Sedgwick, like Latour, was responding to the insistence, almost universally declared, that cultural practice is of value only when it serves the imperatives of *critique*, when the artist (or historian who interprets the artist's work) deploys her craft for the purpose of exposing the structures of domination that lie beneath the surface of what appear to the uninitiated to be nothing more than beneficent aesthetic expressions.[3] In the waning years of the last century, as if to put a final turn to the screw of critique by critiquing critique itself, Sedgwick insisted that "pleasure, grief, excitement, boredom, satisfaction are the substance of politics rather than their antithesis" and that "it's well to attend intimately to literary texts, not because their transformative energies either transcend or disguise the coarser stuff of ordinary being, but because those energies are the stuff of ordinary being" (1–2).

Against the unrelenting demand "always critique!" Sedgwick, Latour, and others (Rita Felski, most recently) cast about for alternative practices.[4] Latour proposes to replace the critic's inclination to debunk and demystify with "the cultivation of a stubbornly realist attitude" that he associates with the constructive (rather than deconstructive) efforts of empiricism (231). Sedgwick, for her part, proposes to replace the critic's unrelenting "paranoia" with the therapist's investment in the *reparative* (24). In a similar spirit, I call for a return to the principle of *affirmation*. I insist on the term "affirmation" not simply because it rubs against decades of critical theory in which so-called affirmative culture (Marcuse) is all but irredeemable, but also, and more substantively, because the first step in any constructive act, any reparative gesture, is the act of affirmation, the act of saying "yes" within an environment in which "no" seems the only reasonable response.[5] Hal Foster has been one of a handful of theorists to raise such a reasonable objection to the critique of critique. Though he is willing to grant that "of course, such critique is never enough: one must intervene in what is given, somehow turn it, and take it elsewhere," he insists, nevertheless, that such "turning begins with critique" (7).

The ghost of affirmation responds in turn with an inquiry into the word "somehow" that made its way into Foster's objection. It is precisely on the question of this "somehow" that the critics of critique have insisted we focus our attention. Indeed, we would do well to ask ourselves, yet again, if indeed critique can do any more than point to problems against which it is wholly impotent. Marcuse lamented as much more than a half-century ago in the final pages of *One-Dimensional Man*. Critical Theory, Marcuse regrets to announce, "cannot offer the remedy." Its truth secured, "the dialectical concept pronounces its own hopelessness" (253). Like Adorno, for whom "[works of art], as eminently constructed and produced objects, ... point to a practice from which they abstain: the creation of a just life" (*Aesthetic* 194). Marcuse's pronouncement of hopelessness proleptically replies to Foster by acknowledging the inescapable limitation of the critical enterprise. Critique can look, but not touch. It can reveal, but cannot change. This would seem to be the source of distress for Benjamin Buchloh, who, like Foster, has devoted his career to detailing the means by which artists of the last fifty years have advanced the critical enterprise. Reflecting on twenty years of brilliant analyses of artists such as Michael Asher, Marcel Broodthaers, and Daniel Buren, Buchloh introduces the republication of his most influential essays with the "painful" recognition that "the sclerotic fixation on a model of reductivist criticality or instrumentalized rationality in artistic practices does not promise to be any more productive than an adherence to the foundationalist myths of the perennial validity of the classical genres and production procedures of painting and sculpture" and that one would do well to focus instead "on the aesthetic capacity to construct the mnemonic experience as one of the few acts of resistance against the totality of spectacularization" (xxv).

In response to Buchloh's proffered alternative to the exhaustion of critique, I would propose that these minimal "acts of resistance" have themselves become compensatory lamentations, and that a more viable solution is to allow the noble dialectics of negation to give way to a program of affirmation, at once more modest and less morose than the critical project to which Buchloh and Foster have pinned their hopes. Indeed, we would do well to make note of the fact that the ghost of affirmation began to haunt theory about the same time as Marxist social formations began to give way to modes of political engagement more readily comprehended within the framework of anarchist thought. Recalling Kropotkin's insistence that "it is not enough to destroy. We must also know how to build" (136–7), the 1999 WTO protests in Seattle, the events of the Arab Spring, and those of the Occupy Movement owe more to what Richard Day has called the "affinity-based practices" of anarchism than to the counter-hegemonic practices of Marxism. Writing in 2005, Day proposed that "what is most interesting about contemporary radical activism is that some groups are … operating non-hegemonically rather than counter-hegemonically. They seek radical change, but not through taking or influencing state power, and in so doing they challenge the logic of hegemony at its very core" (8, 15).

I would go farther even than Day: Social movements like the Arab Spring and Occupy have not only rejected the counter-hegemonic practices of Marxism, they have abandoned the dialectical mode within which the discourse of both critique and counter-hegemony are founded. (This is to say that they go farther, even, than Kropotkin, for whom destruction remains at the forefront, even if it is conceived within a context of construction). As Day himself acknowledges, the foundation of his model of affinity-based practices lies within the writing of Gustav Landauer, an early twentieth-century anarchist who has been gaining increasing relevance in recent years (in no small part because of the prominence Day has given to his writing). Landauer's revolutionary politics were grounded, not in the dialectics of critique and negation, but rather in what he referred to as "an alliance of alliances" (*Revolution* 214). Still more anti-dialectical thinking is evident in Bakunin, who insisted that "freedom can be created only by freedom" ("Statism").[6] Taking Landauer and Bakunin seriously means taking seriously the possibility of an explicitly non-dialectical politics.

What, then, have anarchists proposed in place of the dialectics of negation (of hegemony and counter-hegemony)? By what means are the prevailing conditions of the present supposed to be transformed? For Marx, of course, there is but one moment of change: "total revolution." "Indeed," he writes, in *Misère de la philosophie*, his critique of Proudhon's 1846 book, *Système des contradictions économiques, ou Philosophie de la misère*, "is it at all surprising that a society founded on the *opposition* of classes should culminate in brutal *contradiction*, the shock of body against body, as its final *dénouement*" (Marx 168)? Anarchism, at least in the main, deploys a fundamentally different model of social transformation, one founded on a rejection of the notion that all of social life is but the manifestation of a single unifying conflict. In *The Political Philosophy of Poststructuralist Anarchism*, a book that, like Day's, has played a central role in what is sometimes referred to as "post-anarchism,"[7] Todd May distinguishes anarchism's affinity-based practices from the oppositional practices of Marxism as "the tactical" versus "the strategic." Within the strategic model, social change "must rest upon a transformation at the base. Reducibility, then, lies at the core of strategic political thinking. All problems can be reduced to the basic one; justice is a matter of solving the basic problem." Within the tactical framework, however, "there is no center within which power is to be located" (10–11).

The model sketched here—of an anti-totalizing conception of social change founded on a multiplicity of small, tactical efforts—is not, of course, new to contemporary post-anarchism. It draws upon a legacy that, as Day makes explicit, reaches back to the major anarchists of the late nineteenth and early twentieth centuries, especially that of Landauer. For Day, it is Landauer who most fully articulated an affinity-based model of social change in which the distinction between reform and revolution no longer abides, and in which the tactical supplants the strategic. In "Weak Statesman, Weaker People!" (first published in 1910), Landauer introduced a model of social relations that fundamentally broke with the substantialist conception of entities like states and social classes. The question Landauer posed for himself and those around him who insisted upon a politics of violence and opposition was the following: upon what ontology is such a conception founded? If the State is a thing, an entity like a mountain or a building, one might well be justified in speaking of its destruction. But what if this conception of the State is incorrect? What if it is not, in fact, a thing? How does one do away with it if it cannot be torn down or blown up?

Of all the claims made by early theorists of anarchism, Landauer's insistence that "[t]he state is a social relationship" strikes me as the most radical. Certainly it has had a profound impact on the thinking of subsequent generations. Well before Day appears to have rediscovered Landauer's writing, it was central to Martin Buber, whose *Paths in Utopia* (1949) played a crucial role in bringing

Landauer's work to an English-speaking audience. Buber's reading of Landauer in turn influenced Paul Goodman and, through Goodman, Colin Ward, whose *Anarchy in Action* (1973) opens with an unequivocally affirmative assertion—"How would you feel if you discovered that the society in which you would really like to live was already here, apart from a few little, local difficulties like exploitation, war, dictatorship and starvation?"—and which turns directly to Landauer's conception of the state as a relationship rather than a thing as well as Goodman's tactical and iterative conception of social change as "the extension of spheres of free action until they make up most of social life" (Ward 18).[8] In a related vein, and as if anticipating the subsequent claims of May regarding the non-distinction between reform and revolution, Ward insists that "the choice between libertarian and authoritarian solutions is not a once-and-for-all cataclysmic struggle, it is a series of running engagements, most of them never concluded, which occur, and have occurred, throughout history" (131). In other words, the anarchist conception of social change—at least as inherited from Landauer—is inescapably gradual, iterative, and, quite possibly, unending.

A second candidate for the title of most radical of all those proposed by Landauer, if not all of the theorists of anarchism, is one that follows logically on the heels of his foundational insistence that the State is not a thing but a set of relations. With nothing substantive to destroy or dismantle, the gradual and iterative work of creating new social relations will, of necessity, involve the sorts of affirmative actions that Sedgwick called "reparative" and Latour "constructive": "Therefore let us destroy mainly by means of the gentle, permanent and binding reality that we build." With this, Landauer broaches the question of the relation between aesthetics and politics. The gradual, non-dialectical transformation of the world will proceed at a "gentle" pace and the life of "men together" will thereby manifest a "permanent beauty."

The Ridiculous

Landauer's political project (and, following it, the projects of Buber, Goodman, Ward, and Day) is thus at odds with the critical enterprise—an enterprise founded on the logic of expose-and-negate, debunk-and-destroy. Instead of a dialectical movement of thesis and antithesis, Landauer proposes a *dilational* process, whereby small affirmative acts are linked one to the other in an expanding network of relations. That these relations are at odds with the dominant forces of the moment (the military, the nation state)—and yet contain "a glimmer" of beauty—is, for Landauer, a sign that critique is insufficient and that, in its place, an affirmative project is the only solution. At the same time, Landauer's conception of social transformation explicitly establishes a relationship between politics and aesthetics. And the key to Landauer's understanding of this relationship lies in terms like "gentle" and "glimmer"—to them adheres a sense of the small, the modest, the slow. Against the sublime cataclysm of violent opposition ("the wild, ugly transitional destruction of ugly contemporaneity"), Landauer proposes an aesthetic that would seem almost too small to accomplish anything at all. Indeed, one might well dismiss it as altogether ridiculous.

To get a clearer purchase on the anarchist aesthetics at work in Landauer's affirmation of gentle and binding beauty, we would do well to turn to what is arguably the most renowned of all the anarchist reflections on the relation between aesthetics and politics, Emma Goldman's emphatic proclamation: *If I can't dance, I don't want your revolution!* For Goldman, there will be no delayed satisfaction, no dialectical process by which happiness is held in abeyance, permitted to appear only after the serious work of social change is complete.[9] As she recalled in *Living My Life*, one of her tasks in New York was to "get the girls in the trade to join the strike." And to accomplish that task, Goldman found that one of the most effective means was to organize dances. She loved the dances, but one day, a boy took her aside and, "with a grave face as if he were about to announce the death of a dear comrade," he told her that "it did not behoove an agitator to dance." It was "undignified," he said. Her "frivolity would only hurt the Cause" (Goldman).

Goldman's rebuke at the hands of her male comrades also recalls Kant's reflections on the sublime, for the accusation against her was that she was insufficiently serious, and her insistence upon pleasure lacked a sense of the grand scale of the revolutionary endeavor. For Kant, the sublime is the only aesthetic experience within which to construct a universal ethics (and with it, a rational and sustaining politics). The sublime attracts us, pleases us, because it indicates to us the presence of a universal and all-powerful Law—thus Kant's famous insistence: "Among moral qualities, true virtue alone is sublime" (*Observations* (2011) 22). Other virtues, such as sympathy and love, want for a proper sense of the universal, and thus fall prey to any number of misguided attachments: "For it is not possible that our bosom should swell with tenderness on behalf of every human being and swim in melancholy for everyone else's need, otherwise the virtuous person, like Heraclitus constantly melting into sympathetic tears, with all this good-heartedness would nevertheless become nothing more than a tenderhearted idler" (23).[10]

For Kant, the issue of scale is crucial. The sublime is not simply large, it is *absolutely* large. "We call *sublime* that which is *absolutely great* [schlechthin groß]. ... [Saying] that something is great is also something entirely different from saying that it is *absolutely* great ... The latter is that *which is great beyond all comparison*" (*Power of Judgment* 132).[11] That which is absolutely great—great beyond all comparison—is that which demands our dutiful submission and which is, for Kant, the pivotal step in the transformation of a society of violence into a society of universal laws.[12]

This is well known. What is less apparent, however, is that there exists, in the margins of Kant's reflection on the affective modes of aesthetic experience and their political implications, the outlines of a radically different constellation of aesthetics and politics. For the introduction of the "absolutely great" inevitably provokes the question of its inverse. What is the "absolutely small"? What is the sublime's inverted other? Would it, perhaps, make room for Goldman's dance, Day's affinity-based practices, and Landauer's gentle construction of a community of equals?

Kant's *Critique of the Power of Judgement* does, in fact, broach the question of the absolutely small, and when it does, we find, unsurprisingly, that Kant holds it in the lowest possible esteem: "If ... we say of an object absolutely that it is great, ... in that case we always combine a kind of respect with the representation, just as we combine contempt with that which we call absolutely small [schlechtweg klein]" (*Beautiful and the Sublime* 133).[13] Only once in the *Critique of the Power of Judgement* does Kant use the phrase "absolutely small," but, in its unmentioned condition elsewhere in the book, and even more so in *Observations on the Feeling of the Beautiful and the Sublime*, it haunts Kant's aesthetic theory like a ghost. Though the phrase itself appears only once, the associated aesthetic feeling is mentioned a number of times. Kant calls it *the ridiculous* and its significance is signaled by its antithetical relation to the sublime: "Nothing is so opposed to the beautiful as the disgusting, just as nothing sinks more deeply beneath the sublime than the ridiculous" (*Beautiful and the Sublime* 40).[14]

Throughout *Observations*, Kant identifies a number of things worthy of being called ridiculous. Certain poetic forms are ridiculous, as are men who spend too much time in the company of women (22, 48). Venturing an anthropology of the aesthetic, Kant identifies the French as the most prone to the ridiculous (in contrast to the sublime of the British and Japanese). It is here that readers of Kant confront one of his most problematic utterances, his claim that the most irredeemably ridiculous are the blacks of sub-Saharan Africa. Following

Hume's lead, Kant insists that they "have by nature no feeling that rises above the ridiculous":

> The religion of fetishes which is widespread among them is perhaps a sort of idolatry, which sinks so deeply into the ridiculous as ever seems to be possible for human nature. A bird's feather, a cow's horn, a shell, or any other common thing, as soon as it is consecrated with some words, is an object of veneration and of invocation in swearing oaths. The blacks are very vain, but in the Negro's way, and so talkative that they must be driven apart from each other by blows. (58)

Abhorrent as it is, Kant's distinction between men and women, Germans and Italians, Arabs and Africans, is nevertheless reconceivable in positive terms. Not by insisting upon the falsity of the oppositions, but rather, or in addition, by the revaluation of the opposition itself. In other words, an opportunity appears if we are able to remain with Kant long enough to imagine ourselves taking seriously the aesthetics and politics of the ridiculous. What, we should ask, would come of affirming the ridiculous over the sublime? What would it mean to abide the absolutely small and hold the absolutely great in contempt? What if, like Kant's ridiculous Africans, we insisted upon the sacred value of even the most ordinary of things and renounced all that one would be inclined to describe as noble and just?[15]

Like the ethics of the absolutely large, the ethics of the absolutely small begins with an injunction—not to submit to the transcendent law, but to care for the immanent other.[16] If the first act of the sublime is "respect," the first act of the ridiculous is "intimacy." Here, too, we can glimpse a framework for such thinking in the margins of Kant's thought. Regarding the relationship between individuals of different sizes (think big men and little women), Kant writes: "A grand stature earns regard and respect, a small one more intimacy" (*Beautiful and the Sublime* 20). In other words, the politics of the sublime is framed by *laws*—transcendent and demanding "regard and respect." Correspondingly, the politics of the ridiculous would be a politics constructed of *contracts*—immanent and demanding of "intimacy" (small acts of *trust*). From the former comes universal law and the duty of justice; from the latter comes relational obligations, what anarchists have long referred to as "mutual aid."

The sight of the absolutely small, would thus, as an inverted phenomenon, provoke in us a feeling of absolute power, which is to say, an immediate rush of pleasure. Then, as is the case with the sublime, there comes a second and reverse moment: when one is struck by the awareness of the obligation to do no harm. In this two-step experience, we find the pleasure/obligation pair operating in reverse. In the sublime, the pleasure comes second; in the ridiculous, it comes first. In the sublime, the power of nature is what strikes us initially; in the ridiculous, the requirement that we use our power to nurture comes second, only after the feeling of pleasure subsides.

As I have noted above, the means by which the ethics of the ridiculous is enacted as politics is through the proliferation of contracts. This, too, is an anarchist principle of the first order. For Proudhon, it is the very means by which the State will be made obsolete. A contract, as immanent regulation imposed by the parties themselves, "imposes no obligation upon the parties, except that which results from their personal promise of reciprocal delivery." Unlike the law, contracts are "not subject to any external authority" (Proudhon 53). The concatenation of contractual relations establishes a society iteratively, in absence of any supervening ideal or universal: "The *system of contracts*, substituted for the *system of laws*, would constitute the true government of the man and of the citizen; the true sovereignty of the people, the REPUBLIC" (55; emphasis and caps in original). The politics of the ridiculous is thus the politics of affirmation, a contractual politics in which the new emerges within the old, not as a violent battle for supremacy, but as a gradual displacement of one social arrangement by another.

Sunny Disposition

In connection with my current studies with Duchamp, it turns out that I'm a poor chessplayer. My mind seems in some respect lacking, so that I make obviously stupid moves. I do not for a moment doubt that this lack of intelligence affects my music and thinking generally. However, I have a redeeming quality: I was gifted with a sunny disposition.

(Cage, *A Year* x)

John Cage's "sunny disposition"—as well as the suspicion it inspired in the minds of his critics—ought to remind us of Goldman's insistence that the dance floor belongs inside the revolution. Even more explicitly than his predecessor, however, Cage advanced an art and politics of uncompromising affirmation. When asked, for instance in 1978, if he had been active in any of the political movements of the 1960s, Cage said he hadn't, and then offered the following explanation: "I wasn't interested in critical or negative action. I'm not interested in objecting to things that are wrong. I'm interested in doing something that seems to be useful to do. I don't think critical action is sufficient" (Kostelanetz, *Conversing* 292). Cage's critique of critique, his rejection of the dialectics of negation, was, in fact, the composer's fundamental orientation toward the world, and would find its most renown, and for some notorious, expression in the claim that listeners ought to experience his music as "an affirmation of life, not an attempt to bring order out of chaos nor to suggest improvements on creation, but simply a way of waking up to the very life we're living which is so excellent once one gets one's mind and one's desires out of its way and lets it act of its own accord" (Kostelanetz, *John Cage* 51).

Though seemingly a call for a quiescent acceptance of the world's misery and barbarism, for Cage, the act of excessive affirmation, is, in fact, the origin of an inescapable obligation to the other. What appears at first to establish a politics of total self-interest and thus complete indifference toward all things outside oneself is, for Cage, the foundation of an ethics of infinite care: "Responsibility is to oneself; and the highest form of it is irresponsibility to oneself which is to say the calm acceptance of whatever responsibility to others and things comes a-long" (Cage, *Silence* 139). In Kantian terms, Cage's politics is quite clearly a politics of the ridiculous, of an "inclination that is beautiful in itself but which ... is without self-control and without principles." (Kant, *Beautiful and the Sublime* 24).

To a number of his adherents, such a politics was utterly incomprehensible. Yvonne Rainer, for example, has made it clear that her debt to Cage stops well short of the composer's call for an art of excessive affirmation. For Rainer, Cage's "methods of nonhierarchical, indeterminate organizations" are not to be used to "awaken to this excellent life," but rather, "so we may the more readily awaken to the ways in which we have been led to believe that this life is so excellent, just, and right" (38). Like so many in her generation, Rainer was attuned to Cage's formal inventions—at least some of them—but was unmoved by the politics of affirmation on which they were developed. Instead, Cage's work was pressed to the service of ideology critique and, in the process, stripped of its most radical implications.

Cage was himself an anarchist and identifies the critical year in his political formation to 1954, the year he moved into the Gate Hill Cooperative in Rockland County, New York. The Coop was founded by anarchists Vera and Paul Williams, both of whom met Cage at Black Mountain College (Antliff, "Situating" 54). Two years earlier, Cage performed 4'33", a work that I would argue is exemplary of the anarchist aesthetics of the ridiculous. Like the ridiculous, 4'33" is not only small, but *absolutely* small: the score includes not a single note. Like the ridiculous, 4'33" is "without self-control and without principle": it opens itself to any and all sounds produced over the course of the 273 seconds in which the performance takes place. And like the ridiculous, 4'33" is contractual and relational: the music is performed by listeners as they cough, sneeze, and whisper among themselves. Above all, *4'33"* is affirmative in that it permits all sounds to enter into the composition. Nothing is prohibited. Every sound is musical; every noise aesthetic.

Students of Cage's composition course at the New School for Social Research in New York City practiced an art of affirmation in the mode of the ridiculous. Examples include George Brecht's *Drip Music* (1962), in which the performer pours water from one vessel into another; Jackson Mac Low's *Stanzas for Iris Lezak* (1960), in which deterministic methods yield poems unmarked by the poet's intentions; La Monte Young's *Composition #10* (1960), in which the performer is instructed to "[d]raw a straight line and follow it" (itself an exemplary act of non-dialectical affirmation, since the line, once drawn, guides the action that follows); and Dick Higgins' *Danger Music #15*, which directs the performer to "work with eggs and butter for a time."[17]

Grasping the implications of works like these requires one to set aside Rainer's insistence that radical art be at all times critical. Likewise does it require one to consider the affirmative aesthetics of the ridiculous as different still from Buchloh's call for "mnemonic experience as one of the few acts of resistance." Against this variation on Stendhal's conception of beauty as a promise of happiness (whereby hopeful futurity is replaced by melancholic recollection), the affirmative art of Cage, Mac Low, Higgins, and others begins with Ward's anarchist proposal that "the society in which you would really like to live was already here." Ward's proposal, like Landauer's, Day's, and Cage's, is not to critique, but to shrink—to become small enough to comprehend the ridiculous.

This is to say that there exists an aesthetic peculiar to anarchism, and its main properties can be located in the margins of Kant's aesthetic, despite the fact that Kant himself was utterly dismissive of what these margins contain. The aesthetic peculiar to anarchism is that of the *absolutely small*, the *ridiculous* (or, as the German is sometimes translated, *trifling*).[18] Where the sublime is the aesthetic that attends the feeling of Law in its awesome power and universal dominion, the ridiculous is the aesthetic that attends the feeling of the contract in its small scale and its requirement that the participants act willingly and with care. The aesthetic of the ridiculous also one operates gradually, through expansion and stands opposed to the violence at the core of the critical enterprise. At odds with critique's program of expose-and-destroy, the ridiculous is founded on a program of discover-and-cultivate. It is not, however, without its own risks. That which begins its life as a trifling will surely struggle to grow into something substantial. The waiting may be excruciating. Nevertheless, in its opposition to the politics of critique, a politics that appears to have, as Latour put it, "run out of steam," it at least offers an alternative directive, albeit one demanding a patience of perhaps impossible dimension.

Acknowledgment

This essay is a shorter version of the essay that appeared under the same title in Gage, Mark Foster, editor. *Aesthetics Equals Politics: New Conversations Across Art, Architecture and Philosophy*. MIT P, 2019, pp. 169–93.

Notes

1. "What if explanations resorting automatically to power, society, discourse had outlived their usefulness and deteriorated to the point of now feeding the most gullible sort of critique?" (Latour 229–30).
2. Cristina Ionica's contribution to this volume cautions us against founding a rigorous critique of critique on Sedgwick's celebrated text. Instead, we are best served by treating "Paranoid Reading" as a preliminary sketch of a possible post-critical future rather than a detailed roadmap with all its landmarks and intersections identified.
3. Sedgwick articulated her concern thusly: "[T]he very productive critical habits embodied in what Paul Ricoeur memorably called the 'hermeneutics of suspicion'—widespread critical habits indeed, perhaps by now nearly synonymous with criticism itself—may have had an unintentionally stultifying side-effect: they may have made it less rather than more possible to unpack the local, contingent relations between any given piece of knowledge and its narrative/epistemological entailments for the seeker, knower, or teller" (4).
4. Other significant voices in the affirmative mode include Karen Barad, Jane Bennett, Rosi Braidotti, William Connolly, and Eugene Holland. For a collection of post-critical reflections on contemporary art, see Fraser and Rothman.
5. For a related use of the term "affirmative," see White.
6. That said, the influence of Hegel on Bakunin is incontrovertible, as evidenced, perhaps most vividly in his declaration, "The passion for destruction is a creative passion, too!" (Bakunin, "Reaction" 44).
7. See Rousselle and Evren.
8. Ward dedicated *Anarchy in Action* to Paul Goodman, who had died the year earlier. In light of the persistent misconception of anarchism as a philosophy of disorder, it is perhaps worth mentioning that Ward initially proposed that his book be titled "Anarchism as a theory of organization" (7).

9 For Goldman's influence on the American avant-garde, see Allan Antliff's *Anarchist Modernism*.
10 *Critique of the Power of Judgment* includes a similar identification of the sublime with the virtue of duty: "The consciousness of virtue, when one puts oneself, even if only in thought, in the place of a virtuous person, spreads in the mind a multitude of sublime and calming feelings, and a boundless prospect into a happy future, which no expression that is adequate to a determinate concept fully captures" (Kant, *Power of Judgment* 194).
11 Kant introduces the "absolutely great" in *Critique of the Powers of Judgment*. In *Observations on the Feeling of the Beautiful and the Sublime*, he simply identifies the sublime as large: "The sublime must always be large, the beautiful can also be small" (17).
12 "*Duty!*—you sublime, grand name which encompasses nothing that is favored yet involves ingratiation, but which demands submission" (Kant, *Practical Reason*, 87).
13 Kant's contempt [Verachtung] for the absolutely small has its roots in Augustine's *Contemptus mundi*, itself an indication of Kant's long debt to the legacy of Platonic Idealism and the concomitant denigration of the material world. I thank Gary Steiner for alerting me to this aspect of Kant's thought.
14 Here Kant uses the word "das Lächerliche." Throughout most of *Observations*, however, Kant's preferred term for "the ridiculous" is "das Läppische." It appears more than a dozen times, at least once in each of the book's four sections.
15 My argument here points toward a logic similar to that which Matthew Gannon, in this volume, identifies in Adorno's "tenacious defense of the object" over against the "determining concept" (xx).
16 The role of "care" in my account here parallels that of "responsibility" as articulated in a number of essays in this volume. Of particular relevance is Masami Sugimori's identification of responsible reading as a "morally principled" or "ethical" practice (xx).
17 Young, unlike Brecht, Mac Low, and Higgins, had not been a student in Cage's classes, but did serve as teaching assistant to Richard Maxfield when Maxfield took over Cage's course in 1960 (Grimshaw 57).
18 "Trifling" is John Goldthwait's preferred translation for "läppisch." Though quaint-sounding today, it has two qualities to recommend it over "ridiculous." First, it has a scalar connotation that associates it with the small and thus with Kant's own conception of the ridiculous as "absolutely small." Second, "trifling" was a term frequently used by Hume in his own aesthetic reflections—reflections that were of foundational significance to Kant. See Kant's *Observations on the Feeling of the Sublime*. For an analysis of the gendered aesthetics at work in Hume's critique of what he called "trifling pastimes," see Roelofs (63).

References

Adorno, Theodor. *Aesthetic Theory*, translated by Robert Hullot-Kentor. U of Minnesota P, 1997.

Adorno, Theodor. "Commitment." *Aesthetics and Politics*, translated by Francis McDonagh. Verso, 1977, pp. 177–95.

Antliff, Allan. *Anarchist Modernism: Art, Politics, and the First American Avant-Garde*. U of Chicago P, 2001.

Antliff, Allan. "Situating Freedom: Jackson Mac Low, John Cage, and Donald Judd." *Anarchist Developments in Cultural Studies*, vol. 2, 2011, pp. 39–57.

Bakunin, Mikhail. "The Reaction in Germany." *Anarchism: A Documentary History of Libertarian Ideas, Volume One: From Anarchy to Anarchism (300CE to 1939)*, edited by Robert Graham. Black Rose Books, 2005, pp. 43–4.

Bakunin, Mikhail. "Statism and Anarchism," translated by Sam Dolgoff. *The Anarchist Library*, 1971, https://theanarchistlibrary.org/library/mikhail-bakunin-statism-and-anarchy

Barad, Karen. *Meeting the Universe Halfway: Quantum Physics and the Entanglement of Matter and Meaning*. Duke UP, 2007.

Bennett, Jane. *Vibrant Matter: A Political Ecology of Things*. Duke UP, 2010.

Braidotti, Rosi. *Nomadic Theory: The Portable Rosi Braidotti*. Columbia UP, 2011.

Buber, Martin. *Paths in Utopia*, translated by R. F. C. Hull. Beacon Press, 1949.

Buchloh, Benjamin. *Neo-Avantgarde and Culture Industry: Essays on European and American Art from 1955 to 1975*. MIT P, 2000.

Cage, John. *Silence*. Wesleyan UP, 1961.

Cage, John. *A Year from Monday*. Wesleyan UP, 1969.

Cohn, Jesse. *Anarchism and the Crisis of Representation*. Susquehanna UP, 2006.

Comfort, Alex. "Art and Social Responsibility." *Anarchism: A Documentary History of Libertarian Ideas, Volume Two: the Emergence of the New Anarchism (1939–1977)*, edited by Robert Graham. Black Rose Books, 2009, pp. 103–11.

Connolly, William. *A World of Becoming*. Duke UP, 2011.

Day, Richard. *Gramsci Is Dead: Anarchist Currents in the Newest Social Movements*. Pluto Press, 2005.

Derrida, Jacques. *The Truth in Painting*, translated by Geoff Bennington and Ian McLeod. U of Chicago P, 1987.

Eagleton, Terry. *The Ideology of the Aesthetic*. Oxford UP, 1981.

Felski, Rita. *The Limits of Critique*. U of Chicago P, 2015.

Foster, Hal. "Post-Critical," *October*, vol. 139, Winter 2012, pp. 3–8.

Fraser, Pamela and Roger Rothman, editors. *Beyond Critique: Contemporary Art in Theory, Practice, and Instruction*. Bloomsbury, 2017.

Goldman, Emma. "Living My Life," *The Anarchist Library*. 1931, https://theanarchistlibrary.org/library/emma-goldman-living-my-life.pdf

Graeber, David. *Fragments of an Anarchist Anthropology*. Prickly Paradigm Press, 2006.

Grimshaw, Jeremy. *Draw a Straight Line and Follow It: The Music and Mysticism of La Monte Young*. Oxford UP, 2011.

Holland, Eugene. *Nomad Citizenship: Free-Market Communism and the Slow-Motion General Strike*. U of Minnesota P, 2010.

Joseph, Branden. *Beyond the Dream Syndicate: Tony Conrad and the Arts after Cage*. Zone Books, 2008.

Kant, Immanuel. *Critique of the Power of Judgment*, edited by Paul Guyer, translated by Paul Guyer and Eric Matthews. Cambridge UP, 2000.

Kant, Immanuel. *Critique of Practical Reason*, translated by Werner S. Pluhar. Hackett Publishing, 2002.

Kant, Immanuel. *Observations on the Feeling of the Beautiful and the Sublime and Other Writings*, edited by Patrick Frierson and Paul Guyer. Cambridge UP, 2011.

Kant, Immanuel. *Observations on the Feeling of the Sublime*, translated by John T. Goldthwait, U of California P, 1960.

Kostelanetz, Richard *Conversing with Cage*, 2nd ed. Routledge, 2003.

Kostelanetz, Richard, editor. *John Cage*. Praeger Publishers, 1970.

Kropotkin, Peter. *Kropotkin's Revolutionary Pamphlets*, edited by Roger Baldwin. Dover, 1970.

Landauer, Gustav. "Call to Socialism." *The Anarchist Library*. 1911, https://theanarchistlibrary.org/library/gustav-landauer-call-to-socialism.pdf.

Landauer, Gustav. *Revolution and Other Writings, A Political Reader*, translated by Gabriel Kuhn. PM Press, 2010.

Latour, Bruno. "Why Has Critique Run Out of Steam? From Matters of Fact to Matters of Concern." *Critical Inquiry*, vol. 30, no. 2, Winter 2004, pp. 225–48.

Marcuse, Herbert. *One-Dimensional Man*. Beacon Press, 1964.

Marx, Karl. *The Poverty of Philosophy*. Foreign Languages Publishing House, 1955.

May, Todd. *The Political Philosophy of Poststructuralist Anarchism*. Pennsylvania State UP, 1994.

Proudhon, Pierre-Joseph. "The General Idea of the Revolution." *Anarchism: A Documentary History of Libertarian Ideas, Volume One: From Anarchy to Anarchism (300CE to 1939)*, edited by Robert Graham. Black Rose Books, 2005, pp. 51–8.

Rainer, Yvonne. "Looking Myself in the Mouth." *John Cage (October Files)*, edited by Julia Robinson. MIT P, 2011.

Rancière, Jacques. "The Aesthetic Revolution and Its Outcomes." *New Left Review*, vol. 14, March/April, 2002, pp. 133–51.

Roelofs, Monique. *The Cultural Promise of the Aesthetic*. Bloomsbury, 2014.

Rousselle, Duane, and Süreyyya Evren, editors. *Post-Anarchism: A Reader*. Pluto Press, 2011.

Scarry, Elaine. *On Beauty and Being Just*. Princeton UP, 1999.

Schiller, Friedrich. *Letters Upon the Aesthetic Education of Man*, translated by Reginald Snell. Dover, 2004.

Sedgwick, Eve Kosofsky. "Paranoid Reading and Reparative Reading, or, You're so Paranoid, You Probably Think This Introduction Is About You." *Novel Gazing: Queer Readings in Fiction*, edited by Eve Kosofsky Sedgwick, Duke UP, 1997, pp. 1–37.

Ward, Colin. *Anarchy in Action*. Freedom Press, 1973.

White, Stephen. *Sustaining Affirmation: The Strengths of Weak Ontology in Political Theory*. Princeton UP, 2000.

10

Adorno as a Reader: Writing the Mediation of Literature and Philosophy

Matthew Gannon

This essay, which aims to outline an Adornian theory of responsible reading, is necessarily somewhat anachronistic. The life and work of Theodor W. Adorno largely predate debates about reading in literary theory, which mostly came into focus as an explicit problematic with Louis Althusser and the collective project that resulted in *Reading Capital* in 1965. Adorno, however, was intensely preoccupied with the question of aesthetic experience in general, which, even if not directly synonymous with reading, links up often enough with the question of reading—and in particular reading literature and philosophy, two discourses that share close connections but cannot be collapsed into one another. This question of reading, moreover, is meaningless to Adorno unless it is posed within the context of the writing—or "presentation" as he frequently referred to it—that develops within and out of that reading.[1]

For Althusser, reading is also necessarily linked to writing, as he makes clear when he identifies the origins of this problematic in Spinoza: "The first person ever to have posed the problem of *reading*, and in consequence, of *writing*, was Spinoza, and he was also the first in the world to have proposed both a theory of history and a philosophy of the opacity of the immediate" (14–15). Debates about reading "reflect problems of knowledge production—that is, of writing—as much or more than they do the mere consumption of literary texts" (Wasser 107). But if today's competing understandings of reading more or less agree that the practice in question is neither as self-evident nor transparent as it appears to be—that is, it is not synonymous with simply seeing—that seems to be just about all that is agreed upon. And this notion of reading as a distinct practice with serious stakes—as a problem not to be solved but to be critically clarified—has today become particularly contentious. "The social world—the very fabric of society—depends upon a practice of reading" (Moskowitz 232). Reading is thus the site of significant disagreements about everything from knowledge to pedagogy to politics, and is subject to debates in which various camps argue for their competing version (close or distant, surface or deep, reparative or suspicious, and so on) or advocate for broader paradigm shifts like post-critique and weak theory.[2]

Appropriately enough for the unparalleled thinker of nonidentity, Adorno fits only uneasily into existing debates about reading, and certainly not as some authority who might finally decide which side is correct. But neither is responsible reading intended to serve as yet another option, yet another adjectivally prefixed version of reading to compete in the marketplace of ideas. For Adorno's key insights about reading and writing—and about aesthetic experience more generally—intersect with and deviate from today's concerns in productive ways. Not exactly a close reader by today's standards, Adorno nevertheless scrupulously attended to the singularity of works of art and insisted on interpretation's immanence. While matters of form were always foremost in Adorno's mind, he also thought in sociohistorical terms that could account for the macroscopic perspective of totality by heeding the most minute ephemera. Never content to give up on interpretation and meaning, Adorno also embraced the inconclusive in art and criticism and pointed out the damage done by probing supposedly repressed depths. And though he was a "negative, critical, destructive figure" ("Afterword" 165), as Fredric Jameson recently put it, Adorno never relinquished a hope in art's socially healing power. There is no doubt that Adorno would be unsparing toward today's affirmationist ideologies, and yet he might well have seen in the dissatisfaction with critique what Fabio Akcelrud Durão refers to earlier in this volume as its "unfulfilled promises" (xx): a utopian expression that, in a dialectic twist, sanctions a critique that lives on because the moment to realize it was missed.

What follows, however, is not a scrupulous genealogy that links Adorno's thinking to today's debates about reading. Instead, I will demonstrate what Adorno means by responsibility in aesthetics and tie this to the question of reading. Reading here is understood not in the narrow, conventional sense but as a broader term for the subject's encounter with the singularity of the work of art as object. Adorno notes in *Aesthetic Theory* that "all artworks are writing, not just those that are obviously such" (124), and so aesthetic experience is always tied to something like reading. But though I will not dwell on Adorno's specifically literary insights as such, the word reading here is not purely metaphorical. The literary text is very often the basis for Adorno's conception of aesthetic experience, and so I pay particular attention to one of Adorno's most celebrated essays on a literary work: his famous study of Samuel Beckett's *Endgame*.

In discussing Adorno and the question of reading, it is worth noting that Adorno himself is notoriously difficult to read. "Adorno shunned systematic philosophy and doubted whether true thinking could ever achieve transparency," writes Tom Huhn in his introduction to *The Cambridge Companion to Adorno* (3). Adorno himself is not encouraging here: "True thoughts are those alone which do not understand themselves" (*Minima* 192). But lack of clarity, even self-clarity, is not a barrier to reading but rather its very precondition.[3] And while the carefully constructed and occasionally cryptic chiasmatic formulations that abound in Adorno's writing can make his prose frustratingly puzzling, they are also simultaneously rich with startlingly brilliant speculation. Nowhere is this truer than in his final work, the incomplete, lightly edited, and posthumously published *Aesthetic Theory* that Adorno was working on when he died of a heart attack in August 1969.

But Adorno was always attentive to aesthetic issues—he began his career as a composer and musicologist after all—and the specific ideas for *Aesthetic Theory* can be traced back to a series of lectures on aesthetics that he delivered in the 1950s and 1960s at Frankfurt. This essay cites mainly from these lectures, rather than *Aesthetic Theory*, which were first published just over a decade ago in German and only in 2018 in English. Though less abundant in the aforementioned brilliant formulations than the canonical *Aesthetic Theory*, the more conversational lectures on aesthetics, which are edited from transcripts of taped recordings, are no less "written" themselves, as Adorno carefully prepared these lectures before annotating the typescripts himself for future reference. Moreover, citing Adorno's lectures has several distinct advantages. They are less widely discussed, and this essay provides the opportunity to work through some of their unique and lesser-known insights. Adorno addresses different topics here than his more finished *Aesthetic Theory*—most compellingly for this essay the issue of responsibility—and even familiar topics are treated differently. Furthermore, as Adorno's lectures were often somewhat improvised and delivered between (or in preparation for) major writing projects, we get a picture of Adorno's thinking in motion here, almost in midstride—something that Adorno himself prized greatly.[4]

In Objects Begins Responsibility

Reading for Adorno is one particular term connected to the broader category of aesthetic experience. And yet for Adorno the very idea of aesthetic experience—which he skeptically refers to as "so-called aesthetic experience" in his lectures on aesthetics (*Aesthetics* 116)—is nearly paradoxical. Experience inevitably indexes subjectivity and its affective responses or cognitive faculties. But Adorno's aesthetics is firmly objective—we might even say object-oriented, though Adorno's "objective turn" (202) in aesthetics has little in common with today's philosophical movement by that name[5]—and strenuously resists being collapsed into, or dominated by, "subjective modes of reaction to works of art" (185). The field of subjective aesthetics is wide for Adorno, and names everything from Kant's foundational philosophy to the purely ideological mechanisms of the consumer-centric culture industry.[6] But while Adorno identifies serious problems—both philosophical and political—with subjectivism in aesthetics, "experience" is nevertheless a key term for him, as it was for a number of Frankfurt-affiliated thinkers.

To get past this seeming paradox of an aesthetic experience not dominated by subjectivity, Adorno carefully outlines the conditions for encountering art. He advises that "one should approach the work of art in a certain very delicately rational manner" (185), a manner Adorno elaborates as follows:

> That is, one concentrates on the work in all its aspects, in everything that it brings with it, but that this concentration is not merely a passive concentration, not the kind where one just sits there in a "relaxed" manner, as they say in America, lets things take their course and waits to see what nice things the work will offer; rather, *one takes on that same responsibility as a listener—or a viewer or a spectator—which, as I once told you, the work itself bears at every moment,* and faces it with such concentration that one is capable of carrying out the same synthesis, the same unification, of diverging yet connected aspects of the work that takes place in the work itself. (185–6; emphasis added)

This passage not only establishes Adorno's view of aesthetic experience, it also contains the core of his insight regarding aesthetic responsibility, which, while certainly objective (located in "the work itself" in "all its aspects"), relates also to the subject.[7] Responsibility hinges on the dialectic between subject and object—but, unlike in traditional post-Kantian thinking, the object and subject "have equal status" in Adorno and "the object, for very important reasons, even takes priority over subjectivity" (202).[8] What we, as subjects, must be responsible for—and responsible to—is the work of art as object, or, more radically, the work of art as objectivity as such. From this objective responsibility everything else follows for Adorno: not only his aesthetics but his ethics and politics as well.

Adorno's career is marked by a tenacious defense of the object in the object-subject relation. The very reason that Adorno prioritizes aesthetics over other domains of philosophical inquiry is the special place accorded to the work of art as object. As J. M. Bernstein explains, Adorno's prioritization can be accounted for by the fact that "rather than beginning with a determining concept—the categories or the moral law—in aesthetics we begin with the thing" (1070). Ever since modern philosophy became so relentlessly subject-oriented, art and aesthetics "became the refuge for a suppressed objectivity" (1071). All thinking for Adorno, however, even conceptual thinking, owes a "debt to the object" (Jarvis 81). And it is especially in aesthetics, as Adorno proposes in his *Aesthetic Theory*, that subjective experience encounters its suppressed objectivity: "The experience of art ... is the irruption of objectivity into subjective consciousness" (244–5). Adorno thus prefers tarrying with the reflective judgments of aesthetics rather than the determinative judgments of the understanding and his thinking tends to dwell on singularity rather than rushing to the more general concept. This is more than Adorno's way of dealing with the work of art, as it also authorizes a direct confrontation with objective suffering and injustice that Adorno thinks are too easily rationalized away. Thus, what Gerhard Richter describes as Adorno's "ethico-politically responsible form of aesthetics" ("Portrait" 8) is ultimately a responsibility to this suppressed objectivity of suffering.

This objective mode of aesthetic experience, which entails responsibility, is not only far from "relaxing" then, it is in fact highly demanding. Adorno stresses that the reader—any subject encountering the objective work of art—must be "prepared to renew in yourself, as an observer, that process which is present in the work in a solidified form" (*Aesthetics* 186). This demand, he notes, "deviates from official aesthetics" and "conventional opinion" which hold that "art is also meant to be intuitively appreciable, something that absolves us from effort" (186). Returning to his home field of music, Adorno specifically cites the "demands Beethoven's last quartets still make today," and notes "how small a number of people today are probably at all capable of *following such creations with concentration and responsibility*" (197; emphasis added). That these demands come from "the work itself" is again clear, and Adorno repeats his emphasis on responsibility inhering in objectivity.

While Adorno clarifies that "the notion of an unmediated objectivity in art which has not passed through the subject is precisely not what I have in mind" (175), he nevertheless frequently appeals not only to the object's primacy but to a "freedom to the object" (26). This freedom, which is granted by a "long and uncoercive gaze upon the object" ("Notes" 130), not only forestalls attempts at subjective mastery and domination over the object, but allows for the "experience of self-forgetfulness before the object" (*Aesthetics* 26). Adorno sometimes describes this self-forgetfulness as a sublime experience, but the key here is to abandon efforts to get something out of the work of art: "it is not an understanding experience in the usual sense but rather a surrendering" (128). To surrender is to suspend conventional forms of judgment that subject-oriented philosophical aesthetics typically calls for; yet this surrendering is not anti-intellectual, it does not release the subject from responsibility, and it does not diminish the demand placed upon the subject by objectivity.

In order to be responsible to and with the object that is the work of art, Adorno makes clear that the subject has a particular role to play: that of recreating it. As Adorno puts it most plainly, "artistic experience consists in a particular form of 'doing' or 'making,' namely in co-enacting" (118). This co-enacting is described somewhat paradoxically as "a particular form of active passivity or effortful surrender to the matter" (118). But the work of art is absorptive in Adorno's aesthetics, and it subjects us, rather than the other way around, "by the fact that we enter it and follow it" (120). This is not to say that there is no freedom for the subject here—artistic or critical—but rather that this freedom is "the freedom to submit without arrogance or vanity, and with the utmost concentration, to what the matter wants purely of its own accord" (68). The turns in Adorno's dialectical reasoning can be hard to keep up with, but the basic logic is that responsibility is an acquiescence to the demand that the subject surrender to the object in order to, by co-enacting the work, transform a subjective passivity into an objective activity. As such, Adorno's perspective accords with the idea that any responsible reading, as Masami Sugimori argues in his chapter, must attend to "the object of study" (xx) and vary in method "depending on the given object" (xx). This kind of responsibility, characterized by what Rivky Mondal describes as a certain "aesthetic fidelity" (xx) to the art object in question, also entails the transformation of reading into writing and mere observation into theoretical criticism—crucial transformations that especially bear on the fraught relationship between art and philosophy.

This idea of responsible reading does not perhaps line up neatly with Adorno's reputation—at least his reputation among those who may not have read him entirely responsibly. Adorno, for instance, is singled out by Rita Felski as the very prototype of the "regrettable arrogance" (15) of critique and its "rhetoric of *againstness*" (17).⁹ But while critical negativity is undeniably central to Adorno's thinking, his emphasis on careful attention to singular objects and his understanding of aesthetic experience as re-creation and co-enacting is actually quite close to how Felski herself defines her preferred practice of post-critical reading: "Reading is now conceived as an act of composition—of creative remaking—that binds text and reader in ongoing struggles, translations, and negotiations" (182).¹⁰ Adorno, then, might be more of an ally rather than an antagonist in reorienting hermeneutics away from its more suspicious and even paranoid tendencies. Furthermore, a hermeneutics of responsibility need not fall into the trap of "theological" piety that Felski warns against (29)—in which works of art are approached with undue sensitivity and reverence—but could instead be fairly described, as Paul K. Saint-Amour puts it, as "seeking to know but not necessarily to know better than its object" (444). The difference for Adorno, however, is that rather than leading away from or beyond critique this kind of responsibility is at the heart of the reading and writing of critical theory itself.

Relentless Theory, Speculative in the Best Sense

Among the abiding concerns expressed in Adorno's writings is the vexatious gap between the singular objectivity of particular works of art and the generalizing subjectivity of conceptualization. This gap between singular works and general concepts is the gap between art and philosophy. To facilely bridge this gap by positing a direct relation between the two, to collapse the one into the other, is a fallacy that Adorno cannot abide. It is, in other words, irresponsible. This is not to say that there is no connection between art and philosophy though. Adorno concedes "the very profound connection between great speculative philosophy and the approach of art" (*Aesthetics* 208), and suggests that reading Hegel is "an experience that specifically corresponds to the relationship with art" (124). And yet Adorno cautions that "this should not lead one to aestheticize his philosophy, of course" (124), and he insists that Hegel's writings—and works of philosophy as such—are "not works of intellectual art" (208). Adorno also expresses dissatisfaction with criticism that is "generally content to pick out neatly the philosophical motifs" that seem to have been "sprinkled into or embedded" in works of art (136). Art and philosophy form "radical unity" (78) rather than "an unambiguous, positively given unity" (99) or an "unbroken unity" (103) as romanticism supposed.

But if works of art are not directly philosophical and works of philosophy are not directly artistic, there still must be some connection between the two unless art is to be abandoned to anti-intellectual intuitionism. Adorno repeatedly stresses that art, and especially modern art, is not intuitive or self-evident, and requires not just reflection but self-reflection. The relegating of art to mere leisure in late capitalism, however, ensures that it falls prey to "the aesthetics of 'pure intuition,' whose sublime aspiration [is] to be independent of mere intellectuality" (*Aesthetics* 187). While Adorno rejects the idea that art can be straightforwardly understood—that is neatly conceptualized and therefore liquated into philosophy—there is another practice that retains intellectuality and avoids pure intuition while simultaneously resisting the delusion that art can be straightforwardly understood through complete conceptualization: theory.[11]

The role of theory for Adorno becomes clear when comparing it to philosophy. Hegel's philosophy seems artistic, Adorno explains, because of how it "strives for a very similar interweaving of aspects without reducing them to a single slogan, some ready-made judgement or a conclusion … but rather by seeking the idea precisely in the totality of these aspects" (*Aesthetics* 208). Both art and philosophy—authentic art and philosophy at least—bring together disparate elements and, without coercion, link them together into a totality. It is theory's responsibility to immerse itself in this totality—of art or of philosophy—and co-enact its disparate elements in order to come to grips with its highly mediated relation to social totality. This is expressed most urgently in Adorno's now-infamous letter of November 1938 where, in his "simplest and most Hegelian manner," he chastises Walter Benjamin because his "dialectic lacks one thing: mediation" (Benjamin 101). In this letter, Adorno makes clear that theory does not merely point out mediation, it participates in it.

At stake in Benjamin's essay—his study of Baudelaire—is the relation between literature and history, not literature and philosophy. Yet the collapse of the two distinct categories into each other without mediation creates parallel problems: the former leads to a vulgar materialism while the latter to a vulgar idealism. The role of theory is thus similar, and Adorno's advice to Benjamin bears repeating here. Benjamin is guilty of an "unmediated—I would almost say anthropological—materialism" in Adorno's eyes because of Benjamin's tendency to "relate the pragmatic content of Baudelaire's work directly to adjacent features of the social history of his time, especially economic ones" (101). The mediation Adorno is looking for, in the strictest Hegelian (though really Marxist) sense, is "mediation by the total societal process" (102). But mediation refers to more than this for Adorno and extends to Benjamin's method of presentation as well: "Now, the 'mediation' I find lacking, and obscured by materialist-historiographic invocation, is nothing other than the theorizing from which your work abstains" (101–2). Benjamin's essay "has situated itself at the crossroads of magic and positivism," a site that Adorno warns is "bewitched" (102). The solution? "Only theory could break the spell: your own relentless theory, speculative in the best sense" (102). This is not merely a useful piece of writing advice that Adorno is trying to convey; it encapsulates Adorno's understanding of theory as a crucial mediation between art and its other—history, society, philosophy, and so on. Theory's responsibility, as a reading and writing, is to not only reveal but even speculatively construct their mediating totality.[12]

Art's responsibility is both social and philosophical, and Adorno's idea that "art is the voice of what is suppressed" (*Aesthetics* 49) refers to the histories of suppressed sociality and thinking: the fact that art expresses both "the memory of accumulated suffering" (*Aesthetic Theory* 261) and a "suppressed rationality potential" (Bernstein 1075). But if art is answerable to both society and philosophy, theory's responsibility is to ensure that art does not become directly answerable to them—at least not as they currently are but possibly as they could be. Theory, then, does not posit some secret identity of art and its other; to say that it mediates them is to say that it generates a relation without immediacy by sustaining their nonidentity. As quoted above, responsibility in aesthetic experience entails "carrying out the same synthesis, the same unification, of diverging yet connected aspects of the work that takes place in the work itself" (*Aesthetics* 186). Because the work of art itself, for Adorno, is "the nonviolent integration of what diverges" (*Aesthetic Theory* 190), it requires a certain comportment according to Bernstein: "the judging subject who can reflectively respond to but not conceptually order what is experienced" (1086). This basic idea resurfaces in Jameson too, but Jameson defines it explicitly as reading, perhaps responsible reading: "Reading is then the momentary and ephemeral act of unification in which we hold multiple dimensions of time together for a glimpse that cannot prolong itself into the philosophical concept" (*Valences* 532). Theoretical writing is theory-as-reading and theory-as-mediation then, a status it has assumed in part due to the fate of art and philosophy after romanticism and especially during modernism.[13]

Given Adorno's insistence on the central role of theory in his letter to Benjamin, it is no surprise that in his lectures on aesthetics two decades later we find him praising theory and its analogues. Though the subject surrenders to the work of art, this does not make theorizing subservient to immediate aesthetic experience; theory becomes absolutely necessary for "true artistic experience" which is in fact highly mediated due to "the fact that certain forms, such as that of translation, but most of all commentary and critique, are not parasitic forms that proliferate like weeds growing on art and exploit the primary elements, namely the works, but that these forms too are actually constitutive of art's essence" (*Aesthetics* 129). Concepts and judgments are not sufficient here, as they "go no further than criticism or a position" (207). But there are "higher forms of critique" that Adorno defends: "critiques of works of art that do not follow abstract rules, only their immanent necessity" (152). As he writes elsewhere, these "higher forms of critique" are not a specialist activity, a particular mode of thinking appropriate to certain circumstances only, but rather a basic mode of thinking as such: "one should not just up and start thinking, but rather think of something. For this reason, texts to be interpreted and criticized are an invaluable support for the objectivity of thought" ("Notes" 134). Interpretation and criticism then—or theory, the term does not matter much because at stake is not a concept but a practice—refer to thinking itself, thinking which does not exist without reading, without objects.

Trying to Understand

Even though responsible reading entails a number of aforementioned practices and principles—primacy of the object, subjective surrendering, co-enacting, suspending conceptualization and judgment, and so on—there can be no formula for it. Because the singularity of responsible reading is connected to the singularity of its object, it is helpful to see it at work, as in Adorno's essay "Trying to Understand *Endgame*," which is among his finest essays that directly address a specific literary work and is rightfully counted among his "minor classics."[14] Adorno's theory of reading is not merely posited in this essay but concretized and demonstrated as a practice of reading theoretically. This is evident even in the title of the essay, which foregrounds the importance of not claiming to have already understood, but rather "trying to understand." This is not a great show of modesty for its own sake, nor is it only because Adorno is dealing with Beckett, an author who is notoriously difficult to decipher. This theme of "trying to understand" is constitutive of Adorno's reading practice, and it is also central to "The Essay as Form," another of Adorno's minor classics that in retrospect provides some self-reflective commentary on "Trying to Understand *Endgame*."

The essay, which is "the critical form par excellence" ("Essay 42), is "condemned as a hybrid" (29), Adorno explains, as it is neither sufficiently systematic for modern philosophical methodology nor entirely rhapsodic for those who prefer romanticized reflections. Though the essay does not set about "accomplishing something scientifically or creating something artistically" (30), it shares elements with both science and art. The essay attains "something like an aesthetic autonomy," Adorno contends, "although it is distinguished from art by its medium, concepts" (31). The essay distances itself from positivism, which demands standardization in its presentation. This question of presentation turns once again on the issue of responsibility: "Positivism's irresponsibly sloppy language fancies that it documents responsibility in its object" (31). Adorno does not disagree that bad essays can at times slip into irresponsibility, but the essay honors responsibility in its own way: "Responsibility, however, respects not only authorities and committees, but also the object itself" (32). The essay takes on the responsibility to "the object itself" precisely by its vocation of trying. In dwelling on the word "*Versuch*, attempt or essay" (41), Adorno positions himself in the long tradition of praising the essay for its emphasis on trying, on its "fallibility and provisional character" that "takes place not systematically but rather as a characteristic of an intention groping its way" (41). This *Versuch* is of course the first word in the title of Adorno's essay on Beckett: *Versuch, das Endspiel zu verstehen.*

The opening sentence of "Trying to Understand *Endgame*" demonstrates Adorno's aversion to making direct, unmediated connections between literature and philosophy. "Beckett's oeuvre has many things in common with Parisian existentialism," Adorno writes (237). "But whereas in Sartre the form—that of the *pièce à these*—is somewhat traditional, by no means daring, and aimed at effect, in Beckett the form overtakes what is expressed and changes it" (237). This was a complaint that Adorno often submitted when it came to works of literature, like those by Kafka, that interpreters claimed were obviously "existential." Sartre's literary works—and Adorno makes similar claims elsewhere of Camus—advance a philosophical thesis that is just barely outfitted with literary form and thus aim for philosophical achievements at the expense of literary quality. Adorno opposed all art that "exploited philosophy as a literary subject" (239), and maintained that the overriding attempt to be directly philosophical makes these works inartistic, just as methods of reading that mine works for philosophical content destroy their aesthetic singularity.

The title of Adorno's essay is twofold then, as he is not only genuinely trying to understanding *Endgame* but also assessing attempts to understand *Endgame* and the difficulties and wrong paths that easily mislead interpretation. *Endgame*, as a work of late modernism, is a play written after the demise of the "substantive, affirmative metaphysical meaning that could provide dramatic form with its law and its epiphany" (238). This is a problem for philosophy and a problem for art, as the loss of metaphysical sureties amounts to the loss of the essence of drama: "metaphysical meaning," Adorno somewhat tendentiously contends, "was the only thing guaranteeing the unity of aesthetic structure" (238). When facing such a double loss in which philosophy and art cannot be used to explain one another, there must be a mediating discourse that can contextualize the fate of both but not substitute for this lack: "Hence interpretation of *Endgame* cannot pursue the chimerical aim of expressing the play's meaning in a form mediated by philosophy. Understanding it can mean only understanding its unintelligibility, concretely reconstructing the meaning of the fact that it has no meaning" (238). This concrete reconstructing is co-enacting, and in this case co-enacting the objective unintelligibility of the work of art—a meaninglessness that, through a dialectical twist of speculative theorizing, can be demonstrated to be meaningful.

Adorno's essay carefully considers a number of central motifs of *Endgame*, quotes striking moments of dialogue, and avoids rushing to simple meanings that would turn art immediately into philosophy and philosophy into cheap wisdom. Rather than directly philosophy itself, Beckett's play parodies philosophy. "This is why interpreting Beckett, something he declines to concern himself with, is so awkward. Beckett shrugs his shoulders at the possibility of philosophy today" (239). Adorno has a nose for that which both demands and defies interpretation. "Hence interpretation inevitably lags behind Beckett. His dramatic work, precisely by virtue of its restriction to an exploded facticity, surged out beyond facticity and in its enigmatic character calls for interpretation" (240). Adorno does not try to get out ahead of this lag, but nor does he remain in facticity, as he suggested Benjamin did in his work on Baudelaire where "[m]otifs are assembled but not worked through" (Benjamin 99). Adorno's theory, speculative in the best sense, has a mediating function even as it stops short of an artificial reconciliation that can make sense of everything it gazes upon.

For Adorno, there are objective reasons for this impasse of interpretability: after the Second World War—after the permanent catastrophe that history has become—the conditions for art have been demolished. Culture has turned into "a rubbish heap that has made even reflection on one's own damaged state useless" ("Trying" 240). This is not to say that interpretation is to be avoided, but that the possibilities and potential usefulness of critique must be reassessed. Alluding to Marx and the origins of ruthless criticism, Adorno refers to "the good old days, when a critique of the political economy of this society could be written that judged it in terms of its own *ratio*"—adding that such days have passed because "since then the society has thrown its *ratio* on the scrap heap and replaced it with virtually unmediated control" (240). But even if "bombed-out consciousness no longer has a place from which to reflect" (241), Adorno still traces a few ideas suggested by *Endgame*: the fate of drama, the inadequacies of existential ontology, the extinguishing of subjectivity, unspeakable destruction, bitter humor, the tendency toward silence. Adorno even ends with a sketch of some possible theses that another writer might have led the essay with and then worked out methodically.

"Trying to Understand *Endgame*" is not just an essay then; it is an essay that perfectly matches Adorno's sense of the essay form as such: "It neither makes deductions from a principle nor draws conclusions from coherent individual observations. It coordinates elements instead of subordinating them" ("Essay" 46). Adorno's essay on Beckett is therefore, as is true of any good essay, a constellation in which "the elements crystallize as a configuration through their motion" ("Essay" 38). Adorno does not claim to fully understand *Endgame*, resists immediate conceptualization and even subjectively derived judgments of the play, and refuses a systematic presentation that would eliminate uncertainty and obscure the radically objective otherness of the work of art. Following his own advice on aesthetic experience from his lectures, Adorno "concentrates on the work in all its aspects"—in a way that is "not merely a passive concentration" of course—by "carrying out the same synthesis, the same unification, of diverging yet connected aspects of the work that takes place in the work itself" (*Aesthetics* 185–6). "Trying to Understand *Endgame*," in other words, is a responsible reading.

Conclusion: The Resistance to Reading and the Promise of Happiness

Adorno's reasons for criticizing aesthetic subjectivity are manifold, but the root of the problem for him is that it falls into the trap of what he frequently refers to as identity thinking: assuming that concepts perfectly match their objects and that there is nothing of significance outside cognition, no alterity to subjective consciousness. "Basing aesthetics on subjectivity in the broadest sense in this way," Adorno explains, "means claiming to be largely independent of the supposed randomness of the object and to have recourse to something that is firm and binding because it is immutable, namely the self-identical structure of such a consciousness" (*Aesthetics* 166). We might productively reformulate Adorno's concern here as essentially provoking those who do not want to read: those who evade aesthetic responsibility by refusing to bring the subject into contact with objectivity—or the objective moment of subjectivity itself—by instead fixating on self-identical subjective consciousness and its conceptual or judging apparatuses.[15]

This fundamental complaint about those who seek to avoid reading resonates profoundly today. Though reading is a contested topic and has many defenders—who are often at odds with each other—there is nevertheless a proliferation of theories and methodologies in literary studies that effectively avoid reading or aim to get around it somehow. Instead of confronting the singularity of objects it is preferable, for whatever reason, to substitute for them something self-identical: concepts and cognition, as Adorno himself points out, but also neuroscience or history or culture or data or even abstract definitions of form—frameworks that are preestablished externally to the work of art and then applied from without and imposed on the unread object. Adorno himself, of course, often relies on form or philosophy or history and so on in his interpretations. But he does not use these nonartistic frameworks as a replacement for the unavoidable confrontation with singularity that the subject encounters in the objective work of art. It is disingenuous to immediately replace aesthetic experience with "educational elements," as Adorno puts it: "These educational elements can indeed augment artistic experience, and will perhaps have positive results; but they can also do damage by substituting the mere educational experience ... for the matter itself" (*Aesthetics* 189).

Yet a dialectic is at work here, because Adorno also chastises those who would substitute for conceptual thinking the supposed intuitiveness of a self-identical work of art. Works of art are divided, contradictory, and antagonistic on thematic and, more importantly, formal levels. They are in themselves a broken or uneasy totality, a force field. "To experience or co-enact a work would then mean no more or less than co-enacting in the work all these aspects of the force field which the work constitutes, which it simultaneously is and exceeds" (*Aesthetics* 141). Theory does not aim to explain away, much less resolve or reconcile, these contradictions. Co-enacting is not the reconstitution of a self-identical object, and we cannot evade the demands of the intellect in aesthetics. For Adorno, just as for post-Althusserian thinking, reading is not passive or immediate or transparent, "for we cannot understand any art at all purely with our eyes or our ears" (154). Reading, then, really is part of the active production of knowledge, and therefore "all art actually requires the assistance of theoretical insight" as "a plethora of theoretical preconditions of all kinds ... necessarily contribute to the experience of any work of art so that we can understand this work at all" (154). And even this understanding is really a trying to understand that is neither predominantly conceptual nor wholly intuitive.

If complete understanding is not really within the purview of aesthetic experience then, it is worth concluding with a brief note on something that is, at least in the furthest reaches of Adorno's utopian thinking: happiness. A central dilemma in the politics of Adorno's aesthetics turns on the question of enjoyment, which for him is always reactionary. Enjoyment is the folly of "the amateur and the bourgeois, who turn the work into a plate of pork rib and sauerkraut" (*Aesthetics* 120). Adorno calls this enjoyment a "pre-aesthetic" stance and a "culinary state" (103). Against this ideology of enjoyable consumption, Adorno returns often to happiness as a common refrain in his politico-aesthetic thinking. A seemingly minor concept without many serious stakes, happiness is perhaps not a dominant aesthetic category, but it has deep roots in art. In his *Aesthetic Theory*, Adorno approvingly quotes Stendhal's dictum that *La beauté n'est que la promesse du bonheur*: Beauty is nothing other than the promise of happiness.[16] This happiness, though, is not tied to the enjoyment we supposedly derive from getting something out of the work:

> Rather, the work of art offers happiness because it succeeds in drawing us into it in the way I have tried to show you; that it forces us to accompany it on the paths it traces within itself; and that, at the same time, it thus alienates us from the alienated world in which we live, and through this very alienation of the alienated in fact restores immediacy or undamaged life. (*Aesthetics* 120)

Happiness is perhaps here the twin of responsibility, as Adorno seems to identify in both the possibility of breaking through the deadlock of reification: if we "devote ourselves as purely as possible to the matter without adding too much of ourselves" then "our own subjective needs will be honoured" (*Aesthetics* 4).

These subjective needs are manifold, even overwhelming, when one reflects on damaged life in a false world. Reading—and writing—cannot in itself heal or make true, and to substitute aesthetic experience for political praxis turns art's radicalism into its reactionary opposite. Theory, Adorno said in an interview shortly before he died, "effects change precisely by remaining theory" and cannot "in and of itself recommend immediate measures or changes" ("Appendix" 238). And yet, Adorno adds, "for once the question should be asked whether it is not also a form of resistance when a human being thinks and writes things the way

I write them" (238). The resistance to reading thus finds its dialectical opposition in reading as a form of resistance. But though Adorno's question is asked it is not necessarily answered and the question remains open. The responsibility and the promise of happiness, however, that Adorno describes as at the core of aesthetic experience, and at the core of reading, are nevertheless fundamental to recognizing the nonidentity of a totality in need of transformation.

Notes

1 The Adorno renaissance that began in the 1990s has developed over the last few decades into what is sometimes referred to as the Adorno Industry. In their edited collection *Adorno and Literature*, David Cunningham and Nigel Mapp note that while it is "in relation to questions of aesthetics that much of the most exciting recent work on Adorno has been carried out," even within this surge of interest "Adorno's literary writings have remained severely under-represented" (1). More recently, however, a number of studies in English have directly examined Adorno as a reader rather than simply as a philosopher. Gerhard Richter aims to develop "an Adornean art of reading" in his *Thinking with Adorno* (7), for instance, and Josh Robinson seeks to "make a case for the mutual implication of philosophical reflection and literary criticism" in *Adorno's Poetics of Form* (12).
2 Franco Moretti argues for distant instead of close reading in *Distant Reading*, Stephen Best and Sharon Marcus prefer surface to close reading in "Surface Reading," and Eve Kosofsky Sedgwick outlines reparative reading as opposed to the hermeneutics of suspicion in "Paranoid Reading and Reparative Reading." Rita Felski's recent development of post-critique in *The Limits of Critique* has been influenced by such reappraisals of reading and in turn provides some of the impetus for Paul K. Saint-Amour's "Weak Theory, Weak Modernism."
3 This is the point of Adorno's essay on Hegel's "skoteinos"—his infamous "insufficient clarity" (95)—where he develops an "art of reading" (94) Hegel that has a bearing on Adorno's understanding of reading as such.
4 His "Notes on Philosophical Thinking" aims explicitly to "say something about philosophical thinking, stopping in midstride as it were" (127).
5 Today's undialectical object-oriented philosophies, thing theories, and neo-vitalist materialisms are generally highly scientistic and ontological—two modes of thinking toward which Adorno demonstrated a long-standing antipathy and which he often described as outright ideological. A more sustained elaboration of Adorno's position on subjectivity and objectivity can be found in his essay "On Subject and Object." There Adorno announces the "primacy of the object" (249) while cautioning against a "seemingly anti-subjectivist, scientifically objective

identity thinking" (252) that believes in a "purified object" (253) not mediated by subjectivity (which is in turn mediated by objectivity).

6 See Robert S. Lehman for a well-reasoned elaboration and defense of Kant that takes particular issue with Adorno on this point. Lehman follows Kant in defining aesthetics in terms of "the subjective representation of an object" rather than the object itself in its phenomenal form (252). Of course, for the Hegelian Adorno the work of art may be objective but it is not synonymous with phenomenal form either, as it has a suprasensible, or spiritual, dimension that is more than the sum of its moments or aspects.

7 As is hopefully already clear, the responsibility in question in this essay, and in Adorno's lectures on aesthetics, may be distantly related to but is not is not synonymous with terms like seriousness, maturity, culpability, guilt, and so on. Adorno occasionally explores such synonymous versions of responsibility, and he does address the serious-unserious version of the responsibility-irresponsibility dichotomy in *Aesthetic Theory* where he notes that art cannot be axiomatically cast as either: "The art of absolute responsibility terminates in sterility, whose breath can be felt on almost all consistently developed artworks; absolute irresponsibility degrades art to *fun*; a synthesis of responsibility and irresponsibility is precluded by the concept itself" (39).

8 Adorno actually thinks that even Kant can't help but prioritizing objectivity, even if his thought is directed toward subjectivity: "Despite the Copernican turn, and thanks to it, Kant inadvertently confirms the primacy of the object" ("Notes" 129).

9 Such a view of Adorno is echoed even in this volume. While for me Adorno productively defies easy categorization in today's debates about reading, theory, and critique—neither strong nor weak, not quite surface-oriented nor entirely preoccupied with depths, and so on—Daniel Aureliano Newman singles out Adorno as "one of the strongest of Strong Theorists" (xx) and Roger Rothman characterizes Adorno as embodying the sort of theory that post-critique rejects for its "hopelessness" and "inescapable limitation" (xx).

10 In his chapter, Robert Baines also favorably refers to "creative remaking" (xx), as does Newman (xx). There are other more implicit evocations of this same idea too, such as Yan Tang's focus on how contemporary theorists' writings can, and perhaps should, be "so reminiscent of modernist aesthetics" (xx) in their form. The idea of creative remaking might bind together the otherwise weakly, though productively, diffuse notion of responsible reading within this volume and link it, despite some substantial disagreements on other points, to Felski's post-critical position.

11 The theory referred to here is critical theory broadly speaking, which the Frankfurt School thinkers contrasted with the more positivist and instrumental traditional theory. Adorno himself makes this distinction frequently, but the classic distinction is found in Max Horkheimer's "Traditional and Critical Theory" from 1937.

12 This idea is seconded several times in the chapters of this volume. Durão, for instance, notes that "theory has been converted into a problematically separate realm" (xx) and as a result its vocation is mediatory—specifically a "mediation between philosophy and criticism" (xx) that entails "a textual rearrangement of philosophy and literary criticism" (xx). For Kathryn Carney, theory, as prosthesis, is also a kind of mediation or "interlocution" (xx) between self and other.

13 I follow Carolyn Lesjak's insight that while to some extent theory and reading are seen as opposed today, the defense of one is necessarily the defense of the other (233). Lesjak also notes that "Jameson in *Valences of the Dialectic* (as well as elsewhere) distinguishes between philosophy and theory and aligns reading with the latter" (238).

14 This is Paul A. Kottman's description of "Trying to Understand *Endgame*" in his introduction to the newly published combined edition of Adorno's two-volume *Notes to Literature* (1).

15 This is similar to the "resistance to reading" as Ellen Rooney defines it: "an evasion of the absolutely unavoidable risk entailed in 'reading,' where reading is recognized as a relation among readers, a productive relation, but one that allows for no theoretical guarantee" (184).

16 Adorno quotes the French phrase three times in *Aesthetic Theory*—pages 12, 82, 311—and he uses synonymous phrases (and the terms promise and happiness) many times in that text and throughout his oeuvre. However, he also says in *Aesthetic Theory* that art is "ever the broken promise of happiness" (136) and that, when it comes to the promise of happiness, "this utopic element is constantly decreasing" (311).

References

Adorno, Theodor W. *Aesthetics*, edited by Eberhard Ortland, translated by Wieland Hoban. Polity, 2018.

Adorno, Theodor W. *Aesthetic Theory*, translated and edited by Robert Hullot-Kentor, U of Minnesota P, 1997.

Adorno, Theodor W. "Appendix: Who's Afraid of the Ivory Tower? A Conversation with Theodor W. Adorno." *Language Without Soil: Adorno and Late Philosophical Modernity*, edited by Gerhard Richter. Fordham UP, 2010, pp. 227–38.

Adorno, Theodor W. "The Essay as Form." *Notes to Literature*, edited by Rolf Tiedemann, translated by Shierry Weber Nicholsen. Columbia UP, 2019, pp. 29–47.

Adorno, Theodor W. *Minima Moralia: Reflections from Damaged Life*, translated by E. F. N. Jephcott. Verso, 2005.

Adorno, Theodor W. "Notes on Philosophical Thinking." *Critical Models: Interventions and Catchwords*, translated by Henry W. Pickford. Columbia UP, 2005, pp. 127–34.

Adorno, Theodor W. "On Subject and Object." *Critical Models: Interventions and Catchwords*, translated by Henry W. Pickford. Columbia UP, 2005, pp. 245–58.

Adorno, Theodor W. "Skoteinos, or How to Read Hegel." *Hegel: Three Studies*, translated by Shierry Weber Nicholsen. MIT P, 1993, pp. 89–148.

Adorno, Theodor W. "Trying to Understand *Endgame*." *Notes to Literature*, edited by Rolf Tiedemann, translated by Shierry Weber Nicholsen. Columbia UP, 2019, pp. 237–67.

Althusser, Louis, Étienne Balibar, Roger Establet, Pierre Macherey, and Jacques Rancière. *Reading Capital: The Complete Edition*, translated by Ben Brewster and David Fernbach. Verso, 2016.

Benjamin, Walter. "Exchange with Theodor W. Adorno on 'The Paris of the Second Empire in Baudelaire.'" *Selected Writings, Volume 4, 1938–1940*, translated by Edmund Jephcott and Michael Jennings, edited by Howard Eiland and Michael W. Jennings. Harvard UP, 2003, pp. 99–115.

Bernstein, J. M. "Blind Intuitions: Modernism's Critique of Idealism." *British Journal for the History of Philosophy*, vol. 22, no. 6, 2014, pp. 1069–94.

Best, Stephen, and Sharon Marcus. "Surface Reading: An Introduction." *Representations*, vol. 108, no. 1, 2009, pp. 1–21.

Cunningham, David, and Nigel Mapp. "Introduction." *Adorno and Literature*, edited by David Cunningham and Nigel Mapp, Continuum, 2006, pp. 1–5.

Felski, Rita. *The Limits of Critique*. U of Chicago P, 2015.

Horkheimer, Max. "Traditional and Critical Theory." *Critical Theory: Selected Essays*, translated by Matthew J. O'Connell, Continuum, 2002, pp. 188–243.

Huhn, Tom. "Introduction: Thoughts beside Themselves." *The Cambridge Companion to Adorno*, edited by Tom Huhn, Cambridge UP, 2004, pp. 1–18.

Jameson, Fredric. "Afterword: On Eurocentric Lacanians." *International Journal of Žižek Studies*, vol. 13, no. 1, 2019, pp. 161–8.

Jameson, Fredric. *Valences of the Dialectic*. Verso, 2009.

Jarvis, Simon. "What Is Speculative Thinking?" *Revue Internationale de Philosophie*, vol. 58, no. 227, 2004, pp. 69–83.

Kottman, Paul A. "Introduction to the Combined Edition." *Notes to Literature*, edited by Rolf Tiedemann, translated by Shierry Weber Nicholsen, Columbia UP, 2019, pp. 1–15.

Lehman, Robert S. "Formalism, Mere Form, and Judgment." *New Literary History*, vol. 48, no. 2, 2017, pp. 245–63.

Lesjak, Carolyn. "Reading Dialectically." *Criticism*, vol. 55, no. 2, 2013, pp. 233–77.

Moretti, Franco. *Distant Reading*. Verso, 2013.

Moskowitz, Alex. "Economic Imperception; or, Reading *Capital* on the Beach with Thoreau." *American Literary History*, vol. 32, no. 2, pp. 221–42.

Richter, Gerhard. "A Portrait of Non-Identity." *Monatshefte*, vol. 94, no. 1, 2002, pp. 1–9.

Richter, Gerhard. *Thinking with Adorno: The Uncoercive Gaze*. Stanford UP, 2019.

Robinson, Josh. *Adorno's Poetics of Form*. State U of New York P, 2018.

Rooney, Ellen. "Better Read Than Dead: Althusser and the Fetish of Ideology." *Yale French Studies*, no. 88, 1995, pp. 183–200.

Saint-Amour, Paul K. "Weak Theory, Weak Modernism." *Modernism/modernity*, vol. 25, no. 3, 2018, pp. 437–59.

Sedgwick, Eve Kosofsky. "Paranoid Reading and Reparative Reading, or, You're So Paranoid, You Probably Think This Essay Is About You." *Touching Feeling: Affect, Pedagogy, Performativity*, Duke UP, 2003, pp. 123–52.

Wasser, Audrey. "Spinoza and the Claims of Meaning: 'A Word to the Wise.'" *Diacritics*, vol. 47, no. 2, 2019, pp. 106–27.

11

Writing from Somewhere, Reading from Anywhere: New Criticism and (Neo)liberal Globalization

Sonita Sarker

How does the apparatus of New Criticism that academic-cultural elite in England and the United States manufactured in the first part of the twentieth century become part of the mandatory curriculum for young girls in Kolkata, India, in the latter part of the same century? As one of those girls, I remember my homework assignment was to mimic the methods of reading responsibly, and to consent to do so without necessarily understanding the intentions of T. S. Eliot, I. A. Richards, Cleanth Brooks, William Empson, Allen Tate, John Crowe Ransom, and others, some with the exotic name of the Southern Agrarians. Of course, it was a qualified "consent" since I had neither choice nor countervailing power. Perhaps I shared a certain open-mouthed studiousness with my peers across the seas, in high schools and colleges in England and the United States, Canada and Australia, Kenya and New Zealand.

What was I responsible for, as a reader of New Critical analyses of English poetry? How did that correlate to the responsibilities of New Critics themselves? When Anglophone US and British literatures are framed through the eyes, heads, and hands of white males continents away, a postcolonial, migratory subject's reading of texts that are distributed through colonial circuits of globalization becomes a responsibility that she does not ask to carry but becomes hers to bear. I was ... and still am ... categorized as brown and female in the U.S., no longer so young, no longer in Kolkata but in St. Paul (Minnesota) on the Midwest prairie, on the lands of the Sisseton and Wahpeton peoples, still reading poetry and now teaching it as well. I am not the "Indian" whose "culture [is] 'pattern[ed]' whole," as Eric Aronoff quotes John Crowe Ransom ("Anthropologists" 108–9), in presenting it as a model for New Critic methodology. That "Indian" is admired, exoticized, and objectified for a faux nostalgia based in white colonial privilege, all in one sweeping gesture.[1] Neither Pueblo people nor my multiply-attached identity are, in reality, that "Indian" and neither of us should be mistaken for the other.

From my experience, responsible reading is not a disembodied practice. Felski's idea of "responsible reading" could be extended to ask "responsible reading by whom?" or, less awkwardly, "who reads?" Differently defined identities/bodies, positioned asymmetrically in structures of power, read, and the nature and consequences of that responsibility manifest from these various identities and locations. As it has turned out for me, reading is often a visceral and eviscerating experience. For New Critics, reading is also a similarly dis/embodied experience, but in the theories they produce, the poem becomes the body that is overpowered, occupied, dissected, and delivered for consumption. Reading in these ways, for New Critics and myself, is differently consuming, absorbing, and passing on ways of being. New Critical frames of reading, initially imported into Kolkata, were not just adopted but internalized (digested) as structures of value, discernment, and taste, and eventually passed on to generations of readers, on the prairie and elsewhere. Reading responsibly, à la New Criticism, continues to require both sterile purity and violence—aesthetic appreciation emerges from a surgical excision of emotions which, New Critics would hold, only contaminate the reader's experience.

The focus on the body of the poem and the construction of an architectonics of reading on it had at least two effects in my experience as a reader. For one, I was given the responsibility of forgetting my own identity and location in order to inhabit those structures. For another, the New Critics' responsibility is only to the literary artefact of the poem and their occupation of its internal territories enables a seemingly neutral route away from both critique (antipathy) and post-critique (*pathos*). This route, of "objective" assessment, struck me as a colonizing methodology as a young-er student; from a different position, that kind of assessment may appear to be a third way that disrupts the neat dialectic of critique and post-critique but, on closer scrutiny, is itself not open-ended. In other words, responsibility emerges in a wiggly line from one's embodiment: for white middle- and upper-class masculinity in rural and urban environments located in capitalist-colonial modernity, responsible reading takes particular forms of dis/embodiment.

Taking a representative New Criticism corpus, I discuss how reading, as fashioned by white bourgeois/elite male academics, is delivered through consumable objects that travel on this route between critique and post-critique, and is founded on twin paradoxes. The first is that even as many New Critics, especially the Southern Agrarians, ignore or disavow capitalist modernity and industrialism, their vocabulary is deeply embedded in processes of capital production and ascribes both tangible value and intangible quality to consumable objects. Colonial capitalism is both hyper-marked and elided in their apparatus. It is precisely by adopting colonizing tactics—in absorbing the "other" (the "Indian," for example) and in their absorption with the body of the poem—that they claim a disembodied objectivity. New Criticism is packaged as a priceless set of tools; it is a fetishism of both the critical apparatus and the object on which it exercises itself (the poem). It is an intense preoccupation with the structure of poetry that promises an aesthetic experience bordering on the auratic. The magic of reading in this way seduces a reader to "buy in" to an ethos, much like the cut diamond set in gold does, illuminated by the lights trained on it, in a shop window, an object of desire for those who can purchase it and those who cannot, alike.

The second paradox of the New Critics' being and doing is that, even as they distance themselves from political and historical entanglements, they participate in and even perpetuate a hyper-inflated narrative of modernity. "New" is about making "old" contexts irrelevant, and the frame of aesthetics shifts from the "subjective" and "emotional" to "objective," thus enabling the commodification and distribution of their set of tools. The use of "new" signals their subscription to this narrative, and it is apparent in their writings that "new" also signifies "better" (than the "old" historical or the biographical method). The Southern Agrarians, purportedly opposed to the industrialized US continental North, rely heavily on a romanticized notion of agri-masculinity to counterbalance others in the group who form an urbane, cosmopolitan contingent. Moreover, this masculinity, coded white, that encompasses the urban and the agrarian, presents its "tools" of reading as the only ones that can discern what constitutes supra-historical "value" through the use of pseudo-scientific criteria, at the same time that they protest that literary analysis is not "scientism" (Brooks, "New Criticism" 607).[2]

New Criticism practices in Western European and North American early-twentieth-century modernist times become staples in late-twentieth-century and current neoliberal capitalism. They efface the location of the subject so that the point of view can be universalized, and render the object purchasable (as curriculum, in my context) across cultural and political borders. At the same time, this particular dis-location of the subject which actually amplifies, not diminishes, its influence, rests, in fact, upon the importance placed upon the individual in liberal economies. New Critics' analysis of poetry and commentary on other academics' work creates a self-contained world of Anglophone British and American individual literary, exclusively male, heroes. So New Critics do name specific individuals but make those specificities disappear in their extraction of principles that are suspended from their context and intended as the new universals of analysis. What is presented is innately culturally specific but marketed as attainable everywhere. These dis/appearances of identity and location are further facilitated by two elements: by their own white middle-class maleness as the hegemonic normative, thus invisible and unmarked, and by English as the universal *lingua franca*, itself the result of colonial history. These two elements are, in turn, made possible by sublimating both race and gender into nationality and/or religion: for New Critics, being American or English/British, Catholic or Protestant makes identification as white or male either assumed or unnecessary.

The same mechanism of dis/appearance operates today in neoliberal commodification—the object is produced somewhere but is presented as having value anywhere in the world, whether that object is a car, a film ... or a literary text. However, the circuits of globalization that distribute these objects continue to function on neo/colonial hierarchies of value in which objects from former colonial powers continue to have greater influence. At the same time that individualism is celebrated, the material history of the individual is made irrelevant—the Nobel Prize in Literature is a curious contemporary case in which citations start with an acknowledgment of the author's nationality (or occasionally, regional origins) but emphasize the universality of that individual's achievement, as if to say that something can be written somewhere but can, or should, be read anywhere, now that it has the imprimatur of the Swedish Academy. This particular refusal of the politics of positionality is a prominent feature of New Criticism and remains as residue in our reading, writing, assessing, and adjudicating practices today.

Agro/Urban Masculinity Across the Pond

"Across the pond," a phrase used frequently in Anglophone literary Modernist Studies signifies, to this reader-listener-writer, an affirmation within academia of the "unique bond" (as politicians have called it for the past century at least) between the United States and England. The "pond" is the Atlantic Ocean, the very waters of the Middle Passage that carried peoples to enslavement, the very waters called "kala pani" (the "black waters" in Hindi) over which colonial conscripts traveled to fight for imperial powers on European battlefields. Across these very waters, now addressed with an affectionate diminutive, flow the connections that bind the old British Empire to the new global power of the United States, deepening the fraternal bonds among the band of merry men, the New Critics, worlding a self-contained universe of reference and reading.

The title of Cleanth Brooks's most well-known volume, *The Well-Wrought Urn: Studies in the Structure of Poetry*, is taken from seventeenth-century British poet John Donne's poem "The Canonization" and alludes to the "storied urn" in eighteenth-century English poet Thomas Gray's "Elegy in a Country Churchyard" as well as to nineteenth-century British poet John Keats's "Ode on a Grecian Urn." Brooks comments about the ten poems included in his book that it is "somewhat surprising to see how many items they do have in common" (192), "they" being British metaphysicals and the transatlantic moderns, spanning histories and geographies. In his evaluation of Donne's and Pope's poetry, on what basis does Brooks purport to know the complexity of Pope's attitudes? What allows the unobstructed claim that Southern Agrarians in the United States make to the British Middle Ages, across the pond?[3] In "The Poetry of 1900–1950," Ransom praises T. S. Eliot's perfect use of meters and states quite explicitly: "I name the poets of 1900–1950 who seem as of this moment to have established themselves, and to have good prospect of surviving in our literature for a few half-centuries. They are British or American indifferently" (451). The last word demonstrates most palpably that the complicated histories that bind two white-majority nations is of little significance in his reading.

The sequence of icons of English poetry appears like a collection of objects in a museum, canonized, as it were, to use Donne's image. Yeats is tied to Wordsworth as a "great," though they are very different poets, through qualities selected by the New Critics as supra-historical criteria. At a different place in *The Well-Wrought Urn*, Brooks universalizes these qualities by connecting two very distinct poems, Gray's "Elegy" and Eliot's "The Waste Land" through their common strategy of using "a tissue of allusions and half-allusions" (107). The frames of responsible reading appear clearly defined and only the big powers (an older colonial one and a rising imperial one) across the pond sit comfortably in them. What was a young female reader in Kolkata to do but read from the outside, looking at this magical snow-globe of a world in great wonder?

Brooks strenuously proclaims that he and Robert Penn Warren

> were not out to corrupt innocent youth with heretical views. [Their] aims were limited, practical, and even grubby. [They] had nothing highfalutin or esoteric in mind. [They're] not a pair of young art-for-art's-sake aesthetes, just back from Oxford and out of touch with American reality. (Brooks, "New Criticism" 593)

In this self-description, the claims to the new and the unprecedented coexist with a certain self-effacement, in an intentional counter-positioning to elites and "aesthetes." The implicitly class-inflected vocabulary that shies away from associations with the "ivory tower" by calling itself "grubby," a faux-poor stance, also briefly acknowledges the cultural and material differences across the pond but glosses over them through a gesture of self-awareness.

It is not merely that the New Critical world of references is circumscribed; it also speaks of a specific value system that does not include women or Indians, except as props to display the "new" analytical skills that the members of the group present as revolutionary. To return to the allusions to Pueblo Indian culture mentioned above—Aronoff discusses Ransom's construction of a theory of aesthetic form in poetry; to Aronoff, this is also a theory of regional culture that refers to Pueblo Indian culture as "a model for both a way of life that is itself specifically aesthetic and the structure of which replicates—or more accurately, is replicated in—the structure of the fine poem" which is "internally referential" (108–9). Romanticizing an a-historicized "wholeness" of Indigenous culture enables the vision of the "wholeness" of a literary text and, by extension, the pure integrity of its analysis. Along the same lines, women appear in reductive images and as "figures" that contribute to the structural integrity of the poem. Brooks, in chapter 5 entitled "The Case of Miss Arabella Fermor" in *The Well-Wrought Urn*, referring to Aldous Huxley's "lovers" and Donne's figure of the woman in "The Ecstasy," discusses the functionality of women as exhibiting how "[w]e are disciplined in the tradition of either-or ... the more subtle reservations permitted by the tradition of both-and. Flesh or spirit, merely a doxy or purely a goddess (or alternately, one and then the other)" (81). Later, in the same chapter, Brooks discusses *The Rape of The Lock* and concludes that "though Pope's attitude toward his heroine has a large element of amused patronage in it, ... [he finds] no contempt. Rather, Pope finds Belinda charming, and expects us to feel her charm" (87).[4] He uses the themes of chastity and honor to ascribe nothing but noble motives to Pope and mounts a spirited defense of the poet, again purporting to have knowledge of what might have been in the author's mind.

New Criticism, in this sampling, appears to be responsible only to masculinist English cultural heritage, more specifically the English poem, and to the mission of conveying the values they themselves have ascribed to it.

White Men's Burden: "A Valiant Fight"

The mission of the New Critics starts on contested terrain. Or rather on a terrain that is constructed as contested. Only discontent with "traditional" modes of reading can justify the necessity for new ways of reading and comprehending. The critique of the contemporary state of reading is founded on a number of complaints: that the modern poet has handed his responsibility to convey meaning over to the reader, that the reader is not taught well or at all, that in most cases there is only superficial reading that leads to moral or biographical or historical speculations or, worse, paraphrase, and that English departments have failed in their task. T. S. Eliot, in "The Function of Criticism," delivers his condemnation of the contemporary practices of reading which, in his view, "far from being a simple and orderly field of beneficent activity, from which impostors can be readily ejected, is no better than a Sunday park of contending and contentious orators, who have not even arrived at the articulation of their differences" (69).

Brooks focuses on the question that I asked as a young girl and ask now: Whose responsibility is it to read? In *The Well-Wrought Urn*, he observes that "[n]ow the modern poet has, for better or worse, thrown the weight of the responsibility upon the reader" (76). The latter must now be vigilant about changes in the poet's tone, accommodate "a method of indirection," and be well read in the context; Brooks finds him (the modern reader) deficient in all these skills, ill-equipped, and badly prepared. In "The New Criticism," Brooks indicts the pedagogue who produces "adequate reading" (600) whereas the moment calls for the development of "close" reading. He describes how he and Penn Warren discovered in their teaching that students "had very little knowledge of how to read a story or a play, and even less knowledge of how to read a poem" (593); these readers were either not taught at all or "mistaught," thus implying that there is a correct way of reading that replaces the current tradition of approaching poetry as if it were "an editorial in the local county newspaper or an advertisement in the current Sears and Roebuck catalog" (593).[5] In this crowded scene of readers and analysts, all of whom are presented as misguided and indeed irresponsible, Ransom includes "[t]he Humanists ... and the Leftists or Proletarians [who] create diversions that are "moral" and "intent on ethical values" ("Criticism, Inc." 591). Compounding the problem with reading are the twin errors of biography and paraphrase. In addition, given their affiliations and allegiances to elite academic institutions such as Oxford and Cambridge in England, and Harvard in the United States, it is a particularly distressing to New Critics that English departments should adopt the "atrocious policy to abdicate [their] own self-respecting identity" which would be to "inquire into the peculiar constitution and structure of its product," lose their autonomy, and become subservient to departments of History or Ethics (592).[6] I am quite sure I, in my studious girlhood, would have been perceived by invisible new forces such as New Critics as badly prepared, mistaught, and guilty of paraphrase.

With various readers, including some professionals, dismissed as incapable, the field is clear. New Critics consider themselves the most eligible to occupy this hitherto troubled terrain and take a stand on reading responsibly. As Ransom asserts in "Criticism, Inc.," setting up the basis for the relevance and significance of New Criticism, "[i]t is not anybody who can do criticism" (593). Brooks, in *The Well-Wrought Urn*, laments that analyses of Wordsworth's "Intimations" ode "rush back into biographical speculation" when the task is "to treat the poem strictly as a poem" (126). Later in the same volume, regarding Keats's "Ode on a Grecian Urn," Brooks reinforces the point in stating that "the assertions made in a poem are to be taken as part of an *organic* context [and readers must] be willing to go on to deal with the world-view, or 'philosophy' or 'truth' of the *poem as a whole*" (165–6; emphasis added).[7] His emphasis on "organic" and "whole" resonates with the romanticized wholeness that Ransom ascribed to the "Indian." Decades later, the Kolkata student in India read this through a refracted consciousness and was initiated into a reading practice that aspires to a wholeness, a unity that has always remained elusive to her.

That the "traditionalists" and those who take a stand against them are white, educated, professional (including academic) British and American men, is evident everywhere but explicitly invoked nowhere. Protagonists and antagonists are positioned on the terrain that the New Critics have themselves mapped out. Brooks characterizes the nature of their practices, against those of other white men, as a noble mission (despite calling it "grubby"), as a pitched battle to capture not only the present moment but the times to come. In "The New Criticism," he proclaims that

> [t]he humanities would *abdicate* their function in society if they *surrendered* to a neutral scientism and indifferent relativism or if they *succumbed* to the

imposition of alien norms required by political indoctrination. Particularly on these two fronts the New Critics have waged a *valiant fight* which, I am afraid, must be fought over again in *the future*." (607; emphasis added)

In the new responsibility of reading that New Critics have claimed, the phrase "valiant fight" is significant in describing the nature of their work, couched as it is in terms of combat. To this postcolonial reader, the italicized words evoke the tumult resulting from the missions that white male colonizers carried out. Brooks does not hesitate to draw clear lines in stating that they presented their "questions ... about the poem in a form calculated to produce the battles of the last twenty-five years over the 'use of poetry'" (*Urn* 201–2). In these instances, New Critics appear to use a lexicon without an awareness of its particular resonances in their own past and present, and almost with a fervent anticipation of the struggles to come and the fulfillment of their self-described noble mission. Not only the vocabulary but the very spirit of "the white man's burden," as Rudyard Kipling describes in his 1899 poem of the same name, informs the New Critic mission. The battle against their arch-enemy, the heresy of paraphrase, takes on a quasi-religious tone of a solemn and sacred objective.[8] Paraphrase, in their view, "distort[s] the relation of the poem to its '*truth*'" and brings the poem "into an unreal *competition* with science or philosophy or theology"; asking questions about "the 'use of poetry'... we run the risk of doing even more *violence* to the internal *order* of the poem itself" (201–2; emphasis added). As evident once more in the italicized words, the vocabulary of white colonial masculinity reproduces itself: truth and order, and even peace, are on the side of New Critics, while distortion, competition, and violence are perpetrated by the other side. Reading differently is a pitched battle with winners and losers in the past, present, and future.

New Critic rhetoric continues to be embedded in staples of colonial discourse, carrying the spirit of a mission in terms such as "exploration," "right," "efficient," "elucidation," and "correction." I. A. Richards, in *Practical Criticism*, absolves the poet of the responsibility of delivering meaning, turning us to "wonder if we are reading right" (12). He imagines that if one were to say that one reading is as good as another, his response would be simply, "It isn't" (12). Later, Richards in the significantly titled *How to Read a Page: A Course in Efficient Reading with an Introduction to a Hundred Great Words* asserts unequivocally that "there is a right reading, and unless our business is to find it, we are wasting our time" (11), and the New Critics proclaim victory in having found the "right" way. In "The Function of Criticism," Eliot starts the discussion by quoting himself and then goes on to say that "[c]riticism … must always profess an end in view, which … appears to be the elucidation of works of art and the correction of taste" (69). It is evident that reading must have a telos, otherwise it is irresponsible. The root of the word "elucidation" is "luce," the Latin word that is also the root of the word and the phenomenon, the Enlightenment; the New Critic analysis of a poem aspires to the same status and magnitude of clarity, and thus the New Critic claims to fight "the valiant fight" for himself and for posterity.

In essence, the responsibility of reading, as New Critics would have it, is moral and even quasi-religious, transcending the impermanence of fashion to combat the ravages of history; this aspiration to righteousness as well as lasting power informed imperialism itself. Brooks describes New Criticism as "a technique that yields a standard of judgment that cannot be easily dismissed in favor of the currently popular, sentimental, and simple … A decision between good and bad art remains the unavoidable duty of criticism" ("New Criticism" 607). "Technique," "yields," and "decision" instrumentalize the project for the purposes of reading the right way; for instance, chapter 1 of I. A. Richards's *How to Read a Page* is explicitly titled "How a Reader Might Improve." Brooks asserts elsewhere that "good" and "bad" are subjective "[b]ut in giving up our criteria of good and bad, we have, as a consequence … begun to give up our concept of poetry itself" (*Urn* 216). In "The New Criticism," Brooks quotes René Wellek's 1978 essay "The New Criticism: Pro and Contra" as capturing what they aimed for—it "stated or reaffirmed many basic truths to which future ages will have to return" (607). He issues a serious alert that "[i]f the Humanities are to *endure*, they must be themselves—and that means, among other things, frankly accepting the *burden* of making normative judgments" (*Urn* 235; emphasis added).

When "the valiant fight" is the burden that New Critics bear, when the struggle is for clarity and illumination of an "organic thing," namely a poem, when the object is "to improve," and when the tools—paradox, ambiguity, metaphor, irony, contradiction—have no nationality, the project/product can be easily distributed across the world. On one level, the "valiant fight" is between educated white men, talking across the pond. On another level, the New Critic exerts an easily accessed privilege to equate the "I" with all others in the world. The poem *is* the world and the New Critic mastery of that world is exported and thus extends out into the globe. Richards, in *Practical Criticism*, passionately describes how the exploration of the various internal structures and meanings of a poem, the appreciation of the ways they correlate and depend on each other, and the expression of "the meaning which matter most to *us* form a part of *our* world … [help to see more clearly] what *our* world is and what *we* are who are *building* it to live in" (13; emphasis added). Who is included in "our" and "we"? The New Critics write from somewhere, but as if from nowhere, and can be read anywhere, everywhere.

The Urn and the Engine

New Criticism entangles us all in the mesh created by Art, Science, and Capital, despite the distance it claims from history and politics. This mesh is what I, as a college student, was caught in, without knowing the words for the magnitude of that experience. I read diligently in a curriculum delivered through capitalist circuits of globalization that extended across post/colonial histories and geographies. Aesthetic appreciation, as produced by the New Critics, I apprehended vaguely then and submit today, aspires to the status that both Science and Capital have in early twentieth-century Western European and North American modernity. In these decades, both Science and Capital are fundamentally defined by the processes of colonialism, in England and in the United States. New Criticism, however, easily perceives poetry, and analyses of it, as separate, even antithetical, to the heuristics of both Science and Capital; that legacy still endures to some degree in literary studies. New Critics' subscription to narratives of modernity and progress is already evident in the word "new" in their name and is further underscored in I. A. Richards's remark in his *Science and Poetry* (1926, 1935) published as *Poetries and Sciences* in 1970: "When attitudes are changing neither criticism nor poetry remains stationary" (48).

True, they do not remain stationary but bend toward hegemonic power. The tenets of responsible reading that New Critics craft and hand down through generations of readers simulate the same emphasis on structure and system, form and function, that Science and Capital do. The well-wrought urn, in its symmetry and efficiency, is very much like the well-oiled engine, embodying universally applicable principles. New Critics, particularly the Southern Agrarians, create a cottage industry of reading that distances itself from industrial modernity based in corporate capitalism as well as national culture.[9] Yet, they produce a technology that is truly of its times, welded to the narratives of dominant modernity; one particular feature of such narratives is the reliance on a standard of judgment that survives for all time, as discussed in the previous section. It is precisely their embodied identities, as European and American white male professionals, that allow New Critics' claims of neutrality and objectivity to remain undisputed. It is precisely because white masculinity is deemed the hegemonic norm in the worlds that they inhabit that New Critics' modes of reading can be universalized, and reach colleges in the Bay of Bengal and Midwest prairies equally.

At points in the New Critics' career, the ambivalence about "traditional" and "new" ways of reading coexists with an aspiration to the status of Science. At the same time that Brooks praises Donne for using logic and proof, he insists that "[t]he essential structure of a poem (as distinguished from the rational or logical structure of the 'statement' which we abstract from it) resembles that of architecture or painting; it is a pattern of resolved stresses ... a ballet or musical composition ... a pattern of resolutions and balances and harmonizations" (*Urn* 203).[10] He waxes poetic about "the poem itself [as] ... the well-wrought urn which can hold the lovers' ashes" (*Urn* 17), and asserts that without the "tools" of New Criticism (paradox, irony, wonder) applied to a poem such as Donne's "The Canonization," analysis "unravels into 'facts,' bio-logical, sociological, and economic" (18). In *Poetries and Sciences*, Richards asserts that poetry makes "pseudo-statements" (59ff.) which hold truths that are different from scientific truths. Yet, he later names the goal in analyzing poetry to be the achievement of "unity" and "equilibrium" (207); these words recall the functions and features of a well-oiled engine, or any other material object with shape and balance. He continues on to use quasi-scientific vocabulary to describe the word as "not a discrete particle of meaning, but as a potential of meaning, a nexus or cluster of meanings" (210). Like Richards, other New Critics treat the poem as a precious object, to be handled and handed over with reverence, but one that they can still dissect with authority.

One way out of this ambivalence is the New Critics' attempt to blend the two (scientific and poetic) into a third, so that the methods appear to derive from, but not become subservient to, either Science or Capital. As in other passages of *The Well-Wrought Urn*, Brooks takes care to define a key term, unity, as not "the sort to be achieved by the reduction and simplification appropriate to an algebraic formula. It is a positive unity, not a negative; it represents not a residue but an achieved harmony" (195). Chapter VI, "Poetry and Beliefs," in Richards's *Poetries and Sciences* opens with the observation that "[t]he business of the poet ... is to give order and coherence, so freedom, to a body of experience" (57). Later, in the same work, Richards states that "[t]he nature of the material sets the problem to be solved, and the solution is the ordering of the material" (194). As I mention above, both unity and order read to me as part of the rationale of imperial practice, one that controls territories of difference under the banner of a singular Power, namely, God or Queen. Significantly, Richards argues that order and coherence bring freedom—this belief underscores the logic of domination that promises liberation through control. The student in Kolkata or in Kalamazoo, in the 1980s, may have similarly and differently experienced the acts of reading as disciplining mechanisms operating within a poem's structure as well as upon their bodies and minds; the seductive goal of "freedom" seemed more than enough reason to submit to the responsibility of reading in these particular ways then.

The New Critics' refashioning of the art of reading poetry places the poem, the humanistic object, on par with the mechanistic object that has value because of its utility; yet again, this rests upon a rationale for the relevance of objects in colonial-capitalist structures and systems. In *Theory of Literature*, Wellek and Warren take great pains to delineate the "nature" of literature (chapter 2) and its "function" (chapter 3) in terms of *dulce* and *utile* (18), pleasure and utility. As a reader, I was caught in what New Critics offered as a singular and immersive experience but what I experienced as fractured and refracted: the sensory appreciation of a poem—the *dulce* of melody, rhythm, and sound—and the imperative to produce—the *utile* of structure and objectivity. The "unity" that New Critics found so easily was, and remains, elusive to me.

Both Science and Capital become intertwined with the Art of analyzing poetry; the difference between New Critics' position and my own is that they could ignore the post/colonial contexts in which they (and Science and Capital and Art) were located and I could not. They were responsible to, and for, the English poem—the territory they occupied—and I was made responsible for reading through their eyes. The poem was the engine of their world, and New Criticism became a component of the engine of my readership. Ransom, in "Criticism, Inc.," characterizes the artist, the philosopher, and the professor of literature who have thus far analyzed poetry as "amateurs" (586); in contradistinction, he asserts that "[c]riticism must become more scientific, or precise and systematic, and this means that it must be developed by the collective and sustained effort of learned persons—which means that its proper seat is in the universities" (587). Here the term "amateurs" does not refer to those who hold an informal but deeply felt love for a given art but to those whose skills are not as sharply honed as that of a professional. To an amateur (lover of literature) who happens to hold the title of "professor," such as myself, the distinction is crude and elitist, and does violence to the very "organic wholeness" that New Critics claim that their object (the poem) and their analytical practices possess.

As Ransom goes on to say with some awareness of the implications: "Perhaps I use a distasteful figure, but I think that what we need is Criticism, Inc., or

Criticism. Ltd." ("Criticism, Inc." 588). This statement serves as his preface to present Prof. Ronald Crane at the University of Chicago as just the type of professional to carry on the mission. If the industry were to be developed as a limited enterprise, it would draw all the "alive and brilliant young English scholars all over the country" (589). The comparison to sciences such as economics and psychology, which have today come to be read by critics as "pseudo-sciences," is significant; Ransom predicts that the art of reading poetry will not become an "exact science" but neither will psychology or economics, and asks: are they "sciences or just systematic studies?" (587). "Criticism, Inc." conjures up the image of a corporation based in a professionalized activity that needs (young) workers whose bodies and minds are subjected to a regimentation within sanitized (objective) structures of reading which are then replicated *ad infinitum*. I hover somewhere between "amateur" and "professional," inside and outside "scholar" and "industry," and shudder again at the bloodless violence of the corporate structure imagined by New Critics. I bear the responsibility for which I did not ask but was given to me, to read like the "brilliant young English scholars" whom I can only speculate Ransom envisioned as white male citizens of the United States ... and England.

The paradox, to use a New Critical tool, is that the poem can be thoroughly understood (consumed) but also retains an invincible aura, much like the objects of Science or Capital do. T. S. Eliot, in "Tradition and the Individual Talent," uses the catalyst as an analogy to muster up the magic and mystery of the poetic process which New Criticism renders knowable. As he puts it:

> When ... two gases ... are mixed in the presence of a filament of platinum they form sulphurous acid. This combination takes place only if the platinum is present; nevertheless the newly formed acid contains no trace of platinum and the platinum itself is apparently unaffected; has remained inert, neutral, and unchanged. The mind of the poet is the shred of platinum ... the more perfect the artist, the more completely separate in him will be the man who suffers and the mind which creates. (41)

The magic and the mystery produce the aura, even as the process is tangible and scientifically documentable. The poem becomes knowable through the tools much like the universe does in Science or a product does in Capital, yet it retains an element of unknowability. In "The Function of Criticism," Eliot asserts that "a creation, a work of art, is autotelic; and that criticism, by definition, is about something other than itself ... The critical activity finds its highest, its true fulfilment in a kind of union with creation in the labour of the artist" (74). I labored in Kolkata and

I labored on the Midwest prairie; I studied and worked in Oxford, and conducted research at Harvard, not knowing how remote I was—in terms of gender, race, class, culture, and nationality—from the tutelage of the venerated professor under whom the young scholar labored in the same Oxford and Cambridge (both of them, across the pond from each other). Like Science and Capital, New Criticism enhances the value and desirability of an object, not only the poem itself but the value of its set of tools as well as how the poem is rendered through them. That aura is intended to create reverence: that is how I was schooled, to integrate into my environment an awe for its tools, the use of those tools, and the products of those tools.

And Our Responsibility Now?

Across New Critical texts, there are frequent references to "the reader." As evident in the discussion above, the poet, the critic, and perhaps even the student in any given English Department is understood to be white and English-speaking. Where the New Critic can retain his sovereignty by remaining unmarked, it appears that my body and mind remain hyper-marked in terms of my identity and location. Or is the reader also a white, English-speaking male and is his value system assumed to be the same as that of New Critics? There is also the "common-sense reader" (Brooks, *Urn* 62) who is imagined as wanting clear answers from the poetry that he reads, ones that presumably will be provided by the New Critic. Is this reader, common-sense or not, to surrender to the integrity and self-contained world of the poem as presented by New Critics, and doubt their own capacity to be responsible for their own evaluation and appreciation and understanding?

As I have implied above, New Criticism commits a unique epistemic violence by seeking pleasure in architectonics only, in an engine that navigates past the Scylla and Charybdis of critique (critical dis-assembling) and post-critique (self-understanding, reflection on morality, solace). If New Critical tools—ambiguity, paradox, metaphor, irony—have no nationality and can be used anywhere that English is spoken, it is not clear to me that the tools are intended to be used on objects other than English poetry. Is only English poetry "good" or did the New Critics intend that contradiction, paradox, irony, and the like should carry over to other cultures and languages as tools to apply everywhere, even where English is not spoken or written or read? That portability might imply that the tools themselves are of intrinsic value as gauges for universal poetic excellence. The detail of Brooks's analyses of canonical poems, to take only one example from the New Critical *oeuvre*, is based on knowing English well, an ability that a (native) speaker of a certain education might be expected to have; this certainly excludes the non-native speaker from knowing "good" poetry as determined by New Critics.

In my distance and closeness—cultural, critical, geographical, historical—the fact that we read is only as significant as the question "why do we read?" Moreover, to return to the beginning of this discussion, who reads and where one reads from affect the nature of that responsibility. I find myself reading simultaneously with and against the grain, schooled as I am in, and by, New Critical, New Historicist, Reader Response studies, and recuperations of New Criticism, and I benefit from as well as struggle with all these legacies of reading.[11] My identity as a reader is invariably influenced by changing contexts, and so I wonder what it means for me to read a cultural object as a self-referential entity. In other words, if what I read is meant to stand still, while I move, what is reading? Given my history, responsibility means to decolonize reading, by remaining aware of the constructedness and contingencies of the frames of reading. I remain aware that I have vested interests to either solidify or dislodge ingrained habits of reading, fraught with complications and contradictions as those interests and habits continue to be. Reading has entailed consuming, chewing, digesting, and spitting out interpretation, and it can also entail acts that rise out of epistemological humility, acts that mitigate violence.

After the *stürm und drang* generated by New Criticism, I imagine sitting cross-legged on the grass with my e/book in my lap, anywhere past critique and post-critique, somewhere in the world, and responsible reading beginning again with listening carefully.

Notes

1 See also Aronoff's *Composing Cultures* in which he argues that "modernist conceptions of culture and modernist ideas of literary form—or how to 'read' a culture and how to 'read' a text—are inextricably intertwined" (5). Aronoff appears to minimize the romanticization and exoticization of the "Indian" and Pueblo Culture. Jancovich argues that works such as René Wellek and Robert Penn Warren's *Understanding Poetry* (1938) were intimately tied to cultural context and influenced American academia greatly.
2 See Wyile for a discussion of regionalism and cosmopolitanism in a globalized age. It is worth noting that values attached to "agrarianism" themselves constitute a romanticized construction of industrial modernity.

3 See Karanikas's *Tillers of a Myth* in which he observes: "As New Critics they [the Fugitives] succeeded in doing what they had failed to do as Agrarians: to denigrate the democratic content in American literature, to smother its traditional note of social protest, and to elevate in its stead new literary gods and canons more acceptable to the rightist tradition" (viii).
4 The analysis of the poem's central theme, rape, as "a rude assault" (90) is entirely another matter.
5 It is not the poet's job or lack of skill that prevents the reader from knowing what a poem "communicates"; it is because "so few people, relatively speaking, are accustomed to reading *poetry as poetry*" (*Urn* 76; emphasis in original).
6 Ransom goes on to say that in "economics, chemistry, sociology, theology, and architecture ... it is taken for granted that criticism of the performance is the prerogative of the men who have had formal training in its theory and technique" ("Criticism, Inc." 593). Later, he does mount a defense of "historical scholarship" (596).
7 Ransom in "The Bases of Criticism" has the same issue with "paraphrase."
8 "The Heresy of Paraphrase" is the title of chapter 11 in Brooks's *The Well-Wrought Urn*.
9 See Karanikas's chapter VI, "The Aesthetic of Regionalism" (100–22), and chapter X, "The New Criticism" (187–210), that address the purported rejection of national culture and scientific rationalism. Gerald Graff in *Professing Literature* describes Richards's work as "semantic therapy aimed at mitigating the destructive effects of science and nationalism" (150).
10 The well-tempered clavier as a symbol of harmony, balance, and utility, constitutes the notion, from medieval Western European times, that also relates to the balance of "tempers" in the human body.
11 Fish's "Literature in the Reader," an appendix in *Surprised by Sin*, puts reading within reach of the reader, an act and a responsibility that New Critics had claimed for themselves. Jancovich argues that New Criticism itself has many of the features of post-structuralist analysis. *Rereading the New Criticism* aims to "reevaluate the New Critical corpus ... illuminate its internal heterogeneity; interrogate received ideas about it; and consider how its theories and techniques might be drawn upon toward the reinvigoration of contemporary literary and cultural studies" (Hickman and McIntyre 3).

References

Aronoff, Eric. "Anthropologists, Indians, and New Critics: Culture and/as Poetic Form in Regional Modernism." *Modern Fiction Studies*, vol. 55, no. 1, Spring 2009, pp. 92–118.

Aronoff, Eric. *Composing Cultures: Modernism, American Literary Studies, and the Problem of Culture*. U of Virginia P, 2013.

Brooks, Cleanth. "The New Criticism." *The Sewanee Review*, vol. 87, no. 4, Fall 1979, pp. 592–607.

Brooks, Cleanth. *The Well-Wrought Urn: Studies in the Structure of Poetry*. Harcourt Brace, 1947.

Eliot, T. S. "The Function of Criticism." *Selected Prose of T.S. Eliot*, edited by Frank Kermode. Harcourt Brace Jovanovich, 1975, pp. 68–76.

Eliot, T. S. "Tradition and the Individual Talent." *Selected Prose of T.S. Eliot*, edited by Frank Kermode. Harcourt Brace Jovanovich, 1975, pp. 37–44.

Felski, Rita. *The Limits of Critique*. U of Chicago P, 2015.

Fish, Stanley. *Surprised by Sin: The Reader in "Paradise Lost."* Macmillan, 1967.

Graff, Gerald. *Professing Literature: An Institutional History*. U of Chicago P, 1987.

Hickman, Miranda, and John D. McIntyre. *Rereading the New Criticism*. Ohio State UP, 2012.

Jancovich, Mark. *The Cultural Politics of the New Criticism*. Cambridge UP, 2009.

Karanikas, Alexander. *Tillers of a Myth: Southern Agrarians as Social and Literary Critics*. U of Wisconsin P, 1966.

Ransom, John Crowe. "Criticism, Inc." *Virginia Quarterly Review*, vol. 13, no. 4, Autumn, 1937, pp. 586–602.

Ransom, John Crowe. "The Poetry of 1900–1950." *Kenyon Review*, vol. 13, no. 3, Summer 1951, 445–54.

Richards, I. A. *How to Read a Page: A Course in Efficient Reading with an Introduction to a Hundred Great Words*. Beacon Press, 1959.

Richards, I. A. *Poetries and Sciences*. Routledge & Kegan Paul, 1970.

Richards, I. A. *Practical Criticism*. K. Paul, Trench, Trubner, 1929.

Richards, I. A. *Science and Poetry*. K. Paul, Trench, Trubner, 1935.

Wellek, René. "The New Criticism, Pro and Contra." *Critical Inquiry*, vol. 4, no. 4, Summer 1978, pp. 611–24.

Wellek, René, and Robert Penn Warren. *Theory of Literature*. Harcourt, Brace, 1956

Wyile, Herb. "Ransom Revisited: The Aesthetic of Regionalism in a Globalized Age." *Canadian Review of American Studies*, vol. 28, no. 2, 1998, pp. 99–118.

12

Too Literal Translation: Some Poems of Roger Fry

Rivky Mondal

Assured, then, of an authentic pleasure, Roger Fry's first impulse was to share it: he was charmed, he set himself to translate.
Charles Mauron, coeditor of Some Poems of Mallarmé, 2

*The translation of poetry is often an exercise of great profit
to him who translates and of very doubtful value to those who read it.*
Justin O'Brien, reviewer of Some Poems of Mallarmé, 382

Opening the *Poésies* with a versified greeting, Mallarmé's "Salut" instates the poet as the captain of the ship, the poem as the cup of life, and the reader as the dedicatee of the "salut," or champagne toast. The embarkation motif also introduces Mallarmé's credo that the act of artistic expression reduces the poet to flotsam. Here is how Blake Bronson-Bartlett and Robert Fernandez translate the opening quatrains:

Rien, cette écume, vierge vers	Then nothing, bright spray, hymnal holiday,
A ne désigner que la coupe;	To show us but this skin;
Telle loin se noie une troupe	Dead ahead, impacted sirens
De sirènes mainte à l'envers.	Roll perversely: a log of bodies
Nous naviguons, ô mes divers	We set our course, O rangy
Amis, moi déjà sur la poupe	Friends, I already at aft,
Vous l'avant fastueux qui coupe	You at the glinting fore which breaks
Le flot de foudres et d'hivers;	The sea's membrane of flashes and shivers
(Mallarmé, *Some Poems* 46)[1]	(Mallarmé, *Azure* 3)

Rather than begin their translation with "Nothing" ("Rien"), Bronson-Bartlett and Fernandez choose "Then," a departure which accomplishes two things: "Then" echoes "Rien" and launches the reader into the poem *in medias res*. "Then" is the first of numerous modifications that the translators perform to emulate the motif and music of the original while also mitigating the differences between French and English. For example, "The sea's membrane of flashes and shivers" elegantly evokes the sound and sensation of the eighth line's end word ("hivers"/"winters"). To preserve the delicate balance between euphony and meaning, Bronson-Bartlett and Fernandez have relinquished a portion of Mallarmé's diction, syntax, and punctuation. Their primary aim is to revive Mallarmé for twenty-first-century readers; even in their divagations they honor a "commitment to Mallarmé's sensibility and originality, his freshness and strangeness, and to the poems' ability to stand on their own and to strike, as poems, as the originals do, in English" (*Azure* xv).

Compare Bronson-Bartlett and Fernandez's voguish Mallarmé to Roger Fry's modernist Mallarmé from a century ago:

Rien, cette écume, vierge vers	Nothing! this foam and virgin verse
A ne désigner que la coupe;	To designate nought but the cup;
Telle loin se noie une troupe	Such, far off, there plunges a troop
De sirènes mainte à l'envers.	Of many Sirens upside down.
Nous naviguons, ô mes divers	We are navigating, my diverse
Amis, moi déjà sur la poupe	Friends! I already on the poop
Vous l'avant fastueux qui coupe	You the splendid prow which cuts
Le flot de foudres et d'hivers;	The main of thunders and of winters;

(SP 46–7)

Fry leaves "Nothing" and "winters" in their original position. In fact, he has retained practically every word's placement and declension. Like Bronson-Bartlett and Fernandez, Fry has translated phonetically, although his cognates sound prosaic by comparison: "vers"/"verse"; "troupe"/"troop"; "poupe"/"poop." To be sure, Fry has taken certain liberties—the addition of two exclamation marks for instance—yet they are kept to a minimum in a translation practice that copies the poem word for word. In the introduction to his translations, *Some Poems of Mallarmé*, Fry states that he has "aimed above all at literalness with so much of a rhythmic order in the sound as would not hamper that too much" (302). According to Fry, word order and prosody are the essence of Mallarmé's highly connotative verse networks, which expand and dissipate around subjects like foam or a blank page. However, Fry's "literal-exactitude" does not disseminate tone or mood; it dispels them. Mallarmé's spirit is knocked out of the poem by such lines as: "Nothing! this foam and virgin verse/To designate nought but the cup" (302). The seafaring motif and playfulness of Mallarmé's toast are dashed on literal translations that run up close to the original, and in doing so miss something essential. Whereas Bronson-Bartlett and Fernandez have captured the gist that makes Mallarmé eminently readable, Fry has made up his translation part by part, constructing a poem that looks virtually the same and yields even less meaning than the original. The Fry translation is more literal than the Bronson-Bartlett and Fernandez, but whether it is also more responsible is my central query.

When Fry's translations were published in 1936, they produced ambivalent responses. Some readers, like Harold Nicolson and Justin O'Brien, found them *irresponsible* for the literal technique implemented at the expense of meaning. According to O'Brien, their

> "literalness" ... is not likely to make for beautiful poems in English, nor does it achieve any such. The version is always painfully literal, unrhymed, and, to anyone who can translate the French words himself, contributes nothing to the understanding of the poems since it reproduces the original syntax. Mallarmé has been handled so piously that he is, if anything, more hermetic in English than in French. (383)

For O'Brien being faithful is, ironically, bad for a translator of Mallarmé. He objects to the "piousness" he detects in Fry's method. On the occasion of the translations' 1951 reprinting, Nicolson invokes Fry's determination to translate Mallarmé faithfully while discussing the futility of literal translation. He writes: "Roger Fry in his enthusiasm failed to realise that the purpose of translation is to convey *meaning* from one language to another. When there is no meaning to convey, then there is no point in translating" (7). Notably, for these two readers, the issue is not literal translation alone but the detectability of Fry's faithfulness. In his 1936 preface to *Some Poems*, Charles Mauron explicates this issue in aesthetic terms while passing off the translations' shortcomings to Mallarmé's difficulty:

> This book, as I have said, had in Roger Fry's mind no object but to give others a share in his own pleasure; but whether the reader approaches Mallarmé's poems in the original or in the English translation, he will come up against the same

obstacle—the poet's obscurity. Indeed, it is as though, in spite of the translator's efforts, *or rather in proportion to his fidelity*, Mallarmé, in half his works at least, still persisted in speaking a foreign language. Foreign in French to a Frenchman, he remains foreign to an Englishman in English. Or rather, it is the reader who feels as though he had suddenly become a foreigner. (5; emphasis added)

For Mauron, the issues in Fry's poems are not symptomatic of a translator who lacks aesthetic distance but a poet who interposes too much, pruning away his discursive presence in an impersonal poetics that cedes the initiative to words ("la disparition élocutoire du poëte, qui cède l'initiative aux mots") (Mallarmé, *Œuvres complètes* 366). Fry's "fidelity" may not make Mallarmé's poems clearer, but it does not make them more unclear by transliterating verses designed to obfuscate meaning. Fry translated word for word because it was the least obtrusive course for transmitting the poetry's essence, the word-and-sound networks. By retaining them, Fry believed he could inculcate in others his sensitivity for Mallarmé's "mysterious 'miroitement en dessous'" (SP 2). Fry adapted the translations to serve an ethical imperative of sharing aesthetic pleasure and a pedagogical project of teaching others the operations of Mallarmé's "pure poetry." What O'Brien, Nicolson, and Mauron respectively say of Fry's piousness, enthusiasm, and fidelity points to a striking bifurcation between Fry's process of translating Mallarmé and the experience of reading the translations.

Insofar as Fry respects Mallarmé's word order, are his translations responsible? Can responsibility be encoded in a method? What are we to gain from Fry's ethics of translation if not legible poetry? I approach these questions while examining Fry's equivocally responsible engagement with Mallarmé's work. One irony is the chasm between Fry's aesthetic experience of translating and the ambivalent reception of his results. The other is the imprinting of Fry's exuberance on his translation process, detached as it was from the poems' content and yet, paradoxically, attuned to the emotional intensities of poetic-formal relations. The translations mark a turning point of Fry's career, when he began extending his study of "pure" aesthetic emotion to poetry. They also, however, risk becoming irresponsible to their original; Fry's literal translations confused certain readers and alienated others, including his close friend Virginia Woolf. Drawing out the equivocalness of Fry's ethical endeavor to encourage appreciation for Mallarmé, I do not pretend to overlook the apparent flaws of the translations. Instead, I use the reception to explore how the attribution of responsibility and the ascription of aesthetic value may stand in tension with one another. In this respect, the translations' overt ethics tips the scale, so that the aesthetic badness can no longer be ignored.

Aesthetic fidelity has been a flashpoint in recent literary-critical method debates concerning critics' attachments to their texts. Rita Felski has advanced a model of "post-critical" reading that incorporates aesthetic experiences in order to dispatch "a renewed engagement with art and its entanglement with social life" (191). For Felski, reading method expresses the critic's ethos and ethics. Post-critical reading consists of "structural or formal alignment, moral allegiance, and emotional empathy" (181). While Felski's defense of post-critical reading proceeds under the sign of responsibility in its self-reported fidelity, another vantage shows that her argument's purport is confined largely to the rhetorical transformation of literary critics into characters. As David Kurnick argues, the "covert characterology, a habit of talking about interpretive choices in terms of personalities" (363) renders Felski's (and Eve Kosofsky Sedgwick's) characterological focus irresponsible in its "inattention to the seriousness of queer theoretical critique" (350–1) and its history of truth-telling. There is a striking similarity in the reception of Felski's and Fry's feeling-forward approaches, wherein the operationalizing of aesthetic experience arouses some suspicion when it is turned into a method or speech act. It is as though the semi-public demonstration of aesthetic fidelity, while responsible, cannot be uncontroversial, if a little off-putting. Borrowing Sedgwick's term for the virtual witnessing space around a performative, Kurnick suggests that such displays are "periperformative," citing his own "incomprehension and sometimes irritation" when faced with "the hortatory, cheeriness-mandating critical tradition that has grown up in the wake of 'Paranoid Reading and Reparative Reading'—a tradition that sometimes appears to operate as if the announcement that one speaks reparatively were sufficient to repair anyone in hearing range" (365). The antipathy expressed by Kurnick echoes the responses to Fry's translations, a reception that contradicts Fry's stated intentions to reconstruct Mallarmé responsibly and to assist readers in their pleasure. Fry's poems provide a case study to think through "the performative contradiction—the discrepancy between rhetorical effect and self-report—that characterizes our method conversations generally," which implicates the presupposition that a critic's ethics can be inferred from their method—or, in the context of translation, that words inscribed on a page can transmit a translator's ethical intentions (Kurnick 362). Ironically, readers' tendency to infer Fry's fidelity from his literal method tinged their evaluations of *Some Poems*, leading them to misconstrue Fry's enthusiasm. However, if Fry's efforts adulterate the poems, then they can also justify a responsible rereading.

* * *

Fry's name means little in translation studies, although it stands for far more in art history, where he is remembered for bringing Cubist and Fauve paintings to London with exhibitions in 1910 and 1912, and selling modernist furniture and decoration with a collective of artists in the Omega Workshops. In his scholarly work, Fry promoted a concept of "significant form" that isolates the formal relations of art which viewers experience through pure and detached "aesthetic emotions."[2] Initially, Fry discounted literature from his investigations into aesthetic purity because it was encumbered by representations that pulled the reader out of the work; it could not therefore elicit the "pure" emotion of a Cézanne still-life. For Fry, "the vague and blurred mental images which words call up" prevented poetry from "appeal[ing] more directly and immediately to the emotional accompaniments of our bare physical existence" ("An Essay in Aesthetics" 147, 35). Fry's position that literature could not affect individuals so viscerally as a painting provided grist for many debates with Woolf.

Fry's turn to translation around 1918 undermined some of his most dogmatic claims about modern art. Instead, his translations sought to delineate continuities between literature and painting in their production of aesthetic emotion. In 1914, he wrote that he was "confident that great poetry arouses aesthetic emotions of a similar kind to painting and architecture" ("A New Theory of Art" 159); in 1917, he asserted before Virginia Woolf and Clive Bell that "all art is representative" (Woolf, *Diary* 80).[3] According to Christopher Reed, "the effect is to preserve the formalist belief in the attitude of detached or 'disinterested' contemplation that Fry insisted characterized aesthetic experience, while abandoning the old dogma that only abstract form would provoke such a response" (in Fry, *Reader* 320). No poet better epitomized a detached responsiveness to formal relations than Mallarmé. Around 1918, when Fry first met Mauron and began contemplating the semantic "auras" of words, he started to treat Mallarmé as a demonstration case.

Roused by Mallarmé's reputation as the "first poet to aim consciously and deliberately at purity," Fry declared him "an interesting case for esthetic theory, since we may distinguish more easily in his work than elsewhere the nature of pure poetic form" (SP 289). For Fry the quintessential quality of Mallarmé's poetry, and all poetry as an artistic medium, was the "sequence of word-images and their auras"—a discovery that cued up previous arguments on the moving qualities of pictorial form (296). In a theory elaborated circuitously in *Some Poems*, Fry states that every word in a poem contains an "aura" of associations invoked by "verbal images" (300). The "aura" of one word interacts with others, so that "when a second word is joined to the first (as for instance in apposition, or an adjective to a noun) this changes the aura of the first word, expanding, contracting or colouring it as the case may be" (290). Fry extrapolates this idea to Mallarmé: in his poems, words are placed in unexpected sequences so that verbal images and sounds mingle in surprising ways that are pleasurable to detect. Mallarmé divulges the "essence of poetry" by simplifying its most rudimentary operation: shifting words into relations that "attain the maximum of evocative energy" so that the relations *become* the meaning of the poem (290, emphasis added). In "Soupir"/"Sigh," the poem's structure thematizes its central idea: parted in the middle by a caesura, the poem marks the breathing in and out of a sigh (see Figure 12.1). Metaphorically, the partition conveys the poet's imagination distending toward an unreachable Idea—"vers l'Azur!"—then its expiration as the Idea eludes expression.[4] The "cross-correspondences and interpenetrations" between the cleft structure and the metaphor of a sigh make up the poem's meaning (300). Roger Pearson notes that in "Sigh" and other early

Figure 12.1

Soupir (Stéphane Mallarmé)	Sigh (Roger Fry)
Mon âme vers ton front où rêve, ô calme sœur,	My soul toward your brow where dreams, my calm sister,
Un automne jonché de taches de rousseur	An autumn scattered with freckles of russet
Et vers le ciel errant de ton œil angélique	And the wandering heaven of your angelic eye
Monte, comme dans un jardin mélancolique,	Mounts up as in some melancholical gardens
Fidèle, un blanc jet d'eau soupire vers l'Azur!	Faithful, a white jet sighs toward the Azure!
—Vers l'Azur attendri d'Octobre pâle et pur	—Toward October's tender, pure and pale Azure
Qui mire aux grands bassins sa langueur infinie	Which reflects in great basins its infinite languor
Et laisse, sur l'eau morte où la fauve agonie	And lets, on dead water where the tawny death-throes
Des feuilles erre au vent et creuse un froid sillon,	Of leaves wander windswept and scoop a cold furrow,
Se traîner le soleil jaune d'un long rayon.	The yellow sun creep of a long-drawn-out ray.
	(SP 48–9)

poems "Mallarmé's pursuit of formal symmetry leads to a proliferation of internal linguistic relationships which then threaten to overwhelm the referential, traditionally extra-textual function of language." In this regard, a "Structuralist Mallarmé is born: the creator of texts in which words derive meaning from their relationships with other words rather than from their conventional and arbitrary referents in the world. And a Post-structuralist Mallarmé is conceived: the willing, passive instrument of words which have more to say than he can ever foresee or adequately control" (Pearson 41).

To recreate Mallarmé's expressive design, Fry carries over the "word-image sequence" and its "melodic effect" to render the poem's "cumulative effect" (SP 297). In his translation, Fry hews close to the word order, approximates the syllable count, and achieves an occasional couplet. What are carried out as protocols of a translation that prioritizes literalness also point to an imagination that merges poetry with visual art. Fry rearranges the line following the caesura ("—Vers l'Azur attendri d'Octobre pâle et pur") so that it ends with "Azure" rather than "pale and pure," which would have made for a more exact translation. It is possible that Fry wanted to array each adjective of Azure—"tender, pure and pale"—to foreground their sensuous qualities. Other translation choices indicate a decision pattern that highlights image-like aspects: "taches de rousseur" is translated as "freckles of russet." "The literal translation is, of course, 'an autumn, splashed with freckles,'" Fry states in a note, "but 'taches de rousseur' conveys a colour sensation which is lacking in 'freckles' and 'russet' is necessary to complete the image" (SP 184). It appears that Fry is balancing between literal meaning and something more: a mental image of a poem as a composition of colors and signs. In the same poem, he translates "Se traîner le soleil jaune d'un long rayon" into "The yellow sun creep of a long-drawn-out ray." The sunray seems longer in Fry's version: the translation expresses both its length and the materiality of drawing. These choices are consistent enough to index a strategy that magnifies Mallarmé's visual figures. In addition to translating the word order and rhythm, Fry wrote in his aesthetic experience of the poem's "cumulative effect."

Fry's literalness does not involve simply finding the best equivalent for certain word and rhythm patterns. It also turns words into "word-images." According to Jacques Rancière, the transformation of "figurative particulars into events of pictorial matter" is a mode of "literalization" that places word and image on an equal semantic plane (80, 81). Fry's literalness develops an aesthetic uniformity that moves a Mallarmé poem into an "interface that transfers the images into the text and the text into the images" (89). Counterintuitively, Fry's theory of aesthetic purity does not depend on the particularity of any medium. It emphasizes relations between the arts: the quality that Fry deems essential to Mallarmé's method of arranging words into expressive orders links his poetry to modernist painting. According to Fry, Mallarmé's aesthetic attention to domestic knick-knacks is second only to that of still-life painters (SP 300), and his practice of reconstructing a theme after first breaking it down to pieces "anticipate[s] by many years the methods of some Cubist painters" (301). Fry's translations cast Mallarmé's poetry into a form that is more painterly than sentimental.[5] Given that "the essential quality of [Mallarmé's] method" derives from the "impassioned contemplation of [the] poetical relations" of a subject or a theme that subordinates what is "noble and impressive, or entirely trivial and commonplace," Fry claims literalness as a technique to emulate the neutralizing perspective that treats all words with the same degree of importance or unimportance (300).

What reviewers lamented in Fry's translation—the word-for-word retention of Mallarmé's untranslatable syntax—appears to be the result of Fry's rendering in English the verses he had experienced as aesthetically satisfying. Because Fry believed in the pleasure of inter-art relations, he may have accentuated the sensuous elements so that the reader could perceive what he perceived, demonstrating aesthetic effects by making them. In the "freckles of russet" example, Fry's translation expresses a desire to be image-like, then *literalizes* that desire by pulling out visual elements for the reader to witness. Fry's translations overlap with the "peculiar ideological contradiction" that Lawrence Venuti observes in modernist translation, particularly Ezra Pound's "The Seafarer," in which "the development of textual strategies that decenter the transcendental subject" in the service of poetic impersonality "coincides with a recuperation of it through certain individualistic motifs like the 'strong personality'" (Venuti 29–30). The boundary between impersonality and personality, aesthetic distance and lack thereof, is figured by Fry's literalness. In a translation where all options are ostensibly the same, certain phrases are marked out for the reader's attention. Even as Fry disappears into his inscrutable poems, his personality emanates through the ardor of his introduction and the testimonies in Mauron's preface. Fry's oath to aesthetic emotion and literal translation reemphasizes the ironies of impersonality theory's relationship to modernism's aesthetic production.[6]

Strikingly, Fry's translations want to have it both ways: the pose of aesthetic impersonality—that elevated perspective which sees words as nondiscursive images—with the aspiration that poetic forms could excite the reader as they excited Fry. His theory is not exceptional in its competing interests, however. "Of course it is a minor paradox of modernist impersonality," writes Jed Esty, "that only a poet susceptible to great sweeps and dark depths of feeling need invent, and so rigorously continue to reinvent, such means of distantiation—those masks and poses, those baffled or etiolated desires" (315). The paradox is minor in part because, insofar as impersonality is deployed to purge aesthetic experience of subjectivity and other distracting elements, such avoidance tactics do not hinder the search for alternative ambits of feeling. For Fry, retreating into the purity of aesthetic emotion never meant withdrawing from pleasure, individual or social. Rather it meant finding a similar mediating perspective in Mallarmé. In the translation choices I flag, Fry interacts with Mallarmé's preoccupation to discover a poetic language that "paints not the thing but the effect it produces" ("Peindre non la chose, mais l'effet qu'elle produit."), the keystone of Fry's late aesthetic theory.[7] In cultivating closeness through formal complementarity, Fry stands apart from Pound, W. B. Yeats, T. S. Eliot, and other modernist practitioners of impersonality for whom, in Sharon Cameron's terms, "the perception of difference, of polarity— in its most extreme form, of contradiction—is a means of emerging from a point of view" (14). Working his way into Mallarmé's perspective, Fry re-personalizes Mallarmé's detachment through corresponding formal relations.

The tension in Fry's translations manifests more abrasively in what Cameron calls the "frictive relation between the experiential and the doctrinal," between reading his poems and theorizing about them (176). Fry's literalness offended some not because it misapplied his credo of detachment, but because it produced bad poems while claiming aesthetic fidelity. For certain readers, the translations were saved by Fry's *effort* to conduct them responsibly: the commitments which undermine the translations can also redeem them.

* * *

Fry's literal translations mystified close friends and successive generations of critics. Letters from Vanessa Bell and Virginia Woolf from 1916 and 1920 reveal polite bemusement, tactfully pinning the translations' impenetrability on Mallarmé's French (Caws and Wright 364). "I think the translations are extremely interesting—also very difficult," Woolf writes. "The difficulty may be partly that I've left my Mallarmé in London, and thus can't compare them with the French. But I've no doubt at all that they're very good, and give one the same strange feeling as he does" (*Letters* 439).[8] Reflecting on a day in Fry's company, Clive Bell lists in itinerary that Fry is "back in time for an early tea so that he can drag Vanessa and Duncan to Wilmington to paint landscape; after dinner just runs through a few of Mallarmé's poems, which he is translating word for word into what he is pleased to consider blank verse; bedtime—'Oh just time for a game of chess, Julian'" (Woolf, *Roger Fry* 288). Fry's Bloomsbury readers appear to appreciate the sociality of using translation to share aesthetic enjoyment; meanwhile they insinuate the oddity of the result. A similar splitting happens in the contemporary reception of *Some Poems*. In one of the more even-handed reviews, Morton Dauwen Zabel observes that Fry's aim is to teach others how to read Mallarmé. Calling Fry's book a "primer," Zabel suggests that the translations provide a "practical basis" for understanding Mallarmé and the abstract concept of "pure poetry" that "underlie[s] modern poetics from Coleridge, Poe, and Baudelaire to … Paul Valéry" (354, 351). Zabel appreciates that Fry proffers "actual poetic examples" which show "the connection between this literal verbal content and the poetry achieved for it through sound, rhythm, lyric and symbolic form." At the same time, he finds that "the manner of Fry's translation is the most debatable feature of the book." Zabel surmises thus: "Working on the assumption that of all untranslatable poetry Mallarmé's is the most extreme case, he apparently wanted to give his versions only the typographical appearance of poems" (352–3). That the translations emphasize the poems' visual appearance is a drawback. Their weakness is characterizable in their wanting to make poetry into painting: "the result is neither passable verse nor intelligent English" (353). Even as Zabel affirms Fry's unique usage of literal translation to educate readers in Mallarmé's verse structures, his evaluation breaks off at the aesthetic result that seems to overturn the work's good motives.

Other critics could not help but notice the incongruence of Fry's enthusiasm and the cumbersome method adopted to stoke readers' interest. O'Brien recognizes the fidelity behind the translations without acceding to it, instead reading Fry's promotion of Mallarmé as a careerist move: "And now it is revealed that Roger Fry, who with typewriter and pigment devoted a lifetime to translating Cézanne into English, went to great effort to do the same for Mallarmé" (382). The same goes for Nicolson: "I can see Roger Fry, with his eager entrancing smile, positively crooning over his absurd translations. Did he convert as many people to Mallarmé as he converted to Post-Impressionism? I doubt it, although his enthusiasm was infectious" (7). Nicolson and O'Brien draw on their knowledge of Fry's defenses of post-impressionism to read the translations as a ham-fisted attempt to mainstream more difficult French art. They find Fry's literalness ridiculous, although arguably more displeasing is his certainty that the translations could cultivate appreciation for Mallarmé.

These reported responses to *Some Poems* mark a stark separation from Fry's aesthetic process of translating. For Zabel, the instructional value of Fry's translations is compromised by the results, while for O'Brien and Nicolson, Fry's venture to elucidate Mallarmé appears quixotic. If the word-aura theory behind the translations was lost on reviewers who saw only their literalness, then this set of ambivalent reactions ironically affirms Fry's theory about aesthetic emotion. The reviews *untheoretically* illustrate Fry's argument that a translator must arrange the poem in a way that looks good and sounds right. However, the faithfulness emitted from Fry's literalness is as meaningful as it is meaningless in the reading of the poems. Even though aesthetic fidelity seems to call for an affirmative response, Fry's reception shows that the ethics behind the translations is easily stamped out.

If Fry's intentions do not in themselves warrant calling the translations responsible, then perhaps his enthusiasm, the sweetening effect of his industry, does. More recently, the fact of Fry's meticulousness has led scholars to temper their judgments of the translations. In these scenarios, scholars handle *Some Poems* with ambivalence, to be sure, but evenly account for Fry's effort to translate Mallarmé's "word-image complex" within the joint contexts of his experiential study of aesthetic emotion and his art criticism. In their "collective biography" of the Bloomsbury Group, Mary Ann Caws and Sarah Bird Wright note that "Fry believed, understandably, that translation was the best way of getting to the spirit of a poet, and, less understandably, that the French alexandrian (twelve syllables) could be rendered by the English blank verse (ten syllables) if certain liberties were taken with the syllable count" (274).[9] Caws and Wright appreciate that Fry touches down to earth to examine aesthetic emotion in the company of his familiars, while looking askance at the translations' "blank verse." At the same time, they invoke Fry's convictions to draw out the translations' latent drives: "Reflecting on the complex problems of translation, Roger Fry was fascinated by the mental recasting it forces on the mind … Fry spoke of 'the dangerous ease of French,' arguing that it could eclipse a person's original ideas because of the 'many attractive and ready-made moulds into which one's thoughts can flow'" (351). That Fry used translation to inhabit another artist's mind corresponds with Sam Rose's description of the "introspective detachment" of his art criticism: Fry inferred artists' "forming activity" from the formal elements of their paintings (55, 3). Fry's translations appear to follow the rules of his visual-formalist analyses inasmuch as his insights are "achieved not quite through writing *as if* the artist," but rather "allow the reader to see the work *as* the artist … Fry instead offers a report back to the viewer from the position of one who has examined the work from within the artist's vision, who has time traveled via the apprehension of form and has now come back to tell about it" (58–9).

Fry's responsibility therefore lies in his receptivity to Mallarmé's emulatable model of aesthetic experience. Mallarmé, a poet interested in Impressionist painting and Wagner's music, was exemplary for Fry, who, by the 1920s and 1930s, was working at the junction of arts. Moreover, Mallarmé adopted a literal technique to translate the correspondences between poetry and music in Edgar Allan Poe's "The Raven."[10] Given that Fry used literal translation to orient himself to Mallarmé's process and ethos, how are these translations anything but responsible? The question can be answered succinctly: the translations are bad poems. And yet, instead of pointing automatically to failure, the ambivalent responses bring out the complexity of binding to another artist's point of view and *intentio*. If Fry's enthusiasm creates problems for readers, beginning with translations that are openly responsible yet less compelling as a result, could not this same enthusiasm be what makes the translations readable at all? In other words, could we reassemble the paradox so that the sheer industry behind *Some Poems* diverts some of its aesthetic badness?

In a work titled *Surprised in Translation*, Caws revisits Fry's translations after dismissing them, arguing that Fry's "literal edifice" must be valued alongside "his sustained effort in constructing it. His unchallenged stature as a critic and his enthusiasm for all his projects easily outweigh any hesitation we might have over his results" (48). Caws's stance becomes less absolute when she adds in her doubts about Fry's literalness. Here she recounts her reunion with the translations:

> Roger Fry's immense generosity of spirit meant he had everything to give to what he loved, and you can feel that in his own poems, in his own translations of Rimbaud, Baudelaire, and particularly Mallarmé. I have been poring over the manuscripts of those, and marveling now at their precision. I used to reject their literality, preferring suggestion to statement as I thought Mallarmé would. Yet now I see Fry's mind at work, seeing just how the same sorts of things we lament, and he sometimes lamented in his painting—the static quality, the lack of emotion—show through in his translations, even as his musical ear is just. Let me give an example of that precision, that justness from *Hérodiade*: trying out equivalents for "seul," he tries "solitary," then "lonely," and ends up with "lone." That seems to me just right, like the less ordinary "fierceness" chosen over "ferocity"; for "décroître," he tries "ungrow," then opts for "grow less," tries out "aether" before settling on "azure." If God is anywhere in the details, it is certainly in such translations. (49–50)

Caws's self-report marks her initial failure to treat Fry's translations with the same industry with which they treat themselves. Confronting her skepticism, she sees the translation with new eyes and with Fry's re-enchanting touch. Note that "literality" becomes "precision" and finally "justness"; the bad aesthetic of the poems is absorbed into Fry's palpable effort to find the word that is right for Mallarmé and right for *us*. Much like Robert Baines applies post-structuralist concepts to puzzle out the "equivocity" of Joyce's manuscripts in his chapter in this volume, Caws turns to genetic criticism to account for the multivalent senses and significations in Fry's process of translating.[11] From the negligible difference between "ungrow" and "grow less," Caws infers the workings of a mind stretching to find the conclusive "word-image" with which to stimulate the reader. As Fry does with Mallarmé, Caws takes over the poems, empirically discovering the author's *intentio* in his writing tics and finding justifications for Fry's thinking within her own.

Insofar as "Mallarmé has been handled so piously that he is, if anything, more hermetic in English than in French," then the translations have succeeded, despite much self-problematizing, to render the effects of Mallarmé's obscurity (O'Brien 383). However, Fry's poems are impenetrable in ways that perhaps Mallarmé's poems are not: their difficulty lies not in their intellectual profundity but in their overzealous intellectualizing. To begin understanding them, two paths are laid open to us: examine the ways in which they do (or don't) realize Fry's aesthetic fidelity or meet Fry halfway and match his efforts in re-personalization. I prefer the second. It is as if we need to make a project out of inhabiting Fry's mind to make sense of his poems. To an extent, *Some Poems* challenges us to better define and defend the reports of aesthetic experience that Fry believed to be self-evidently persuasive. The translations are interesting for their oddly overdesigned-yet-makeshift quality, which prompts the reader to accompany Fry in examining the differences between his poems and the originals. They therefore require an interpretative labor that is not primarily concerned with determining what the poems mean but why they are aesthetically significant to a particular person. Fry's translations place the reader in the same position as Mallarmé's poems by making the task, in the words of Mauron, "less to solve riddles than to get used to a way of thinking which is very unlikely to be his own" (SP 13). Fry used literal translation to direct the reader's attention to what he deemed noteworthy. In the end, he shows that literal translation proves better at revealing things about the original than the original is itself.

* * *

Acknowledgments

This essay has taken on many shapes over the years and crossed the desks of many attentive readers. Thank you to Christopher Reed for overseeing the first draft in a graduate course on the Bloomsbury Group and for sharing precious archival materials. I appreciate the many audiences furnished for the essay by various panels, workshops, and reading groups: no amount of gratitude could repay the support of Jonathan P. Eburne and the Modern and Contemporary Studies Initiative; the Berkeley-Stanford graduate conference on "Mimesis and Mutation"; the Modernist Studies Association panel organized by Laura Hartmann-Villalta; and the 20th/21st-Century Workshop convened by Jean-Thomas Tremblay and Nell Pach. Thank you especially to Rachel Galvin, Sianne Ngai, Julie Orlemanski, and Jennifer Scappettone for their electrifying feedback, and to Madison Chapman, Jacob Harris, Sarah McDaniel, Brandon Truett, Rebeca Velasquez, and Michal Zechariah for their encouragement. This essay will encounter new readers because of Stephen Ross. My most emphatic thanks go to him.

Notes

1 Hereafter referred to as "SP" in the text.
2 See Bell ("The Aesthetic Hypothesis" 3–37). Fry's specifications for "significant form" and "aesthetic emotion" were consonant with but never identical to Bell's; see Rose (20–5). For a definition of significant form mediated through affect theory, see Yan Tang's essay in this volume. Tang provides an excellent overview of the varieties of aesthetic emotion bolstered by Virginia Woolf, W. B. Yeats, and Ford Madox Ford to conceptualize the ethics of externalizing private aesthetic experiences. Tang argues for the "imbrication of affect and ideology" within both modernism and the affect theory of Silvan Tomkins vis-à-vis Eve Kosofsky Sedgwick and Adam Frank (xx).
3 Qtd. in November 22, 1917 diary entry of Virginia Woolf.
4 Marie Rolf provides an exhaustive close reading of "Soupir" that includes a diagram which visualizes the poem's "arch form" and the structural mirroring between the first "inhalation or upbeat followed by an exhalation or release of tension" (194). See her remarkable essay on "Semantic and Structural Issues in Debussy's Mallarmé Songs."
5 I have Jennifer Scappettone to thank for this brilliant insight.

6 For the "ideological tension as well as a conceptual instability" of modernist impersonality, see Ellmann. For a recontextualization that multiplies the theories as well as the ontologies of impersonality, see Rives.
7 Mallarmé in a letter to Henri Cazalis, October 1864, qtd. in Œuvres complètes, 1440.
8 Letter to Roger Fry dated August 13, 1920.
9 In his introduction to the translations, Fry acknowledges the misalignment between meter and word order with a "note of failure" (SP 302).
10 See Lukes (745–63). Fry's approach to translation bears a striking resemblance to Mallarmé's. According to Lukes, "Rather than focusing on the reproduction of form or the rendition of content, translating, for Mallarmé, consists of developing relations and correspondences, which put into the words of a foreign language the sonorous effects of the original" (761). Neither Fry nor Mauron mentions Mallarmé's translations in *Some Poems*.
11 See Baines, "The Positive of the Negative: Joycean Post-Structuralism as Felskian Critique," this volume, xx.

References

Bell, Clive. "The Aesthetic Hypothesis." *Art*. Chatto & Windus, 1914, pp. 3–37.

Cameron, Sharon. *Impersonality: Seven Essays*. U of Chicago P, 2007.

Caws, Mary Ann. *Surprised in Translation*. U of Chicago P, 2006.

Caws, Mary Ann, and Sarah Bird Wright. *Bloomsbury and France: Art and Friends*. Oxford UP, 1999.

Ellmann, Maud. *The Poetics of Impersonality: T.S. Eliot and Ezra Pound*. Edinburgh UP, 2013.

Esty, Jed. "All that Consequence: Yeats and Eliot at the End of the End of History." *Yeats and Afterwords: Christ, Culture, and Crisis*, edited by Marjorie Howes and Joseph Valente. U of Notre Dame P, 2014, pp. 314–36.

Felski, Rita. *The Limits of Critique*. U of Chicago P, 2015.

Fry, Roger. *Letters of Roger Fry*, vol. 1, edited by Denys Sutton. Random House, 1972.

Fry, Roger. *A Roger Fry Reader*, edited and with introductory essays by Christopher Reed. U of Chicago P, 1996.

Fry, Roger. *Vision and Design*. Chatto & Windus, 1920.

Kurnick, David. "A Few Lies: Queer Theory and Our Method Melodramas." *ELH*, vol. 87, no. 2, Summer 2020, pp. 349–74.

Levenson, Michael. *A Genealogy of Modernism: A Study of English Literary Doctrine 1908–1922*. Cambridge UP, 1984.

Lukes, Alexandra. "Dictionary and Divination: Mallarmé Translating, Back-Translating, and Not Translating." *MLN*, vol. 134, no. 4, September, 2019, pp. 745–63.

Mallarmé, Stéphane. *Azure: Poems and Selections from the "Livre,"* translated by Blake Bronson-Bartlett and Robert Fernandez. Wesleyan UP, 2015.

Mallarmé, Stéphane. *Œuvres complètes de Stéphane Mallarmé*. Gallimard, 1951.

Mallarmé, Stéphane. *Some Poems of Mallarmé*, translated by Roger Fry, edited by Charles Mauron and Julian Bell. New Directions, 1951 [1936].

Nicolson, Harold. "Associations." *The Observer*, February 24, 1952, p. 7.

O'Brien, Justin. "Review of *Some Poems of Stéphane Mallarmé*." *Romanic Review*, vol. 28, no. 4, December, 1937, pp. 382–4.

Pearson, Roger. *Unfolding Mallarmé: The Development of a Poetic Art*. Clarendon Press, 1996.

Rancière, Jacques. *The Future of the Image*, translated by Gregory Elliott. Verso, 2009.

Rives, Rochelle. *Modernist Impersonalities: Affect, Authority, and the Subject*. Palgrave Macmillan, 2012.

Rolf, Marie. "Semantic and Structural Issues in Debussy's Mallarmé Songs." *Debussy Studies*, edited by Richard Langham Smith. Cambridge UP, 1997, pp.179–200.

Rose, Sam. *Art and Form: From Roger Fry to Global Modernism*. Pennsylvania State Press, 2019.

Venuti, Lawrence. *The Translator's Invisibility: A History of Translation*. Routledge, 2008.

Woolf, Virginia. *The Diary of Virginia Woolf, Volume 1: 1915–1919*, edited by Anne Olivier Bell. Harcourt Brace Jovanovich, 1977.

Woolf, Virginia. *The Letters of Virginia Woolf: Volume 2, 1912–1922*, edited by Nigel Nicolson and Joanne Trautmann. Harcourt Brace Jovanovich, 1976.

Woolf, Virginia. *Roger Fry: A Biography*. Harcourt, Brace, 1940.

Zabel, Morton Dauwen. "A Mallarmé Primer," *Poetry*, vol. 49, no. 6, March, 1937, pp. 350–4.

13

Afterword: Necessary–Impossible and Responsible–Irresponsible Reading

Paul K. Saint-Amour

Responsible reading. I was deterred by the phrase at first: there's a bit of wrist-slap and finger-wag in it, as if the reader had been caught veering off a narrow path and were about to be brusquely set back on it. The expression seemed to me to promise either a set of indisputable claims about academic integrity or a load of interpretive norms heavy on Thou-shalt-nots. Imagine my chagrin, then, at learning that the contributors to this volume had drawn the adjective "responsible" from, among other sources, an essay of mine. There I expressed my hope that the special journal issue I was introducing would irritate the field of modernist studies into a state of self-scrutiny that might generate "fresh methods and collaborations, needed forms of humility and responsibility, unforeseen kinds of projects, and renewed or new reasons for undertaking them" (442). The term came into sharper focus when I characterized two kinds of expansion in the field: one animated by a sense of responsibility to move beyond the conventional modernist canon, and the other by a sense of entitlement to expand into any disciplinary space one wished. Responsibility, I suggested, could act variously as a warrant for and as a restraint upon the exercise of entitlement. In the spirit of restraint, I asked, "[H]ow might an ethics of humility help us to responsibly weak ways of engaging works, persons, subjects, and areas that we aren't entitled to engage strongly?" (454). But what, exactly, were these responsibly weak ways of engaging works? Was the responsibility in weak engagement the same as the responsibility to open up the modernist canon? Were only weak things responsible?

That a term so weakly theorized—in that essay, at least—could help catalyze such a varied and compelling collection as the present one is a tribute to Stephen Ross and the other contributors to *Modernism, Theory, and Responsible Reading*.

It also supports my argument in the same essay that weakly defined terms and concepts can, under the right circumstances, serve more readily as centers of collective attachment and innovation than strenuously defined ones. But rather than respond to this volume from the perspective of "Weak Theory, Weak Modernism," I'd like to engage the concept of responsible reading in some of the ways it's explored, modeled, and theorized in the preceding pages, giving it as full a consideration as space and my own capacities allow.

The first portrait of responsible reading that one encounters, in Ross's introduction, is of a "middle ground" or "third way" between critique and post-critique, "a principled way forward, a dialectical progression that can at once cancel and preserve" both adversaries in the stalemate (xx). Such a middle way is necessary, in Ross's account, because critique and post-critique exhibit failures of responsibility. Critique, at its most bloody-minded, can be "but little concerned with the responsibility to the wider complexity and challenge of cultural objects, their producers, and their consumers" (xx). Post-critique, for its part, can be so bent on reading as a site of attachment and reparation that it declines to consider whether some readerly attachments and their objects may be irreparably complicit in morally indefensible worldviews. (Ross implies this in wondering aloud "what it would look like to try a post-critical reading with *Heart of Darkness*" [xx].) Responsible reading would cancel the excesses of critique and post-critique while preserving their more defensible attributes. It would keep the operation of critique but wrest it away from the critic-as-heroic-revolutionist, siting it in the cultural object itself. It would retain post-critique's with-the-grain orientation toward its objects but not its wholesale animus toward critique. Responsible reading would proceed in a way Ross describes in measured, modest terms: as "fair"—a word he rescues from throwaway comments by Bruno Latour and Rita Felski—and "principled" (xx).

The first thing that strikes me about this portrait of responsibility is how absolutely it seems to depart from the post-structuralist models that largely powered the "ethical turn" of the 1990s and 2000s. Touched off in literary studies by Derrida's writings on Levinas and developed further by Judith Butler and many others, these models figured responsibility in terms that were anything but measured or modest, and certainly uninterested in a middle ground or third way. They understood responsibility to be extreme to the point of limitlessness, and therefore to produce several kinds of impasse. Because I have limitless responsibility to the singular other but limited resources of time and attention, they held, responsibility will only ever be an asymptote I approach, and seldom very nearly. Even more terribly, my limitless responsibility to the other may require me to act in ways that are irresponsible to others. To invoke a key instance in Derrida's *The Gift of Death*, Abraham's responsibility to God required him to commit an act of child-murder irresponsible—indeed monstrous—in the eyes of the ethical order to each member of which and to whose totality he was also responsible. What condemns the concept of responsibility "*a priori* to paradox, scandal, and aporia," according to Derrida, is my owing every subject a responsibility no less absolute for being incompatible with my other responsibilities: "I cannot respond to the call, the request, the obligation, or even the love of another without sacrificing the other other, the other others" (69). Given that in everyday life I must sacrifice ethics in even attempting to behave ethically toward a particular other, I can never pride myself on having acted responsibly. Much less am I justified in preaching to others about the nature and dimensions of their ethical responsibility, as those whom Derrida dubs "the knights of good conscience" like to do (68).

This volume's framing of responsibility-in-reading as sublating critique, post-critique, and their opposition through dialectics may come across, then, as an attempt to advance us to a new opposition: between post-structuralist notions of responsibility and a more practicable, less paradoxical conception of responsibility. We could even express this opposition as one between a strong theory of responsibility (as limitless and aporetic) and a weak theory of responsibility (as measured, unblocked, and principle-oriented). In that case, the contributors to *Modernism, Theory, and Responsible Reading* would appear to advocate a weak theory of responsibility. But the preceding essays, in fact, draw repeatedly on the dynamics and insights of post-structuralist ethics, if not always on its vocabulary. We encounter one such engagement when Fabio Akcelrud Durão posits that to read "Theory" responsibly is to de-instrumentalize it, a move that follows Theory's lead in declining to know or seek to know everything about its objects. We meet another when Kathryn Carney, drawing on the work of philosopher Alia Al-Saji, characterizes hesitation as "the moment of responsibility's emergence," the portal or pore through which an unending practice of responsibility enters the critical act (xx). In Masami Sugimori's "Weak Theory, 'Responsible' Reading, and Literary Criticism," we find the central paradox of post-structuralist ethics—the aporia of the necessary–impossible—in "the dilemma that a critic *has to work* on the *impossible* mission of fully capturing the infinitely multifaceted object" (xx; emphasis added). Ross, for his part, invokes Levinasian ethics in the introduction's second half in order to advocate "resting uneasily in incomplete knowledge" of a cultural object rather than to certify its "ultimately untouchable otherness" (xx). Here, as in the other instances, responsibility veers not toward the measured but toward the limitless, the scholar being "compelled to respond to [the cultural object] without ever being able to do so adequately" (xx).

Fascinatingly, all of the passages I've just cited imagine responsibility as an obligation not toward other *subjects* but toward cultural *objects*. In some of these cases—Durão, perhaps Sugimori—the writer may simply be using the analogy of ethics to urge scholars to practice epistemological humility toward their objects. Matthew Gannon places the object at the center of Adornian aesthetic responsibility but only briefly alludes to its analogous place in Adorno's ethics. Ross, however, states plainly that the artwork *is* an ethical other: "We must accept that works have the status of actors: they are others toward which we are oriented, which regard us (in the dual sense of seeing us and pertaining to us), and to which we owe a just response" (xx).[1] This is to go well beyond post-critical invitations by Sharon Marcus and Stephen Best, Heather Love, Rita Felski, and others to read with the grain of the cultural object. It's also to exceed Bruce Robbins's recent reminder, in a response to Felski, that "critique is often unambiguously organic to the texts themselves" (372).[2] Although Ross elsewhere declines to outfit the cultural object with an "ultimately untouchable otherness" (xx), the formulation quoted above implies that cultural works are possessed of the same radical singularity and ethical faciality—a "regard" that obliges—as persons, and are therefore owed the same limitless responsibility that persons are. Levinas, who doubted that even snakes have faces in the ethical sense, never went this far, and one doesn't have to share his avowed anthropocentrism to wonder about the ramifications of treating inanimate objects and animate beings as ethically coplanar (171). Eric Hayot has argued that Western humanists' tendency to conflate the singularity of the artwork with that of the person is at least as old as the homologies between Kant's aesthetics and ethics. But the methodological questions that follow from a view of cultural objects as ethical singularities can only have grown more numerous as literary methods have continued to multiply. If artworks are singular others, what happens to critical approaches that understand individual works as participating in abstract sets such as genre or the commodity form? How does one responsibly study the historical, sociological, demographic, and economic forces that shape a work? Can any quantitative methods be considered responsible by these lights? As Hayot puts it, "At the limit of the ethical relation to the singular, each object would have to produce a completely unique method, even a unique language" (473).

You'll wrestle as you will with the claim that we owe a just response to cultural works, and with the ethical and epistemological frameworks in which that claim participates. As for locating that claim within current theoretical developments, the ethical coplanarity it implies between inanimate objects and animate beings clearly partakes in the flat ontologies explored by recent new materialist work, which has itself been an important tributary to post-critique via figures such as Latour and Felski. But I'd like to suggest that this volume's invitation to consider cultural objects as obligingly singular in the manner of persons might also lead us back to modernism, specifically, and thus to a sense of what the title words *modernism, theory,* and *responsible reading* might signal together. For what is distinctive about the "high" modernist artwork if not the tendency to assert its own alterity—and, by means of that assertion, to demand that its reader or beholder or translator (see Rivky Mondal's essay on Roger Fry's Mallarmé translations) accord it limitless responsiveness and attention? Together, the ancillary documents of literary modernism—the agenda-setting prefaces and manifestos, the annotations and schemata—frame reading as a scene of unprecedented encounter with a singular work. (Significantly, one doesn't find Victorianists these days demanding that we encounter *Middlemarch* or "In Memoriam A. H. H." as ethical subjects.) To be sure, the field of modernist studies has moved away in recent years from the narrow, maximalist canon that once sponsored this portrait of the artwork. The scene of reading, meanwhile, has been pluralized and arguably deconsecrated by modernist scholarship in a range of subfields, from periodical studies and genetic criticism to work informed by sociology and economics. Yet, judging by its recurrence in these pages, the portrait of the artwork as a singular other to which one owes a kind of limitless responsibility still appeals. For all that it's been lit anew by post-critique, new materialism, and the nonhuman turn, the portrait itself is an artifact of high modernism's own self-mythmaking. Insofar as it remains with us, it may be a sign of an older, stronger theory of modernism persisting, undialectized, within the new modernist studies.

None of which is to suggest that this volume fails to consider our responsibility, in the scene of reading, toward animate beings, especially human ones. If we should treat the cultural object "as something like a subject in its own right," says Ross, it's in part because such objects are "a product not just of impersonal forces … but also of a living breathing person capable of inconsistency, contradiction, passion, and change over time" (xx). Being a repository of its maker's singularity, the artwork, too, obliges us. Overall, however, *Modernism, Theory, and Responsible Reading* manifests less concern for the scholar's responsibility toward creators of cultural works than toward other scholars. For Ross this means "not just citing one another accurately but doing so generously and productively," registering our affective reactions to others' work in our own and contacting other scholars to praise their writing when it really resonates with us (xx). For Amy Tang, more pointedly, it means seeking more diverse citational practices. "Cultivating citational practices informed by historically anchored and more diverse theoretical accounts of political affect," writes Tang, "helps modernist studies to not only 'go beyond the merely descriptive' but also activates the self-awareness of one's complex attachment in encountering modernist aesthetic affects" (xx). According to Tang, citing the work of Wendy Brown, Lauren Berlant, Christina Sharpe, Sara Ahmed, and other recent theorists of affect can both extend important earlier work on affect and ideology in the field and draw needed attention to attachment's imbrication with racism, sexual violence, heteronormativity, and neoliberal ideology (xx).

Tang calls for more diverse citation practices principally to help scholars of modernism take responsibility for the role of affective attachments in their work and field. But by bringing Sara Ahmed's work on affect alongside the question of citational practices, Tang implicitly asks us to consider Ahmed's influential work on citation as speech act by which one may, variously, acknowledge or suppress one's debts, bolster or supplant established genealogies, and perpetuate or interrupt the reproductive technologies of our disciplines. One thinks especially of the introduction to *Living a Feminist Life*, where Ahmed announces her strict policy, while writing the book, of not citing any white men so as no longer to "conflate the history of ideas with white men" (16)—of citing only "those who have contributed to the intellectual genealogy of feminism and antiracism" (15). Ahmed's boldly political decision insists—indeed relies—on the fact that the performative space of citation always answers at least two questions: To whom does the author respond? To whom does the author *not* respond? If one were to cite all of one's inputs and influences, citation would stop precisely nowhere. It's specifically because citation must stop somewhere that it is performative, and what it performs is at once a facing and a facing-away. In other words, in being responsive and responsible to those we cite, we are necessarily unresponsive, even irresponsible, to those we decline to cite—those other others from whom we turn away. This turning away, as Ahmed's gesture illustrates, may be the result of implicit bias, of explicit bias, or of a principled decision to counteract both biases. But in recognizing one set of interlocutors, we unavoidably shun others. To cite is to cut. By these lights, a responsible citation practice without unresponsiveness, without at least tactical irresponsibility, is as chimerical as ethical responsibility without violence.

These questions about responsibility and citation open out on a broader question that's implied by this volume's title: responsible as opposed to what? Does a theory of responsible reading need to define that practice or aspiration in contrast to some stipulated notion of "irresponsible reading"? Are there cases in which this opposition itself must be complicated, such that responsible reading might be understood to entail irresponsible reading rather than simply to avoid or negate it? Does a theory of the responsible need to include and preserve some notion of responsible irresponsibility?

Understandably, the contributors to this volume are reluctant to offer itemized examples of irresponsible reading. No one is eager to sound like a knight of good conscience. Ross may be most willing to risk it when he writes, "Simply to focus on what we interpret as an individual person's, work's, or object's ideological errors so we can reduce them to those errors, compartmentalize them, and be done with them *is just not responsible*" (xx; emphasis added). But this reprimand seems unlikely to box any actual ears. No one, from critique's most committed practitioner to the most fervent advocate of post-critique, describes their own work as a game of reductive ideological "gotcha." Still, if one allows that a fully just response to a particular person, work, or object is both necessary and impossible—is a limit to which we *must* aspire and *can only* aspire—then some reductive misreading is unavoidable. What's more, some reductive misreading may be productive, even necessary, in advancing debates and unsettling habits of mind. Rita Felski's dictum "Context Stinks!" doesn't do full justice to the varieties, stakes, and limits of contextualization; to the contrary, it loudly and theatrically forgoes the obligation of full justice-doing in order to plant a provoking elbow in the ribcage of cultural studies (Felski, "Context" 573).[3] Like the entrenched citational genealogies that Ahmed rejects, methodological conventions are powerfully self-perpetuating. As with any massive object in motion, they take a great deal of energy to turn or to slow. In that sense, we might consider Felski's slogan a means of generating force through reductivism in order to reduce historicism's momentum. "Context Stinks!" would then be an irresponsible formulation that fulfills a different order of responsibility, an instance of responsible irresponsibility. Felski's is an especially vivid example of tactical reductivism for the sake of provocation. But I'd submit that a partial or tendentious account of one's scholarly interlocutors—even allied ones—is the rule rather than the exception in our discipline. Recognizing that this is so could serve as a first step toward addressing the existence of distinct, discordant, and sometimes mutually incompatible orders of responsibility in our work. Such a project could offer us the chance to debate two further questions: How do we recognize when responsible irresponsibility shades into irresponsible irresponsibility? And how do we know when, if ever, we are being "responsible enough" to the arguments and positions of others?

The question of when a scholar or scholarly field has taken enough responsibility grounds the final section of Ross's introduction, which invites practitioners of modernist studies to consider their responsibilities to the victims and legacies of imperialism, genocide, slavery, and other macroscale atrocities of modernity. Ross writes, "For the captured Africans who chose death by drowning over slavery in the Middle Passage to the too-many who still die because they 'can't breathe' under contemporary policing practices, modernity—modernist studies—is responsible" (xx). Modernity's not solely responsible, one imagines, but it's not *not* responsible either. Some readers may want to slow the equation of modernity with modernist studies (by way of the elided enthymeme, modernism) and to ask whether these are sites of the same kind of responsibility. Others may find that this summons back to the historical contexts of the field's emergence implies an unwelcome re-elevation of critique and critical detachment over affective attachment. But it would be a pinched theory of attachment that let it compass only love, that failed to see responsibility as a form of attachment that love may be alloyed with. For to love an object, field, or community of inquiry may be to attach yourself by way of that love to its complicities in historical trauma, and to recognize your responsibility for those complicities as a concomitant form of attachment.

Is there a way of knowing when you have discharged your responsibility for modernity's atrocities, your responsibility to their victims? Or of knowing when your responsibility cannot be discharged through academic life alone but must flow in other, more activist channels? I'd hazard that for the contributors to *Modernism, Theory, and Responsible Reading* there is not. By the lights of this volume, the questions "How far am I responsible?" and "When will I have acquitted myself, once and for all, of responsibility?" can neither be avoided nor answered conclusively. Indeed, to do either would be abhorrent. Whether we call this ethics post-structuralist or not, it is no middle ground or third way. Earlier, I characterized it as a strong theory of responsibility in its refusal to name limits. But in at least one crucial way it embodies a weak theory of responsibility. To hold yourself responsible without limit for past atrocities and their legacies is to accept a state of epistemological humility with respect to that responsibility—a state of not knowing how much responsibility is enough, of not having a theory that tells you the upper limits of your responsibility. It's to find yourself at the cliff face of the necessary–impossible without knowing the dimensions of the pore or portal through it—without knowing whether an opening is coming at all—and yet not to turn away.

Notes

1 Similar formulations occur at several points in Stephen Ross's introduction. "[R]esponsible reading presupposes an ethical obligation to honor the complexity, dynamism, and even incoherence of the cultural object" (xx). "Responsible reading opts … to treat [the cultural object] as something like a subject in its own right" (xx).
2 For Robbins, attacks such as Felski's on the critic as heroic agent of critique often fail to accord the text a critical agency of its own.
3 Felski is quick to point out that her title is a citation of Bruno Latour, who is himself citing the architect Rem Koolhaas.

References

Ahmed, Sara. *Living a Feminist Life*. Duke UP, 2017.
Best, Stephen and Sharon Marcus. "Surface Reading: An Introduction." *Representations*, vol. 108, no. 1, Fall 2009, pp. 1–21.
Derrida, Jacques. *The Gift of Death and Literature in Secret*, translated by David Wills. U of Chicago P, 2008.
Felski, Rita. "Context Stinks!" *New Literary History*, vol. 42, no. 4, Autumn, 2011, pp. 573–91.
Felski, Rita. *The Limits of Critique*. U of Chicago P, 2015.
Hayot, Eric. "What Happens to Literature if People Are Artworks?" *New Literary History*, vol. 48, no. 3, Summer 2017, pp. 457–82.
Levinas, Emmanuel. "The Paradox of Morality: An Interview with Emmanuel Levinas." Conducted by Tamra Wright, Peter Hughes, and Alison Ainley. *The Provocation of Levinas: Rethinking the Other*, edited by Robert Bernasconi and David Wood. Routledge & Kegan Paul, 1988, pp. 168–80.
Love, Heather. "Close Reading and Thin Description." *Public Culture*, vol. 25, no. 3, Fall 2013, pp. 401–34.
Robbins, Bruce. "Not So Well Attached." *PMLA/Publications of the Modern Language Association of America*, vol. 132, no. 2, March, 2017, pp. 371–6.
Saint-Amour, Paul K. "Weak Theory, Weak Modernism." *Modernism/modernity*, vol. 25, no. 3, September, 2018, pp. 437–59.

Contributors

Robert Baines is Associate Professor of English at the University of Evansville where he teaches twentieth-century British and Irish literature. He received his BA from Oxford University and his MPhil and PhD from Trinity College Dublin. He has published articles on James Joyce in journals including the *Dublin James Joyce Journal*, the *Journal of Modern Literature*, and *European Joyce Studies*. He is currently completing a monograph on the role of philosophy in Joyce's *Finnegans Wake*.

Kathryn Carney is a doctoral student in the History of Art and Architecture at the University of Pittsburgh. Her current research explores the historical fungibility of race, disability, and social deviance in turn-of-the-century German visual culture and medicine. More broadly, she is concerned with posthumanist modernisms and the biopolitics thereof, regularly drawing on the insights of critical theory, crip and queer theory, critical phenomenology, and more in her art-historical research. Carney holds an MA from the Centre for the Study of Theory & Criticism at Western University.

Fabio Akcelrud Durão is Professor of Literary Theory at the State University of Campinas (Unicamp). He is the author of *Modernism and Coherence: Four Chapters of a Negative Aesthetics* (2008), *Teoria (literária) americana* (2011), *Fragmentos Reunidos* (2015), *O que é crítica literária?* (2016), and *Metodologia de Pesquisa em Literatura* (2020), among others. He is also the editor *Culture Industry Today* (2010) and the coeditor *Modernist Group Dynamics* (2008). His essays appeared in journals such as *Critique, Cultural Critique, Parallax, Wasafiri*, and *Luso-Brazilian Review*.

Matthew Gannon is a doctoral candidate in the Department of English at Boston College. His research investigates the politics of aesthetics and pays particular attention to questions of form in modernism. He is especially interested in aesthetic autonomy, literary responses to major political events like general strikes, and the politics of historiography. Matthew's dissertation, "Modernity against Itself," is predominantly informed by the theoretical intersection of Marxism and psychoanalysis. Focusing mainly on Wyndham Lewis, Virginia

Woolf, Hope Mirrlees, T. S. Eliot, and James Joyce, "Modernity against Itself" traces the ways that modernism was simultaneously related to and antagonistic to capitalist modernity.

Cristina Ionica teaches English, Film, and Advanced Writing and Communication courses at Fanshawe College (London, Canada). Her research articles on Martin Amis, Gilles Deleuze/Félix Guattari/Samuel Beckett, *South Park*, Donald Barthelme, Kathy Acker, and Ian McEwan have been published in *English Studies in Canada*, *Angelaki: Journal of the Theoretical Humanities*, *Modern Language Studies*, *Critique: Studies in Contemporary Fiction*, *Literature Interpretation Theory*, and *Horror Studies*. Her book *The Affects, Cognition, and Politics of Samuel Beckett's Postwar Drama and Fiction* was published this year as part of a series entitled New Interpretations of Beckett in the Twenty-First Century.

Rivky Mondal is a doctoral candidate at the University of Chicago. Her writing is published or forthcoming in the *Henry James Review*, the *Journal of Modern Literature*, *Post45*, and *3:AM Magazine*. Her undergraduate course, "Women of the Avant-Garde," received a fellowship from the Center for the Study of Gender and Sexuality in 2020. She has performed editorial work for a range of academic publications, including *Reading Sedgwick* (2019), edited by Lauren Berlant; *1922: Literature, Culture, Politics* (2015) and *A Handbook of Modernism Studies* (2013), both edited by Jean-Michel Rabaté; and *Critical Inquiry*. She is completing a dissertation on the micro-social forms that undergird and frustrate the transmission of aesthetic judgments.

Daniel Aureliano Newman is Assistant Professor (Teaching Stream) of English at the University of Toronto, where he is also Director of Graduate Writing Support in the Faculty of Arts & Science. He is the author of a book *Modernist Life Histories: Biological Theory and the Experimental Bildungsroman* (2019), as well as articles in journals including *Style*, *Twentieth-Century Literature*, *Configurations*, *Journal of Narrative Theory*, and *American Journal of Botany*.

Stephen Ross is coeditor (with Kirby Brown and Alana Sayers) of the forthcoming *Routledge Handbook to North American Indigenous Modernisms*, and of a special issue of *Modernism/modernity* on "North American Indigenous Modernisms and Modernities" (2021). His most recent book is

Youth Culture and the Post-war British Novel (2019). Often perplexed, he is thankful to find that confusion can be productive (though it need not be).

Roger Rothman is Professor of Art History at Bucknell University. He is the author of *Tiny Surrealism: Salvador Dali and the Aesthetics of the Small* (2012) and coeditor, with Pamela Fraser, of *Beyond Critique: Contemporary Art in Theory, Practice, and Instruction* (2017). Among his recent publications is "Anarchism," a special issue of the journal *Modernism/modernity* (2020), for which he served as editor and contributor.

Paul K. Saint-Amour is Walter H. and Leonore C. Annenberg Professor in the Humanities and currently chairs the Department of English at the University of Pennsylvania. He is the author of *The Copywrights: Intellectual Property and the Literary Imagination* (2003) and *Tense Future: Modernism, Total War, Encyclopedic Form* (2015). Paul has edited *Modernism and Copyright* (2011) and co-edits, with Jessica Berman, the Modernist Latitudes series at Columbia University Press. He served on the Board of the Modernist Studies Association from 2010 to 2014 and now sits on the supervising committee of the English Institute. In 2018, he edited a special issue of *Modernism/modernity* on weak theory.

Sonita Sarker has published essays in post/colonial and trans/national modernisms, subalternity, literary theory, and early twentieth-century and Cold War women's writing, and on Virginia Woolf, Rokeya Sakhawat Hossain, Antonio Gramsci, Michel Foucault, and Walter Benjamin, among others. Her work has appeared in *Cultural Studies*, the *NWSA Journal*, and *Modernism/modernity Print Plus*, among others, and in her coedited collection *Trans-Status Subjects: Gender in the Globalization in South and Southeast Asia* (2002) and edited volume *Sustainable Feminisms* (2007). She is currently writing on indigenous modernisms as well as authoring a volume on Modernist Studies and Whiteness and a monograph titled *N/native* (forthcoming). She teaches in WGSS and English at Macalester College, St. Paul, Minnesota, United States.

Masami Sugimori is Associate Professor of English at Florida Gulf Coast University, where he teaches nineteenth- and twentieth-century American literature and culture. He is currently working on a book manuscript about racial passing and American modernism, chapters of which have appeared in *Faulkner Journal* and *MELUS*.

Yan Tang is Assistant Professor of English at the University of the Fraser Valley. Her research interests include twentieth-century British and Irish literature, critical theory, and the environmental humanities. Some of her writings have appeared in *LIT: Literature Interpretation Theory*, the *Routledge Encyclopedia of Modernism*, and *Modernism/modernity Print Plus*.

Index

Adorno, Theodor W. 54, 68, 154, 165 n.15, 169–84, 184 nn.1, 3, 5, 185 nn.6–9,11, 228
   Aesthetic Theory 170–1, 173, 185, 186 n.16
   "Commitment" 73
   Dialectic of Enlightenment 5
   "Essay as Form, The" 178
   Notes to Literature 186 n.14
   "Trying to Understand Endgame" 178–81
   Versuch, das Endspiel zu verstehen 179
aesthetics 9, 26, 28, 74, 144, 158, 157–60, 162–3, 170–4, 176–7, 181–3, 184 n.1, 185 nn.6, 7, 10, 191
affect 4, 5, 7, 10–11, 15, 59–60, 62–4, 67–75, 82–5, 114–15, 117, 121–2, 139, 230
Affective Materialities Reorienting the Body in Modernist Literature 73
affirmation 123, 153–5, 158, 161–3, 192
Ahmed, Sara 70–2, 82, 230, 231
   Cultural Politics of Emotion, The 72
   Living a Feminist Life 230
Alber, Jan 101
Allen, Woody
   Deconstructing Harry (film) 46
Al-Saji, Alia 79–83, 87, 88 n.4, 227
Althusser, Louis 120, 169
Ammons, Elizabeth 148
anarchism 155–7, 163 n.8
Anderson, Amanda 3, 12
Anker, Elizabeth 2, 3, 15
   and Rita Felski
      Critique and Postcritique 18 n.18, 54 n.1
anti-realism 27
anti-Semitism 3, 9
Arab Spring 155
Aronoff, Eric 189, 194, 196

Composing Cultures Modernism American Literary Studies, and the Problem of Culture 204 n.1
Asher, Michael 154
Ashtor, Gila 126 n3.
Ayers, David 123

Baines, Robert 185 n.10, 220, 222
Bakhtin, Mikhail 42, 99
Bakunin, Mikhail 155, 164 n.6
Balzac, Honoré de
   "Sarrasine" 85
Barad, Karen 164 n.4
Barnes, Djuna
   Nightwood 80, 84–6
Barthes, Roland 26, 30–2, 36, 53, 54 n.9, 85
   "From Work to Text" 30–2, 36
Baudelaire, Charles 42, 176, 180, 217, 219
Beckett, Samuel 18 n.6, 60, 93, 96, 105, 178–80
   "As the Story Was Told" 93, 105
   Endgame 171, 179
   Watt 60
Bell, Clive 216
   "Aesthetic Hypothesis, The" 221 n.2
   Art 64
   Significant Form 64–5, 212, 221
Bell, Vanessa 216
Benjamin, Walter 42, 176–7, 180
Bennett, Jane 164
Beresford, J. D.
   Imperfect Mother, The 98
Bergson, Henri 74 n.2, 81
Berlant, Lauren 63, 70–3, 88, 230
   and Lee Edelman
      Sex, or the Unbearable 88 n.3
Bernstein, J.M. 173, 177
Bersani, Leo 117
Best, Stephen 3–4, 119–20, 228
   and Sharon Marcus

"Surface Reading: An
    Introduction" 54 n.1, 184 n.2
Bewes, Tim 54 n.1
binarism 47, 123, 126
Bloomsbury Group 217–18, 221
bodily ecology 79
Bowen, Elizabeth
    House in Paris, The 104
Braidotti, Rosi 164 n.4
Brecht, George
    Drip Music 163
Bronson-Bartlett, Blake 207–9
Broodthaers, Marcel 154
Brooks, Cleanth 189, 193–8, 200, 203
    "New Criticism, The," 198
    *Well-Wrought Urn, The: Studies in the
        Structure of Poetry* 193–6, 200,
        205 n.8
Brown, Wendy 70–3, 230
    States of Injury 70
Buber, Martin 156, 157
    Paths in Utopia 156
Buchloh, Benjamin 154–5, 163
Buren, Daniel 154
Butler, Judith 1, 73, 88 n.3, 116, 118, 226
    Gender Trouble 116
Butor, Michel 98
    modification, La 100
Butts, Mary 9, 10

Cage, John 161–3, 165 n.17
Calvino, Italo
    *Se una notte d'inverno un
        viaggiatore* 100
*Cambridge Companion to Adorno,
    The* 171
Cameron, Sharon 216
Camus, Albert 179
capitalism 10, 176, 191, 199
Carney, Kathryn 107, 123, 186 n.12, 227
Castiglia, Christopher 18 n.3
Castronovo, Russ 148 n.6
Caughie, Pamela L. 146–7
Caws, Mary Ann 218, 219–20
    and Sarah Bird Wright
        *Bloomsbury in France Art and
            Friends* 218
        Surprised in Translation 219
Cazalis, Henri 222 n.7

Chen, Mel 73
Christianity 80, 106, 112–13
Communism 136, 167
Connolly, William 164 n.4
Conrad, Joseph 10
    Heart of Darkness 4, 226
    Secret Agent, The 16
Cousset, François 46
Crisis (magazine) 143
critical disability studies 79
Critical Theory 59, 67, 68, 70–2, 74, 154,
    185 n.11
criticism
    eco- 73
    genetic 28–38, 220, 229
    paranoid 121
critique 1–3, 4–7, 10, 13, 15, 17–18 nn.3,
    5, 26, 28, 32–5, 37, 41, 49–50, 63,
    68–9, 71, 74, 96, 99, 106, 111, 115,
    119–20, 122–5, 153–6, 158, 161–4,
    164 nn.1, 2, 170, 174, 178, 180, 185
    n.9, 190, 195, 203–4, 226–8, 231–3
    anti 94
    biopolitical 89
    corrosive 2–5, 10, 11, 13, 17
    Felskian 23, 25, 27–9, 37
    Marxist 72, 94
    New Historicist 95
    paranoid 80, 83
    political 3
    queer 211
Culler, Jonathan 54 n.9
Cunningham, David
    and Nigel Mapp
        Adorno and Literature 184 n.1

Day, Richard 155–7, 159, 163
del Pílar Blanco, Maria 15
Deleuze, Gilles 42, 46, 113, 117
Deppman, Jed 29
Derrida, Jacques 23–6, 30, 33, 42, 46, 53,
    62, 226–7
    *Edmund Husserl's Origin of
        Geometry: An Introduction* 23–5
    Gift of Death, The 227
    "Two Words for Joyce" 24
Detloff, Madelyn 147 n.1
Dimock, Wai Chee 4, 113, 132–4,
    136, 138–9

Index

"Weak Network: Faulkner's Transpacific Reparations" 133–4, 147 n.1
disability 80, 83
dissemination 147
Docter, Pete
  Inside Out (film) 72
Donne, John 193, 200
  "Canonization, The" 193, 200
  "Ecstasy, The" 194
Dostoyevsky, Fyodor 42
Dreadnought Hoax, the 9
Dukas, Reuven 94
Durão, Fabio Akcelrud 5, 59, 83, 87 n.2, 88, 107, 170, 186 n.12, 227–8
dynamotropism 82

Eburne, Jonathan P. 221
Edelman, Lee 88 n.3
Egan, Jennifer 100
Ekman, Paul 73, 74 n.2
Eliot, T. S. 3, 8, 10, 97, 189, 193, 216
  "Function of Criticism, The" 195, 197, 202
  "Tradition and the Individual Talent" 202
  "Waste Land, The" 193
Ellmann, Maud
  Poetics of Impersonality, The: T.S. Eliot and Ezra Pound 222 n.6
empiricism 14, 154
Empson, William 189
equivocity 24, 220
Esposito, Roberto 89
  Bíos 88 n.6
Esty, Jed 216
experimentalism 99

Fascism 64, 67
Faulkner, William 99, 132–4, 136–41
  Soldiers' Pay 139, 141
  speech at Nagano 133, 136, 139–41
Fauset, Jessie Redmon 141–6
  Comedy, American Style 142
  Plum Bun 142
  "Sleeper Wakes, The" 105, 132, 141, 143–4
Felsch, Philipp
  Der lange Sommer der Theorie 44
Felski, Rita 2–7, 11, 12, 15, 18 n.1, 23, 25–9, 31, 34–5, 38, 54 n.1, 68–70, 94, 119, 121–2, 124, 126, 132, 148, 153, 174–5, 185 n.10, 190, 211, 226, 228–9, 231, 233 nn.2, 3
  Limits of Critique, The 11, 23, 29, 54, 68, 184 n.2
Fernandez, Robert 207–9
Ferrer, Daniel 29–32, 35
fiction
  feminist 100, 105
  modernist 99–100, 105
  post-colonial 105
  post-modern 100
Fish, Stanley 205 n.11
Ford, Ford Madox 65–6, 73, 221 n.2
  English Novel, The 66
Fordham, Finn 35
  Lots of Fun at Finnegans Wake 35
Forster, E. M. 97, 99
Foster, Hal 154–5
Foucault, Michel 1, 42, 116, 118, 123–4
Frank, Adam 60–1
Frankfurt School, the 1, 67, 74 n.1, 185 n.11
Fraser, Pamela
  and Roger Rothman
    Beyond Critique: Contemporary Art in Theory, Practice, and Instruction 164
French Revolution, the 66
Freud, Sigmund 1, 42, 94, 97–8, 115–16, 118, 120
Friedman, Susan Stanford 11, 69, 96, 123–4, 147 n.3
Fry, Roger 207–20, 222 nn.8–10
  and Charles Mauron
    Some Poems of Mallarmé 208–9, 211, 213, 217–20, 222 n.10
  Significant Form. See Clive, Bell
Fujita, Fumiko 140
Fuss, Diana 122

Gabler, Hans Walter 36
Gannon, Matthew 5, 107, 165 n.15, 228
Garland-Thomson, Rosemarie 87 n.1
Gelder, Tim van 126
Genetic Criticism: Texts and Avant-Textes 29
Genette, Gerard 48, 93, 99–100
Gente, Peter 44

Goethe, Johann Wolfgang von 42
  Elective Affinities 42
Goldman, Emma 158–9, 161, 165 n.9
  "Living My Life" 158
Goodman, Paul 157, 165 n.8
Graff, Gerald 43
  Professing Literature An Institutional History 205 n.9
Granovetter, Mark 132
Gray, Thomas
  "Elegy in a Country Churchyard" 193
Gregg, Melissa
  and Gregory J. Seigworth
    Affect Theory Reader, The 74 n.2, 75 n.3
Groden, Michael 29–32, 35
Guattari, Felix 113, 117

Hall, Radclyffe
  Adam's Breed 103
Haraway, Donna
  "Situated Knowledges: The Science Question in Feminism and the Privilege of Partial Perspective" 88 n.4
Hardt, Michael 113
Hawking, Stephen 95
Hawthorne, Nathaniel
  "The Haunted Mind" 100
Hayot, Eric 228
Heath, Stephen 25–6, 28, 31, 36
  "Ambiviolences: Notes for Reading Joyce" 25–6, 28, 30
Hegel, Georg Wilhelm Friedrich 164 n.6, 175–6, 184 n.3
Heidegger, Martin 55 n.15
Heller-Roazen, Daniel
  Echolalias 51
Hensley, Nathan 73–4
Herman, Peter C. 43
hermeneutics of curiosity 96
hermeneutics of responsibility 175
hermeneutics of suspicion 3, 6, 94, 106, 116, 164 n.3, 184 n.2
Higgins, Dick 163, 165 n.17
  Danger Music #15, 163
Hitler, Adolf 9
Holland, Eugene 164 n.4
Horkheimer, Max 5, 54 n.10, 67, 69

"Traditional and Critical Theory" 67–8, 74 n.1, 185 n.11
Huhn, Tom 171
humanism 14
humanities, the 5, 8, 13, 44, 48, 59–61, 69, 73, 74 n.2, 106, 123, 126, 134, 146, 196, 198
Hume, David 160, 165 n.18
Hurston, Zora Neale 99
Husserl, Edmund 23
Huxley, Aldous 194

imperialism 13, 198, 232
industrialization 14
International Joyce Symposium 27
interwar era 79
Ionica, Cristina 5, 69, 80, 88 n.5, 95, 133, 164 n.2
Ishiguro, Kazuo 73
  Unconsoled, The 73

James, David 15
James, Henry 4, 97, 99
James, William 148 n.5
Jameson, Fredric 53, 116, 120, 124, 170, 177, 186 n.13
Jarry, Alfred 98
  pataphysics 98
Jay Gould, Stephen 107
Jelliffe, Robert A. 140
  "Meeting with Nagano Citizens" 137
Johnson, James Weldon
  Autobiography of an Ex-Colored Man, The 142
Jones, Gayl
  Corregidora 72
Joyce studies 23, 26–9, 32, 37–8
Joyce, James 23–9, 32–8, 99–100, 220
  and equivocity 23–4, 33
  and post-structuralism 23–6, 27–30, 32–4, 37
  Finnegans Wake 25, 23–8, 32–7, 47
  Portrait of the Artist as a Young Man, A 99
  Ulysses 27, 36, 93
Julius, Anthony 3

Kafka, Franz 18, 42, 179
Kajima, Shozo 140–1

Kant, Immanuel 1, 34, 158–60, 163, 165 nn.13, 14, 18, 172, 185 nn.6, 8, 228
 Critique of the Power of Judgement 159, 165 n.11
 Observations on the Feeling of the Beautiful and the Sublime 159
Karanikas, Alexander 205 nn.3, 9
Keats, John
 "Ode on a Grecian Urn" 193, 196
Kenner, Hugh 99–100
 Uncle Charles Principle, the 99
Kincaid, Jamaica 100
King, Jr., Martin Luther 16
Kipling, Rudyard
 "White Man's Burden, The" 197
Klein, Melanie 80, 116–19, 126 n.3
Koolhaas, Rem 235 n.3
Kottman, Paul A. 186 n.14
Kristeva, Julia 26, 117
Kropotkin, Peter 155
Kurnick, David 211

Lacan, Jacques 42–3, 53, 55 n.15, 116, 117–18, 120, 124
Laird, Holly 112, 123
Landauer, Gustav 155–9, 163
 "Weak Statesman, Weaker People!" 156
Larsen, Nella
 Passing 142
Latour, Bruno 2–3, 5, 7, 11, 94–6, 122, 153–4, 157, 163, 226, 229, 233 n.3
 "Why Has Critique Run Out of Steam?" 54 n.1, 96, 153
Le Corbusier 9
Lehman, Robert S. 185 n.6
Lehmann, Rosamond
 Dusty Answer 101, 103
Leitch, Vincent
 Living with Theory 55 n.12
Lernout, Geert 27–8, 32
 French Joyce, The 27, 32
Lesjak, Carolyn 186 n.13
Levenson, Michael 99
Levinas, Emmanuel 11–12, 14, 88, 136, 226, 228
 "Ethics as First Philosophy" 11
Lewis, Wyndham 8–10, 99
Leys, Ruth 61, 70, 73, 75 n.5

Libet, Benjamin
 "Unconscious Cerebral Initiative and the Role of Conscious Will in Voluntary Action" 61, 75 n.5
Locke, John 88 n.6
Love, Heather 3, 94–5, 119, 121, 228
Lukes, Alexandra 222 n.10
Lyotard, Jean-François 117

Mac Low, Jackson 163, 165 n.17
 Stanzas for Iris Lezak 163
MacCabe, Colin 26–7, 36
 James Joyce and the Revolution of the Word 26
Mallarmé, Stephane 207–20, 222 nn.7, 10
 "Salut" 207
 "Sigh" 214
Mandela, Nelson 16
Maoism 117
Marcus, Sharon 3, 119–20, 228
Marcuse, Herbert 67–8, 154
 "On Hedonism" 68
 One-Dimensional Man 154
Marinetti, Filippo Tommaso 8
Marx, Karl 1, 97–8, 116, 118, 120, 155, 180
 Misère de la philosophie 156
Marxism 72, 155–6, 176
masculinity 85, 191
 white colonial 190, 197, 200
Massumi, Brian 61–4, 69–70, 74 n.2, 75 n.5
 "Autonomy of Affect, The" 60–3, 70
Mauron, Charles 207, 209–10, 212, 215, 220
mauvaise conscience 11–12, 16, 136–7
May, Todd 156–7
 Political Philosophy of Poststructuralist Anarchism, The 156
McInerney, Jay
 Bright Lights, Big City 100
Merleau-Ponty, Maurice 81–2, 87–8 n.3
Merve Verlag 44–5
metanarrative 87 n.2, 134
Micir, Melanie 147 n.2
Miller, D. A. 116
 Novel and the Police, The 116
modernism 5, 8–10, 13–16, 18, 59–63, 67, 70–1, 73–4, 96–7, 99, 123, 131–2,

134, 142, 144, 177, 179, 215, 229–30, 232
  high 10, 59, 142, 229
  weak 10, 13
Modernism/modernity Special Issue Weak Theory, September 2018 79, 111, 123
modernist studies 8–10, 14, 60, 70–1, 73–4, 79, 87, 111, 131, 225, 229–30, 232
Modernist Studies Association 16, 221
Mondal, Rivky 60, 174, 229
Mondrian, Piet 9
Moore, Lorrie 100
Moretti, Franco 48
  Distant Reading 184 n.2
Moses, Omri 123
Murphet, Julian 123

NAACP 143
Nail, Thomas 113
narration
  first-person 102
  free indirect 144–6
  mixed-voice 100–5, 107
  second-person 97, 100–5
  third-person 102–5, 139, 144–6
narratology 97, 99
nativism 69
Negri, Antonio 113
neoliberalism 49, 50, 107, 191–2, 230
New Criticism 189–204, 205 n.11
New Critics 189–205 nn.3,11
New Historicism 41, 204
new materialism 73, 229
New Negro Renaissance 142
Newman, Daniel Aureliano 17, 18 nn.5, 7, 69, 185 nn.9, 10
Ngai, Sianne 61, 221
  Ugly Feelings 73
Ní Chonchúir, Nuala 100
Nicolson, Harold 209–10, 217–18
Nietzsche, Friedrich 1, 71, 116
Nobel Prize in Literature 192
Norton Anthology of Theory and Criticism 42
Nuwās, Abū 51–2

O'Brien, Edna 100
O'Brien, Justin 209–10, 217–18
Occupy movement, the 155

Omega Workshops, the 212
Orientalism 137
Orwell, George 64
  "W.B. Yeats" 64

paranoia 94, 115–16, 154
paranoid inquiry 114–16, 118, 124
Pearson, Roger 213
Perkins, David 126
phenomenology 79, 82, 88 nn.3, 4
physiognomy 142
Piketty, Thomas 113
Platt, Len 27
Poe, Edgar Allan
  "Raven, The" 219
Pope, Alexander 193
  Rape of the Lock, The 194
porosity 79–80, 83, 88 n.3
post-anarchism 156
postcolonialism 41
post-critique 1–5, 10, 13, 17, 18 n.5, 41, 86, 93–6, 132, 142, 170, 184 n.2, 185 n.9, 190, 203–4, 226–9, 231
posthumanism 79–80, 86
post-structuralism 23, 25–30, 31–8, 220, 226–7
Potts, Jason 54
Pound, Ezra 8, 10, 93, 216
  Seafarer, The 215
prison-industrial complex 14
prosthesis 80–7, 88 n.6, 89, 107
prosthetic thinking 79–84, 86–7
Proudhon, Pierre-Joseph 161
  Système des contradictions économiques, ou Philosophie de la misère 156
Proust, Marcel 42, 60, 99–100

queerness 83
Queneau, Raymond
  Exercices de Style 98
  Hundred Thousand Billion Poems, A 99

Rabelais, Francois 42
Racine, Jean 42
racism 9, 13, 15, 230
Rainer, Yvonne 162–3
Ransom, John Crowe 189, 194–5, 201–2, 205 n.7

rationalism 14
reading
　adequate 195
　Adornean 184 n.1
　allegorical 107
　casual 41
　close 1, 41, 46, 107, 134, 139, 170, 184 n.2, 195, 221 n.4
　critical race 1
　deep 41, 84, 170
　distant 1, 41, 48, 170, 184 n.2
　ethical 12
　fair 2
　feminist 1
　figurative 107
　genetic 33, 35
　historicist 1
　irresponsible 231
　literal 107
　Marxist 1, 28
　mere 1
　micro-sociological 1
　middle 1
　mimetic 52
　new historicist 1
　nonfigurative 94
　paranoid 1, 18 n.6, 94–5, 97, 106–7, 114, 121, 164 n.2, 211
　phenomenological 1
　postcolonial 28
　post-critical 4, 26, 34–5, 175, 211, 226
　post-Marxist 1
　post-structuralist 1, 23, 25–6, 28, 33, 35
　prosthetic 80
　psychoanalytic 1
　reductive 133
　reparative 1, 4, 69, 118, 132, 136, 140, 170, 184 n.2, 211
　responsible 1–2, 5–13, 17–18, 41–2, 51, 73–4, 96–8, 105, 107, 131, 134, 136, 139, 141, 146–8, 169–70, 174, 177–8, 181, 189–90, 193, 196, 199, 204, 212, 225–6, 229, 231, 233
　superficial 195
　surface 1, 41, 84, 120, 170
　suspicious 18, 124, 170
　symptomatic 120, 132
　unproductive 51

　weak 119
　with-the-grain 41
Reagan, Ronald 63, 69
Reaganism 116
realism 27, 120
Reed, Christopher 212, 221
Residential Schools 14
Rhys, Jean 102, 103
　After Leaving Mr. Mackenzie 101–2
　Voyage in the Dark 101, 103
Richards, I. A. 189, 200–1, 205 n.9
　"How to Read a Page: A Course in Efficient Reading" 197–8
　Poetries and Sciences 199–201
　Practical Criticism 197–8
　Science and Poetry 199
Richardson, Samuel 66
Richter, Gerhard 173
　Thinking with Adorno 184 n.1
Ricoeur, Paul 3, 116, 148 n.4, 164 n.3
ridiculous, the 157–64, 165 nn.14,18, 217
Robbins, Bruce 228, 233 n.2
Robinson, Josh
　Adorno's Poetics of Form 184 n.1
Robinson, Marilynne 107
Rodowick, D. N. 43
Roger, Jacques 48
Rolf, Marie 221 n.4
Rooney, Ellen 120, 186 n.15
Rorty, Richard 135–6, 148 n.5
Ross, Stephen 123, 136, 221, 225–33
　Modernism and Theory 16, 99
Rothman, Roger 54 n.1, 81, 185 n.9
Rousseau, Jean-Jacques 42
Russian Formalists 43, 99
Ryan, Judith 46

Said, Edward 15
Saint-Amour, Paul K. 6–10, 16, 80, 82, 111–13, 116, 126 n.2, 131–2, 134–5, 142, 175
　Weak Theory, Weak Modernism 17, 54 n.1, 79, 86, 131–2, 184 n.2, 226
Sanders, Mark A. 142
Sartre, Jean-Paul 179
Scappettone, Jennifer 221, 221 n.5
Schofield, Dennis 101

Schuyler, George
   Black No More 142
Sedgwick, Eve Kosofsky 2, 3, 60–4, 69–70, 74, 80, 88 n.5, 94, 111, 114–19, 121, 124, 126 n.3, 132, 148 n.5, 153–4, 157, 164 nn.2, 3, 211
   and Adam Frank
      "Shame in the Cybernetic Fold" 60–3, 67, 70, 74 n.2, 221 n.2
   Bathroom Songs 61
   "Paranoid Reading and Reparative Reading or, You're So Paranoid, You Probably Think This Essay Is About You" 184 n.2
   "Paranoid Reading and Reparative Reading or, You're So Paranoid, You Probably Think This Introduction Is About You" 153
   Touching Feeling 69, 114
Sharpe, Christina 70–2, 230
   Monstrous Intimacies 72
Shklovsky, Victor 75 n.4
Simpson, James 7
Sinclair, May 102
   Life and Death of Harriet Frean 102–3
   Mary Olivier 100–2
slavery 14, 15, 72, 112, 192, 232
Slote, Sam 24
Smith, Zadie
   On Beauty 106
Sollers, Philippe 25
Southern Agrarians 189, 191, 193, 199
Spinoza, Baruch 74 n.2, 169
Spivak, Gayatri Chakravorty 46
Stalinism 117
Stanley, Kate 148 n.5
Stein, Gertrude 60, 61
Stendhal 163, 183
structuralism 29, 30, 44, 46–8, 61
Sturm, Hertha 61, 75
Sugimori, Masami 5, 12, 18 n.7, 54 n.1, 69, 74, 95, 105, 126 n.1, 165 n.16, 174, 227–8
Symons, Arthur 75 n.6

Tang, Yan 5, 18 n.5, 83, 126, 185 n.10, 221 n.2, 230
Tate, Allen 189
Tatsunokuchi, Naotaro 140
Tel Quel (magazine) 25, 44

theory
   affect 59–65, 69–71, 73–5, 114, 132, 135, 148, 221 n.1
   crip 79
   critical 119
   Foucauldian 116
   Freudian 98
   gender 120
   High 99
   Lacanian 124
   Marxist 116, 120
   narrative 99
   prosthetic 79, 84
   psychoanalytic 120
   queer 126
   Reader Response 204
   strong 53, 95, 106, 114–15, 119, 121, 124, 227, 232
   strong affect 142
   weak 6, 8–9, 13, 70, 88 n.5, 95–6, 105, 111, 113–16, 119, 121, 123, 125, 126 nn.1, 2, 131–5, 142, 147 nn.1–3, 148 n.5, 170, 227, 232
Theory 41–3, 45–55, 59, 88, 95, 107, 153
Tóibín, Colm 4
Tolstoy, Leo 75
Tomkins, Silvan 60–2, 64, 69–70, 73–4 n.1, 114–17, 121, 132, 142, 148 n.5, 221
   "Left and Right a Basic Dimension of Ideology and Personality" 70
Totalitarian regimes 125
translation 26, 34, 108, 136, 139, 171, 175, 178, 207–20, 229
Triangular Trade, the 14
Trump, Donald 125

Vadde, Aarthi 147
Van Hulle, Dirk
   James Joyce's "Work in Progress": Pre-Book Publications of Finnegans Wake Fragments 37
Vattimo, Gianni 6, 114, 132
Venuti, Lawrence 215
Vieira, Padre Antônio 53

Ward, Colin 157, 163
   Anarchy in Action 157
Warren, Robert Penn 194–5
weakness 6–8, 10, 80, 95, 111–14, 123–4, 131–4, 217

Weed, Elizabeth 120
Wellek, René
   and Robert Penn Warren
      Theory of Literature 201
      Understanding Poetry 204 n.1
   "New Criticism,Pro and Contra,
      The" 198
White, Stephen
   Sustaining Affirmation: The Strengths of Weak Ontology in Political Theory 164
White, Walter Francis
   Flight 142
Williams, Garrath 148
Williams, Jeffrey 113, 132
Williams, Paul 162
Williams, Raymond 65
Williams, Vera 162
Willmott, Glenn 4
Windrush Generation, the 14
Wollaeger, Mark 7

Woolf, Virginia 9, 10, 65–6, 73, 97–9, 145, 147 n.2, 210, 212, 216, 221 nn.2, 3
   "Freudian Fiction" 98
   "Modern Fiction" 98
   "How Should One Read a Book?" 98
   Mrs. Dalloway 97, 98, 99
   "Professions for Women" 65
   To the Lighthouse 65
Wordsworth, William 193
Wright, Sarah Bird 218
Wyile, Herb 204

Yeats, W. B. 64, 73, 193, 216, 221 n.2
   "Symbolism of Poetry, The" 64
Young, La Monte
   Composition #10 163

Zabel, Morton Dauwen 217–18
Zambreno, Kate 147
Zerilli, Linda M. G. 70
Žižek, Slavoj 43

www.ingramcontent.com/pod-product-compliance
Lightning Source LLC
Chambersburg PA
CBHW041730300426
44115CB00021B/2966